AUBREY TAYLOR
HONEY UNDONE

Copyright © 2025 by Aubrey Taylor

All rights reserved. No part of this publication may be reproduced, stored or transmitted in any form or by any means, electronic, mechanical, photocopying, recording, scanning, or otherwise without written permission from the publisher. **This work is never to be used in AI training or anything that involves such. It is illegal to copy this book, post it to a website, or distribute it by any other means without permission.**

For permission requests, contact Aubrey Taylor, Aubreytaylorauthor@gmail.com

This novel is entirely a work of fiction. The names, characters and incidents portrayed in it are the work of the author's imagination. Any resemblance to actual persons, living or dead, events or localities is entirely coincidental.

Aubrey Taylor asserts the moral right to be identified as the author of this work.

Aubrey Taylor has no responsibility for the persistence or accuracy of URLs for external or third-party Internet Websites referred to in this publication and does not guarantee that any content on such Websites is, or will remain, accurate or appropriate.

Designations used by companies to distinguish their products are often claimed as trademarks. All brand names and product names used in this book and on its cover are trade names, service marks, trademarks and registered trademarks of their respective owners. The publishers and the book are not associated with any product or vendor mentioned in this book. None of the companies referenced within the book have endorsed the book.

Book Cover by Aurora McGaughey

Editing and Proof Reading by Becky Clapham and Jessica Norton

Illustrations by Aubrey Taylor

First Edition 2025

Love, I think.
And that love can be for a boy or a girl
or a place or a way of life or even for a family.
But where you find it is up to you.
So where are you gonna find that love?
B.D.

THIS ONE IS FOR THE LOVER BOYS,
PLEASE NEVER STOP MAKING TIK TOK THIRST TRAPS.
YOU'RE WRITING THE BOOKS FOR US.

OFFICIAL PLAYLIST

TRAINING SEASON - DUA LIPA
ALL THAT I'M CRAVING - AIDAN BISSETT
SEX - EDEN
WHAT IT IS (BLOCK BOY) - DOECHII, KODAK BLACK
SPEED OF LIGHT - THE GLORIOUS SONS
THE START - AMBER RUN
OH NO - BIIG PIIG
SHIRT - NIGHTLY
GOOD FOR YOU - SELENA GOMEZ, A$AP ROCKY
SWEET MOMENT - MACKENZY MACKAY
CHERISH YOU - MIKKY EKKO
EVERY SIDE OF YOU - VANCE JOY
WURLI - DOMINIC FIKE
HEAVEN - NIALL HORAN
TEETH - MALL RAT
HOMESICK - MICO
LOVE ME NOT - RAVYN LENAE
UNDRESSED - SOMBR
PILLOWTALK - ZYAN
NOTICE ME - ROLE MODEL, BENEE
GUN-SHY (GIRL LIKE YOU) - JACOB FITZGERALD
MAN EATER - NELLY FURTADO
HEART TO HEART - NOW MORE THEN EVER
SHE'S GOT THAT - WE THREE
MONA LISA, MONA LISA - FINNEAS
MARRIED IN VEGAS - THE VAMPS
THOSE EYES - IRIS JEAN

Sexual Content
The End of an Era
**Take breaks, get some water,
snuggle your loved ones and pets.**
Be kind to yourself, being a human being is tough.

Contents

1. SARAH — 1
2. JENSEN — 9
3. SARAH — 15
4. SARAH — 22
5. JENSEN — 29
6. JENSEN — 36
7. SARAH — 43
8. SARAH — 49
9. JENSEN — 56
10. SARAH — 64
11. SARAH — 70
12. JENSEN — 77
13. JENSEN — 82
14. SARAH — 89
15. JENSEN — 95
16. SARAH — 104
17. JENSEN — 112
18. SARAH — 124

19.	JENSEN	131
20.	JENSEN	138
21.	SARAH	144
22.	SARAH	150
23.	SARAH	158
24.	SARAH	164
25.	JENSEN	172
26.	SARAH	179
27.	JENSEN	185
28.	SARAH	196
29.	SARAH	205
30.	SARAH	214
31.	JENSEN	220
32.	JENSEN	228
33.	JENSEN	234
34.	JENSEN	240
35.	JENSEN	246
36.	JENSEN	253
37.	SARAH	259
38.	JENSEN	267
39.	SARAH	273
40.	JENSEN	279
41.	JENSEN	283
42.	SARAH	289

43.	SARAH	296
44.	SARAH	301
45.	JENSEN	305
46.	JENSEN	310
47.	JENSEN	317
48.	JENSEN	323
49.	EPILOGUE	329
50.	ACKNOWLEDGEMENTS	334

SARAH

"Addy!" My name was called through the thick crowd of people that flooded the concourse, but Cosy's voice traveled through the noise and carried me toward them. Kaia was waving a piece of licorice in Sunday's face, laughing as it hit her in the nose. Her brown hair was cut short around her jaw, and her smile was infectious as Sunday tried to swipe the candy out of the air with only her teeth.

She was wearing a Hornet's jersey under her jean jacket and her long dirty blonde hair was pulled into a ponytail and through her baseball cap.

"Look who showed up," Sunday said, her head turning to look at me as I approached them. Cosy scowled at her and threw her arm around me. Her dark red hair brushed against my cheek as she pulled me in for the hug.

The stadium was buzzing with playoff energy as we wandered down through the sea of bodies to our seats. It wasn't often that we got our hands on spare tickets so when Cosy's brother Van offered them up it was rare we passed on them.

"We're here." She pointed at the four seats that were sandwiched between the Hornet's dugout and the fence. The view of the in-field from this position was insane but I always preferred our normal seats further back. I liked to see all the action, from here all we would see was the batter's box and the pitchers mound. Even the view of the third was obscured.

"So excited to stare at the catcher's ass for three hours," I said, sinking down into my seat between Cosy and Kaia.

"Are you complaining about baseball pants right now?" Kaia scoffed. "We come here to objectify men, Addy. It's the main reason."

"I come to cheer for my brother." Cosy shook her head, but the smile on her face gave away the amusement.

"And your *brother,*" Kaia said, a wicked grin building on her face. "Has a top ten Hornet ass."

"You have a list?" I asked.

Kaia was the kind of pretty that made me envy every inch of her. From her high cheekbones and bright smile, to her dark almond eyes and thick brown hair that complemented her golden skin. Even worse, she was a boy's worst nightmare, wild and unchained. She said what she meant and always meant exactly what she said.

"Of course I do," she said, reaching down between us as she grabbed the roster card that was shoved between the sheets. "Do you have a pen?" She turned to Sunday, who dug one out of her small purse with a tiny giggle.

"Colton Todd, flat, needs to do more squats. Dougie, too white there's nothing there. Mattheson, Hamilton and Reyes… shameful. Louis…" She tapped the paper and then pointed to second base. For a moment, I thought we might have gotten to the good stuff. "Cute ass but not a *good* shape." She moved her hands in a loose circle and pouted, "There's no grab-ability."

"That's not a word," I said but continued to listen.

"It is now," Sunday said, ripping open her bag of M&Ms and dropping the lot of them into her popcorn.

"Now, top five, Cael Cody, shortstop, fifth place. Do you want to know why?" She asked me with a serious tone in her voice.

"You're going to tell me anyway," I guessed.

"Correct," she said, booping my nose with the pen, "he's got a great ass, but it doesn't hold up in sweatpants. That's a waste."

"Does he know this?" I laughed.

"Van Mitchell," she continued, and Cosy pretended to gag.

"Fourth place, really nice but he's just too tall. No offense," she said to Cosy.

"None taken, you aren't ogling my ass," she huffed.

"I have before, you're top three Hillcats," Kaia said to her.

"Awe, really?" Cosy cooed, suddenly a little more into the conversation.

"Yeah right behind Rhea and this fat ass." She winked at me. "Thighs for days," she added with a smile when I stared at her. "Back to the list, Dean 'Golden Boy' Tucker," she emphasized. "That man is built like a brick wall and his ass is proof that a higher power exists."

"The first baseman?" Sunday asked, and Kaia nodded before continuing.

"Then there's Arlo," she sighed wistfully.

"Isn't he retired?" I asked and Kaia shrugged.

"The list is timeless, and his ass is Harbor legend in baseball pants. The calendar tells no lies and memorializes it for all of eternity," she said.

"So who's number one then?" I asked.

"Jensen." Kaia's smile widened as her head turned to the field. The pen slipped between her teeth, and she sighed as her eyes found a player standing with his helmet under his arm chatting with the Hornets' Coach. "*That's* an ass."

She wasn't wrong. His other hand was on his hip as he looked at whatever was on the clipboard. He had insanely strong legs that pushed the boundaries of his ball pants in every way possible, leading up to the conversation piece at hand.

"Okay, yeah. That is a really nice ass," I said, swallowing tightly as he turned to look out to the field where the Coach pointed.

His dark hair was messy and sticking off the front of his head in damp peaks that moved every time he nodded. The sun bathed across his olive skin and his jaw tightened as he squinted into the bright light with a focused expression on his face. I leaned forward in my seat to admire the way his nose swooped and how his brows pinched together.

He pointed in the same direction and his tattooed-covered arm flexed tightly. I couldn't help the smile that formed on my lips or the heat that crept up my neck at the sight of his bicep and strong forearm. It wasn't just his ass that he had going for him.

He was *everything*.

"Oh, we're leaning?" Kaia sat back from me with a smile on her face, "do you think Jensen is cute?" she lowered her voice like he was in ear shot and I laughed at her, pushing her shoulder playful.

"No," I said, shaking my head yes.

Very much so.

"You shook your head yes and you've glossed over like that time we did LSD," Sunday said, her head tilting sideways.

"Oh she absolutely has the hots for the Catcher," Kaia said, louder this time and I reached over to pinch her.

"Shut up," I warned her and she just laughed, turning back in her seat as the game started.

"Jensen is one of the older players," Cosy said as Kaia became distracted with cheering. "He's kind of a floater, but Van always has good things to say about him. I guess he's never had a serious girlfriend. Four years of college. I don't know if he's a serial booty call or what."

"Really?" I asked, watching as he sank low behind the batter's box. He focused on the pitcher, their silent communication was fun to watch as they readied to throw the first pitch. I looked over at Cosy again, "that feels so weird. Aren't Catchers supposed to be playboys?"

"Yeah. Van is always trying to set him up with girls and he never takes the bait," Cosy popped a piece of popcorn in her mouth. "He's so polite though, he came to our house for Easter last year, he did all the dishes after dinner."

I looked back to the field as the Ump called the strike. Jensen stood to his full height and I heard Kaia sigh as her head cocked to the side to admire his ass.

Cosy's insight did nothing to quell the butterflies in my chest. It had been a long time since the mere sight of a man had any effect but there was an air about him that acted like a magnet.

Two whole innings went by and still every time he came out it was like something had come over me. When he took off his mask to wave to people in the crowd we were greeted by a smile that could cut glass. Sharp and bright, it was perfectly lopsided and did unspeakable things to my nerves. I stuffed it down and chalked up the lightness in my chest to nausea.

"I'm going to go get something to eat," I declared as the third inning started.

The Hornets gave up two runs in the second but the kid at the concessions counter promised me that it was a strategy and they'd come back in the third. He handed me the bag of gummy cola bottles and a bottle of water with a huge smile on his brace filled face. When I finally sank back into my seat the Hornets were up to bat in the bottom of the third.

"What happened?" I asked Kaia.

"They went down one," she said, "but you got back just in time." She nudged me with her elbow. "Have you ever seen a real life angel?" She asked as I caught sight of who she was talking about.

Jensen was free of his catcher gear.

"Wow," I huffed quietly, pausing, I held a piece of candy between my teeth as he rolled out his shoulders. We were granted peeks of more tattoos as his jersey stretched and shifted over his chest and biceps with the stretches.

He came up to the box and gave his bat another swing.

"Hey, twelve! Did it hurt?" Kaia stood up in her seat and yelled.

Jensen turned and it felt like everything was moving in slow motion when his eyes landed on mine. His expression shifted from focused to what might have been marvel. "Huh?" he said from his spot in the dirt, dropping his bat but never his gaze.

There was no way he didn't hear her.

"When you fell from heaven, did it hurt?" Kaia asked him loudly enough for the Ump to shush her. "Oh buzz off," she stuck her tongue out.

"Number twelve," the Ump warned and Jensen's attention shifted but his goofy smile remained as he turned on the base.

As the pitcher threw the ball he turned around again, the ball whizzing by his head into the catcher's mitt.

"Jensen!" The Coach barked from the dugout, "what the fu—"

His curse was drowned out by the Ump calling the strike.

"Do I know you from somewhere?" He asked me over the sound of everyone screaming.

I shook my head, a small amused smile forming on my lips.

His brows pinched together and he looked like he wanted to ask another question but he slowly fixed his position as the pitcher readied for another throw. Jensen dropped his bat at the last moment and spun around again.

"Are you sure? You were at Delta last weekend, weren't you?" He pointed it at me and I shook my head again.

"Hey dipshit! Stop fucking around!" Dean Tucker yelled from the dugout, his body leaning over the banister to scream at Jensen on the plate.

Jensen looked more confused than ever but also like he was enjoying it?

"He's losing his shit," Kaia laughed at my side.

"Him and everyone else," Cosy said over the sound of the stadium growing restless.

Jensen missed his third swing, completely striking out. He turned to look at me as he walked backward off the plate. For a man that just cost his team a run in the playoffs he didn't look like it bothered him for a second. He was smiling like an idiot.

"Is he drunk?" Sunday asked, her confusion palpable.

He was accosted the second he stepped down into the dugout and disappeared under the covering but the screaming could be heard even over the fans. When they came back out on the field in the fourth, the team had recouped and were up by three.

"What's your name?" Jensen asked, pulling my focus to him from the scoreboard.

"Why do you need my name?" I asked back.

He inhaled like he had been holding his breath and that stupid grin returned.

"Cause I swear I know you," he said. His coach was barking at him again and he looked over his shoulder quickly before looking back at me. "And if I don't, I want a proper introduction."

"You should probably worry about the game," I suggested and sat back in my chair.

I could see the thoughts turning behind his eyes as he pulled the cage over his face and got ready for the inning.

"You're going to get us kicked out," Kaia huffed with a pride-filled smile and it only made me laugh.

"Can they do that?" I asked, looking at Cosy who just shrugged.

The batter struck out twice before he repositioned and hit a ball into the outfield and took second. The second the play was dead Jensen turned and ripped off his mask.

"How can I take you on a date if I don't know your name?" He yelled up to me and I swear the entire Hornets dug out hollered as a collective.

He pulled his cage back down and returned to the game.

"You'd think he'd be frustrated?" Kaia smiled down at him.

"I think… it's turning him on…" Sunday added with a burst of laughter.

It definitely was. It was vibrating off him with every play, like he was itching to get back to being a flirt. I shifted in my seat and chewed on the candy to settle my nerves. It was getting harder and harder to deny him. His smile and impressive willpower seemingly ate away at my resolve with every turn, glance, question.

I was a goner.

But I had gotten a taste for driving him insane and the way it made me feel was like a rush of adrenaline. I wasn't quite ready to give up just yet. The inning went by fast, the defense shut them down hard and the opposing team only brought in two runs before they were switching out. Every inning got harder to watch as the teams traded runs and the sun dropped in the sky. The last inning came around and as the lights in the stadium flickered on with a resounding buzz the Hornets were up for their last bat.

It was hard fought and by the time Jensen came out to bat, the bases were loaded, and Harbor needed every single run to win the game. He didn't even bother to set up on the plate that time, he walked toward the fence and stared across the distance at me. His hair was sweaty and stuck up in messy brown peaks as he curled his fingers into the cage.

"Let me take you on a date," he pleaded instead of being phased by the rowdy crowd and even more pissed off teammates. "You say we've never met, prove it, let me take you on a date!"

"Jensen, I will bench you!" His coach hollered from the dugout.

"You aren't a very good baseball player," I said with a smile.

"Ouch," he said in a lower tone that stirred an unknown heat in the pit of my stomach as his brows furrowed together and a smirk formed on that unreasonably handsome face. "Give me one chance," he said, that same husky tone carrying through all the noise.

"Fine." I looked out at the bases, ignoring the desperate pleas for Jensen to play the game before he got fined or kicked off the plate.

"Yeah?" he smiled, his body pressing against the cage.

"I'll go on a date with you if you bring everyone home," I challenged him, and he looked behind him at the bases.

"Child's play," he said, his cheeky smile growing confident.

"With a bunt," I added, leaning on the railing that separated us. "And I get to pick the date!"

"Get in the box, Number Twelve or you can leave the game and give your team an out," the Ump ordered but Jensen just stared me down with that dumb look on his face.

"Deal."

JENSEN

"Jensen I swear to—"

It didn't matter what Coach said next, the entire stadium was silent when she smiled at me. I could have sworn I heard her agree to the terms, but anything after she said fine was just useless details.

Deal came out of my mouth in between the rapid beats of my heart, and it only hit me after I said it, that I realized the gravity of my decision. *Shit.* I turned back to the plate and surveyed the field. Van was on third with a tight jaw, Cael on second with an unreadable expression and Louis was a bag of nerves on first. The three fastest guys on the team. It could work. I was screamed at as impatience got the best of the dugout. I looked over my shoulder at her again and couldn't help but grin seeing her leaned forward in her seat watching.

If the prettiest girl in Harbor wanted a game-winning bunt, *I'd give her one.*

Dean hissed from my left as I delicately planted my feet in the loose sand. Looking at him was a death wish. He would burn a hole through what little confidence I had to pull off the move. I rotated my hands on the bat, it felt heavy in my hands, but the weight made me feel at home in the batter's box.

All I had to do was hit the ball.

Colhan stared at me like I was an easy out, rolling the ball in his pitching hand with a nasty smirk on his face that meant trouble. I had one shot to get the swing right. I tapped my foot on the plate and inhaled. Timing it exactly to how he pulled his arm back and released the ball with power behind it.

As the ball came at me, I turned my back like a flicker, sticking my arm out straight and tapping the ball with just enough force. In the same second, I pushed off my back foot and took off running as fast as I could. It didn't matter where I made it. The second the ball bounced, everyone scrambled. Colhan tripped over his step in the panic, missing the ball as it rolled through the infield. The entire crowd was screaming as Van made it home with Cael on his tail. Coach was screaming at Louis from the dugout as the infield finally got control of the ball. I slid across the divide and crossed second before Louis slid home just beneath the hard whip of a ball from pitcher to the catcher.

As I collided with the third baseman, the ball hit his mitt, and the Ump called me out. The baseman shoved me hard, flying off insults as I scrambled backward to the dugout with my arms in the air. I didn't want a fight, I just wanted the girl.

I stumbled a step, the smile on my face so big it was starting to hurt as I looked over at her. Puffing up my chest and rolling back my shoulders, I pressed my lips into a knowing smirk and gave her a wink.

The girls beside her burst into laughter and screams as she stood there staring at me. Her head shook gently in disbelief and my chest lit up with fireworks as the stadium ceased to exist around us.

A hand cracked across the back of my head and I knew that Arlo had met me at the entrance of the dugout from the way it stung in the back of my eyes.

"That was ballsy." His bite was definitely worse than his bark that time. I rubbed the spot he slapped with a smile on my face. "Good job," he added, the serious look still pulled tight across his face.

"A bunt?" Coach was the next in line for the berating, the bridge of his nose between his fingers as he worked to control himself. Other players clapped me on the back and celebrated. "You're an idiot, Jensen."

"It worked." I shrugged, narrowly avoiding the daggers flying from Dean from across the dugout. He wasn't actually mad he was just putting on his best Captain glare to make me think he was.

"It was a fluke," Coach corrected and tossed his clipboard on the bench behind him. "Handshake," he snapped at everyone. "This conversation isn't finished."

Cael and Van shuffled me out of the dugout, jostling me between them in celebration as we made our way up the small set of stairs to the field.

"What the hell was that?" Van asked, throwing his arm over my shoulder.

"That," I said, my eyes trailing up to where she still stood with her friends. "Do you think Cosy will vouch for me?"

"With her?" Van barked out a loud laugh that turned his cheeks red. "There's not a chance you ever get with that, Jensen. You're good, but you aren't that fucking good." He pressed his hand to the back of my head and ruffled up my hair even more than it already was.

"Best let that one die and be grateful that play worked or you'd be single *and* a benchwarmer for the rest of the season," Cael joked, jogging up to get ahead of us and waving to some people in the crowd.

"The second one might still be a possibility," Josh said, sauntering past me with his arms crossed over his chest and his hat low on his brow line.

My eyes trailed up to the stand as I stood in the back of the line to shake hands with a very sour NYU team. Cosy lifted her arm in the air and tapped her wrist like she was wearing a watch as her eyes drifted to the smallest blonde shuffling from her seat to the end of the aisle.

Shit.

I was going to miss my only shot at getting her number. I pushed in front of Van and dodged my way through a few bodies, shaking random hands and offering 'good game' to those who made eye contact until I was closer to the front of the line right behind Dean who took his sweet time to talk to Colhan about the play. I interrupted with a stupid smile and patted him on the shoulder.

"Rough end to a good game buddy, catch you later," I blurted in a string of words that all rolled together at the end as I ran back through the huddle of players to the edge of the field.

"Hey!" I called out as she reached the stairs and my breath caught in my chest when she looked over her shoulder at me. "Where are you going?" I asked her and she paused on the step. "Come here." I called her back down.

"I'm okay here," she said, a tiny smirk playing on her perfect lips.

"You never gave me your name!" I linked my fingers around the barrier that separated the stands from the field. Her friends, including Cosy, were giggling around her and I could feel my heart creeping into my throat with every second that passed as the stadium emptied.

"When you figure it out, come find me," she said, shoving her hands into the pockets of her jacket. Her dark waves hung over her shoulder and I wanted to tug on the chunky pieces of hair that curled wildly around her heart-shaped face.

"What about your number, at least give me that so I can text you my guess!" I tried again, my feet lifting off the grass.

She shrugged her cute little shoulders at me, the smile growing as she drove me insane with her teasing. "I didn't bring my phone," she said and hissed something at the brunette behind her as she offered up a phone.

"That's a shame," I said, licking my bottom lip. I gripped the barrier tighter just trying to keep her here by any means necessary. I looked around and took a second to mull over my options... She never took her eyes off me but I could feel her starting to retreat. Whatever game we were playing, I was about to lose.

And I hated losing.

"Wait!" I said as she went to step up behind Cosy. I roughly tugged on my jersey until it came loose over my head and ran to the dugout.

"What the fuck are you doing now?" Arlo grumbled as I snatched the permanent marker from the clipboard and jogged out. I climbed over the barrier and ran up the stairs completely out of breath and half naked with my jersey in my fingers.

"Here," I scribbled my number across it with my name and held it out to her. "Now you can text me when you start to miss me."

She looked down at it, her tongue playing nervously with one of her sharp top teeth as her brows pinched together.

"What makes you so sure I'll miss you?" She asked.

"Take the jersey..." I held it up to her, using the railing to lean forward. "*Please.*"

Her lips twitch in amusement, "Only because you're embarrassing yourself groveling like this."

"You'll *know* when I'm groveling," I said, I let my eyes trace the expanse of her skin, stopping on the little sliver of skin above the jeans she wore. She cleared her throat and my eyes flickered up to her lips. "Use the number, you owe me a date."

She nodded, holding the jersey up as she backed away up the stairs after her friends and out of sight. I stayed on the stairs for a second, smiling like an idiot before my name was shouted for the hundredth time that evening.

"Locker room!" Coach glared, "now."

"Coming Coach," I hollered back and jogged down the stairs toward him.

Delta was packed as we all found spots on the ratty furniture in the living room. Todd was losing in Mario Kart to Ella who was barely paying attention to her controller as she talked to Zoey about something.

"What's she like?" I kicked Van with my sneaker and sat forward on the couch. He pressed his lips to his beer and smiled over at me, it was bright and mischievous, and made me feel like I was being left out of some secret.

"Adeline?" He said, distracted by the way Zoey was stepping over people to get to him.

"God, she would have the prettiest name." I leaned into the sound of it and if I thought about her long enough I could smell the warm flowery scent of her perfume in my nose. "She plays rugby right, with your sister?"

"Yeah, and she's out of your league," Van said, his hand wrapping around Zoey's tiny throat to gently pull her deeper onto his lap for a kiss. I took his sudden interest in his girlfriend as a cue to leave the issue alone but my mind wouldn't stop wandering to her.

"Earth to Jenny!" Cael tossed an empty can at me. I swatted it away at the last second and downed the rest of my own before throwing it back. A few people groaned as the can sprayed the foamy bottom around the living room as it flew through the air.

"What?" I ignored them all and slid off the couch to the floor, gagging when my hand hit something sticky. "Do the Delta guys ever clean?" I grumbled and moved closer to Cael.

Clementine handed me another beer with a soft smile.

"Thanks," I said, cracking it.

"What's wrong with you?" Cael asked over the intense booming of music, "you won the game today. You'll be in the highlights for at least a month with that bunt."

"Hey M-Clem," I corrected. It was still weird calling her by her real name after we had been addressing her by Mary. She perked up, her brown eyes giving me their full attention. "What do you know about Adeline, she plays for the Hillcats."

"Adeline Sarah," she said, ignoring Cael's protests not to get into it with me. "I don't know a lot about rugby but her name is in constant circulation. She's one of the faster wingers on the team."

"Anything else?" I asked her but she just shook her head.

"That's all I got, sorry Jensen," she said, her voice sincere before Cael distracted her with his mouth. I sighed, curling my knee up and looking around the packed living room. Ella had successfully beaten Todd and was on her knees flirting with Arlo. Dean was sunken into an old chair and Josh was perched on the side engaged in hushed conversations.

"Hey you wanna go get wasted and do illegal shit?" Todd asked me in passing but I just shook my head. I wanted company that didn't smell like day-old beer and sweat.

I wanted Adeline.

SARAH

Kaia chucked a ball at me from my left and I hurled it back to her in a smooth spiral motion. She followed the pattern of our drill, pushing off her right foot and moving in a one eighty behind me to toss the ball from my right.

I stumbled on the grab, and it bounced wildly in my hands before I gained control and threw the ball into the dirt with a frustrated grumble. "I can't take it from the right." I ran my hands over the tight braids that held my dark hair in place and squatted down on the balls of my cleats.

"Coach said to run it until our fingers are numb," Kaia warned but she rolled across the grass in a somersault and flopped on the ground next to me with a smile. "You know that the Bears run wide right with their defense, the pocket is on the right, we throw right. You have to get it down before Friday."

"Just let me swap with Sunday, she can take right, I'll take left wide." I laid back in the grass and stared up at the clouds. Not that I didn't want to perfect my skills, it was that I was wholeheartedly distracted for the first time in my entire life. And worse, it was by a boy.

"Good luck getting Sunny to agree to that," Kaia huffed, "unless you're prepared to get a lesson in karmic intervention and how switching is bad luck..." She rolled her head to the side to look at me. "It's not the pass bugging you," she poked at the open wound that festered from my distraction. "It's the *Catcher*."

"Am I that transparent?" I clutched my chest and looked over at her finally.

Kaia smiled brightly, a little lopsided, and her bottom lip jutted out in the sweetest way. I sighed, knowing I was *exactly* that see through.

"Hey Minty." Rhea came across the field in her gear, the shorts she wore stretched tightly around her strong thighs. "You got that extra tape around?" She asked and I pointed to my duffle by the benches. "Thanks baby," she smiled at me and jogged in the other direction.

I got the nickname Minty one season after making the highlight reel for hitting a girl so hard the gum she forgot to spit out went flying across the pitch mid-game. It just stuck. I couldn't complain much, it wasn't the worst of the nicknames that had been given on the Hillcats over the years. They used to call one girl '*dumpster*'.

"What the fuck is this?" Rhea called out. She was Reaper, and for a good reason. She was like a bullet train of death on the field. Big *and* fast.

"Oh, God." I wanted to disappear into the grass.

"You put it in your practice kit?" Kaia lost it laughing when Rhea held up the white home jersey with Jensen's number written across the back shoulder. "Stupid, stupid girl with a stupid, stupid crush," Kaia said with a shake of her head. "No one can save you now."

"Is this like *the* guy?" Rhea chucked the jersey at me and I rolled it up in my hands before looking at the number on the back. I set it in my lap and nodded as she sat down in front of us and threw the roll of tape to Kaia who was already crawling into a knelt position to help.

"Which one of you told her about that?" I asked as Kaia handed me the tape roll. She tore off a piece and started to tape Rhea's knee to give support. I mindlessly ripped off similar length pieces.

"How dare you expect Sunny to keep a secret," Rhea said, and kicked my cleat with her own. "Spill."

"He's a guy, he's cute," I said, picking at the tape and not making eye contact as I fought to keep my voice neutral.

"The bullshit pouring from her lips right now," Rhea scoffed and slapped Kaia on the shoulder. "You're beet red and can't make eye contact!"

"It's Jensen," Kaia said.

"Snitch," I hissed.

Kaia laughed, unbothered by the insult and continued to press the tape flat to Rhea's tanned skin. When she was finished she looked down at the jersey in the grass.

"You have to call him eventually," she said, "you made a bet and lost."

"Wait back up," Rhea said with a smile, "a bet?"

"She bet him that he couldn't pull off a game-winning run with a bunt and she *lost*." Kaia pushed the jersey closer to me. "And when he tried to get her name and number, she froze up like a deer in headlights."

"I did not," I defended myself.

Kaia's breath quickened and her eyes widened like she was nervous.

"Shut up." I shoved her shoulder and set the tape down. "I don't have time for that kind of shit," I said simply. "I need to focus on this, on the team."

"The team needs to focus on getting you a date," Kaia argued.

"Didn't I tell you to shut up?" I laughed.

"I'm a terrible listener," Kaia said.

"Have you texted him?" Sunday joined the conversation, standing with her arms crossed behind Rhea.

"No," I said, "a pretty boy is not a priority right now you guys."

"You're selling him short," Kaia purred, "he's fucking gorgeous."

"Unhelpful," I frowned at her and she flashed a wide smile that crinkled at the corners of her eyes. *He in fact was the most beautiful boy I'd ever seen.*

"So you're just going to leave him hanging?" Rhea pushed off the grass with her fingers and rolled into a stretch that would warm her thighs and calves.

"Do you think he's a *hanger?*" Kaia whispered, and used her hands to mimic a dick swinging between her legs.

"Easy way to turn a six into a ten." Sunday noted.

"He's at least an eight," Kaia sounded offended for me.

"He'd be cuter blonde." She shrugged her tiny shoulders. Sunday was built for speed. She was the only player on the team faster than me, *even though Kaia would argue against that with her dying breath,* her legs made up eighty percent of her body and it showed. When she found a pocket it was very rare that the opposing team caught her before she scored a try.

"Not everyone wants to date someone that would pass for their sibling, Sunday," Kaia clipped at her.

"Ew," Sunday pretended to gag. "Whatever. Text him, he's cute and from what I've heard all those baseball boys fuck like animals."

"She's right," Kaia said. "Last summer, when me and Christian were on that break, I got drunk and fucked Louis, the second basemen?"

"I remember..." I said to her with a sigh.

"You think dirty talk is hot? Wait until you hear it in a different language," Kaia faked a dramatic moan.

"What does that have to do with me?" I swallowed tightly, staring down at the jersey. I tried to hide it but the memory of him jogging up the stairs, sweaty and glistening under the lights of the stadium, was burned into my brain. Every muscle tight from overuse and his stomach taut from breathing heavy.

I couldn't forget the sight even if I tried.

"You, out of any of us, need a good *dicking*," Kaia said.

I looked to the other girls for help but Rhea clearly agreed and Sunday was spaced out on something in the distance.

"Repeat after me." Rhea waved her hand in a lazy circle in front of me. "Call him, fuck him, ghost him," she said.

That wasn't exactly my style.

"It hurts no one," Kaia said, "but you will hurt my feelings if you don't at least find out what's under those ball pants."

"For science," Sunday said with a smile.

"Yeah, science!" Kaia raised both hands in the air.

"Screw every one of you," I said, "we have to get back to practicing before Coach loses her shit." I pushed out of the grass, picking up the jersey with me. I left Kaia and Rhea gossiping to put it back in my duffle at the edge of the field.

"You're still stumbling into that pass, Sarah," Coach wandered over to me with her hands in her pockets. "One, two, step into it." She mimicked the movements, "breathe and be ready for the ball."

"You make it sound easier said than done, maybe I do have my limits?" I questioned.

"I don't believe that and neither do you," she scowled at me and her bright blue eyes glared at me until I nodded in agreement. "Go, practice until—"

"My fingers are numb, yeah, yeah." I cut her off and backed away from the bench to rejoin the team. I flexed my hands, shaking them out as I went back to running drills with Kaia. After an hour or two, I started to get it down, *one, two, step into it.* I pocketed the ball from the right with more confidence and pushed off my left foot into a hearty sprint. We did it over and over again until we couldn't breathe and sweat poured down our faces.

"I'm done," Kaia called time out. "I could throw that pass in my sleep if I had to."

"I still couldn't catch it in mine, but it's better." I placed the ball down and tried to convince myself.

I looked around and realized that it was just her and I left on the field and the sun was hanging low in the sky. The frustration was quick to mount because in the silence and slowed movements I realized that the second I pushed his stupid smile from my thoughts—my focus returned.

But there he was, like a cricket in the dark.

Fuck.

"I'm going to go shower, I have a date tonight." Kaia swung her bag over her shoulder and made her way into the building adjacent to our practice pitch. The Shore Center for Athletes was newer, made of glass and navy steel beams that matched most of the other buildings that kept popping up around Harbor.

It was insane to think about how much they owned but I had no complaints, they kept us supplied with gear, a well-kept field and whatever support we needed to play the game. And all I ever wanted was to play rugby.

I sat down on the bench, digging through my bag. I pulled out my phone and then the jersey and laid it across my knee. It bothered me how neat his handwriting was and how quickly my mouth got dry at the thought of him.

My phone lit up and the background of my girls mocked me. Maybe they were right? I needed to relax and who was I to deny a hot guy if he wanted to help me do that...

It could just be fun, *temporary.*

I stared at my phone trying to think of a way to start the conversation knowing that didn't make me sound pathetic and needy. Which I wasn't but the way my heart was racing argued that I was a little nervous.

"Just do it you coward," I cursed myself and started typing.

> **Have you figured out my name yet?**

I went to set my phone down and it vibrated in my hand.

> **It took you four days and six hours to start missing me Adeline.**

> **That hurts.**

A traitorous smirk formed on my face, and I couldn't push down the tingling feeling that flickered across my chest. I forgot how much I hated that feeling. Uncontrollable and it made me giggly with anticipation. It would have only taken him a few asks to figure it out but the effort was noted and made me feel special that he was still trying.

> **My friends call me Addy.**

> **I don't want to be your friend.**

He was smooth, I would give him that.

> **How does tomorrow sound?**

I laughed, he was also eager. I sighed, tapping my thumb against the screen and trying to come up with a response that kept him on his toes.

> **I have practice.**

> **After?**

"Adding *persistent* to the list," I said to no one but myself. I swiped out of our messages to give myself a moment to think without his words staring up at me. It was like I could see his expression, it was the same one from the game.

His big brown eyes staring up at me, practically begging me to take his number with a goofy *kissable* grin on his face. I cursed myself for wanting to know if he was good at it, he had to be with lips like that. My mind wandered to all the inappropriate places he could put them. My shoulders dropped and I laid back on the bench to look at the sky, maybe relaxing was easier than I thought it would be.

> **I play a real sport, pretty boy. It's not all flirting and showboating.**

> **You're mean today.**

> **I like it.**

I pressed the phone to my chest and pulled my bottom lip between my teeth as I squealed into the chilly air. It was becoming obvious that he was ready for anything I threw at him and he was enjoying every second of it.

> **I'll get that date eventually, Adeline.**

SARAH

JENSEN:
We have a game tonight.

Too bad, it's hair washing day.

What kind of shampoo do you use?

That's creepy.

No it's not, I want to know what you smell like.

His texts stop for a second and it's almost like I can hear his realization as the little dots pop back up at the bottom of the screen.

Okay that did sound creepy but...

I think it's some blue bottle, it's Amika.

I don't even know why I told him that, maybe the sick need to feel something took over. Even if it meant being stalked by some cocky baseball player. I was tempted to google the statistics of baseball players being horrible people. Did I really want to know if the cute guy that was flirting with me about what kind of shampoo I used was a stalker? Or did I just want to be stalked because it meant someone was giving me attention.

"Stop chewing your nails." Tyson leaned over from his desk with a dirty look on his face.

I was going to argue with him but to do so I had to take my fingers out of my mouth. I set my phone in my lap and spun in my chair to face him.

"Talk to me," he leaned back on his own. It was hard to concentrate because he was wearing a vintage band shirt with two naked women riding a motorcycle on it today that literally demanded all the attention in the room.

Tyson had been working with me as an app developer at Clarity for two years and we had trauma bonded over bad dates and even worse bosses. I rarely ever saw him outside of the office. His desk was covered in weird trinkets he found thrifting and his wardrobe was made up of click bait vintage t-shirts and obnoxiously bright Hawaiian button-ups. He was made up of all the weirdest things, a curly ginger mullet, dark green eyes and more freckles than a normal person with a crooked smile and a dramatic flare.

Work would be boring without him and he proved it every time he opened his mouth.

I held out my phone to him with the messages open.

"Addy there's like *hours* of interactions here." He scrolled through it and with each swipe his big green eyes widened even more. "Who is this guy?"

"He plays for the college baseball team," I said, taking my phone back.

"Ooh, a younger man," he smirked. "You know, in two years of working together you've never once brought up a boy. I was starting to get worried."

My phone vibrated again and I looked down to see it's just my brother making sure that I remembered about dinner next week.

"Oh you're in deep," Tyson hummed and leaned forward with his mouth half open. "Tell me more."

"We have to get the pitch out before Friday, we don't have time for this," I reminded him.

He rolled his eyes, turning around in his chair, typed on his computer for a total of three minutes before turning back to me. "Pitch sent."

"Tyson!" I gasped. "There was—"

"Nothing to be done with it, you were being a perfectionist again, the client will love it." He brushed off my worry, "now tell me about the cute younger man."

"I don't actually know a lot," I confessed.

"You're killing me," he groaned and dragged his chair across the floor to my computer. He pushed me out of the way and started to type things into google. "What's his name? You have him on your phone as J."

"Uh Jensen, he's the Catcher..."

"The Catcher?" Tyson turned to look at me, "Those boys are good with their hands."

I laughed, "How the hell would you know that?"

"Freshman year, I had a stint with one. Hot sex, but he was stupider than a captivity-bred panda bear," he scoffed.

"There he is. M. Jensen." He brought up his roster stats and the picture that went with it. "Holy shit, Addy..." he fanned himself playfully. "Is he Greek?"

"I don't fucking know, Tyson. That's the problem," I said between a bout of laughter.

"Okay..." he shrugged and cracked his knuckles, "more research."

He continued to type away on the computer, bringing up different tabs as he found more information on him. With every article it was becoming apparent that he was good, *really* good. He had a shot to go pro if he wanted but he was still playing college level for some reason.

Why wouldn't he take the chance?

"Oh look!" He nudged me, "that's where I know that handsome face from. His mother."

The website was for a bed and breakfast chain that had over one hundred and thirty locations across the United States. The picture on the main page was of an older, beautiful woman with a thick bundle of dark curls. A man with salt and pepper hair and a softer look to him alongside a younger-looking Jensen, who stood beside the woman with a mirrored smile.

"They're like *The Jensens*," Tyson emphasized. "That's one of the most badass women in Harbor. By the age of sixteen she had already opened the first location right here in Harbor."

"Yeah, I know the place. My Dad loves staying there when he's in town," I nodded. It was down past main street.

"It was a heritage building that she won in an estate sale bid and redid on her own while going to school, and raising a brand new baby." He read the bio below the picture and my interest peaked. "Holy shit, she's only forty... I think I'm in love."

"Shut up," I laughed. "Does it say anything about Jensen in there?"

"Nothing really, his father helps run the business, and it just says they're proud of their son for all he's accomplished in life so far," he shrugs.

"Does he have an Instagram?" I asked finally and Tyson held up his hand before switching tabs to another page. There wasn't much on it, and for the majority it was all shitty taken photos of him and his friends. But there was one that caught my eye, "that one," I said, pointing to it.

Tyson brought it up and it was a photo of him in a graduation gown smiling with his arms around his parents. "He's graduated?"

"That can't be right," I said, "how is he still playing baseball?"

Tyson shrugged, "looks like a masters in business... maybe?" He titled his head to try to read the certificate he was holding but it was too small and too blurry even zoomed in. "He's a smart Greek God? I don't know what you got yourself into but God damn am I glad to be along for the ride."

"So we're going right?" Kaia was laid across my couch with her feet propped up over the arm and an intense look on her face. Her hair was braided back and it made her usually sharp, beautiful features blinding.

"I don't think so," I shook my head and closed my laptop on the island. My studio apartment wasn't exactly spacious but it was enough for me. The exposed brick wall and hardwood floors had called to me the first time I saw them. It was now decorated with neon signs and weird art that framed in a tv that hung across from the long, thrifted sectional in the center of the loft.

"This is bullshit, why are you fighting it so hard?" She rolled to sit up so she could really glare at me and I avoided the harsh gaze by grabbing a beer from the fridge.

"I'm not fighting anything," I laughed, popping the top and flicking the bottlecap at her. "I'm just not ready to become some brainless bat bunny because a cute guy smiled at me."

"There's literally nothing wrong with a good brainless fuck from an *extremely* attractive baseball player, you're just insulting a demographic to make yourself feel better about being a coward!" Kaia declared.

"Alright alright, calm down Killer," I said, raising my hands in surrender. "What the hell has gotten into you?"

"I'm pretty sure Christian is cheating on me," she blurted and I instantly handed her my beer as I sank on the couch beside her. "He's been doing that *I'm working late. I can't come over* bullshit, and he bailed on the last three dates."

She and Christian had been together for years but they had the worst relationship I'd ever seen and yet...

"Why the hell do you entertain that?" I asked her as she chugged back the beer.

"Because he's sweet when he wants to be, and it's the only love I've ever had. It's about commitment okay." She shrugged and set down the empty bottle.

"Who's the coward now?" I raised an eyebrow at her.

"I'm not just going to quit. I've been at it too long," she said.

"No one is going to call you a quitter," I said to her.

"I will," she argued. "Stop deflecting the conversation, we're going to the game tonight."

"Won't that give him hope?" I asked and leaned over to rest on the back of the couch with my shoulder and head.

"We're actively trying to give him hope, we need to get you laid." She smiled and pushed off the couch, "come on you need to get cleaned up and you need shorter shorts."

I grumbled and followed her toward my closet. She helped me clean up a little, and redid my hair with some clips before she disappeared and returned with the jersey.

"No." I shook my head. "Absolutely not, that's *too* much hope."

"Put it on."

I knew I wasn't going to win the argument so I slipped the jersey over the tight black cropped t-shirt and did the middle button up. I hated how cute I felt in it and how proud Kaia looked when she surveyed the finished product.

We took a cab over to the stadium, stealing two seats higher up in the stands tucked between some drunk college students and a few girls who kept giggling about Cael Cody. Kaia handed me a bag of cola bottles and I ripped them open, popping one between my teeth nervously.

"He can't even see you up here, relax." Kaia leaned over with a piece of licorice pressed to her tongue.

The game started and despite how much I wanted to put on a cool and collected front, the second I saw him that tingling warm feeling blistered across my chest and my fingers curled around the bag as I shoved my hands between my thighs to keep still.

"It's like the sunshine makes him prettier," Kaia swooned and I giggled because she wasn't wrong. It licked at his exposed muscles and made his tawny skin glow and highlighted every dark swipe of permanent ink that covered him. "How dare you deny that," she scolded under her breath as the game started.

I finally relaxed going into the bottom of the fifth inning. Starting to think that Kaia was right that we could make it through the game without being spotted. When Jensen came up to bat and knocked the ball out of the park with a resounding crack that echoed over the crowds screaming, everyone jumped up in excitement as Jensen carried himself to first. His head was turned up in the crowd and for a second I thought he wasn't looking too hard but he shifted, jogging backwards to second base and pointed directly at me.

My cheeks turned a shade of red that burned at the touch as Kaia wrapped her hands around them and pulled our noses together.

"Are you convinced yet?" She asked loudly over the sounds of cheers. "Because that man is down bad!"

I gripped her wrists as she squeezed my face and smiled at her. I was screwed and I liked it.

JENSEN

I was still riding the high of the home run from the night before and even more so the look on Adeline's face in the crowd when she realized I knew she was there. I had been checking with Susanna, bribing her with pastries, to see if anyone used their Harbor Sports card to purchase tickets. It was a program that the Shores created to help the athletes support each other. We got discounted tickets to all the games, NCAA and professional, as long as they were home games.

Kaia Keegan had purchased two tickets that morning.

When I stepped out onto the field my eyes went directly to her but she was too busy shoving candy in her mouth and laughing with Kaia to even notice. It wasn't until the home run hit that I made sure she knew that I saw her.

"Mom?" I closed the door behind me, calling out as I kicked off my shoes.

"We're in here!" I heard Dad call from the kitchen. I rounded through the living room peeking at the puzzle they were in the middle of before sliding into the kitchen in my socks. "Hey kid," Dad chucked a can of soda at me and I caught it mid air as Mom appeared from the pantry.

"Don't throw soda in my house," she grumbled and set a container of pasta on the counter.

My phone vibrated in my pocket and I pulled it out.

> **UNKNOWN:**
> What are you wearing?

"Kai?" I looked up at the sound of her voice.

"Sorry, I think one of the guys gave my phone number out, I keep getting weird perverted texts..." I set my phone down, disappointed that it wasn't Adeline.

"Is vodka sauce ok? We ran out of the other stuff you like," she asked, holding up a jar of homemade sauce.

"I don't care Mom, anything you make is delicious." I looked over at Dad who was working on something on his laptop. "How many pieces is the new puzzle?" I asked.

"Ten thousand," Mom answered, putting a pot on the stove. "It's a picture of Niagara Falls your grandmother sent so every piece is just blue," she grumbled.

Grandma lived in Ontario, which is where my Mom was from but they moved to the states when she was little and Grandma moved back after Grandpa died a few years ago.

"I swear she sends those just to piss you off," I laughed and popped the tab on the can.

"Language," Mom said and I rolled my eyes at her. "What was this about your number, do we need to get it switched?"

"No," I said too fast and she looked over from the pot with her usually bright brown eyes narrowed on me with the token Mom glare.

"Out with it," she demanded and put her hands on her hips. Her head cocked to the side and she looked at me. It wasn't out of the ordinary for Mom to read me like a book, but I felt like it might be a little soon for me to be discussing a crush with her. *Is that weird?* I paused, chewing the inside of my mouth when the smile crept up on her face. I know I'm in trouble. "What's her name?"

"Huh?" I tried to play it off with a shrug.

"I know that look," Mom crept forward.

"What look?"

"Every single crush you've ever confessed about has resulted in you turning a funny shade of pink and chewing a hole in your lip. What's her name?" She asked me again with a soft smile on her face. *She was too good.*

"Adeline," I said, leaning against the counter.

"That's pretty," Dad responded without looking up and pushed his glasses up on his nose.

"You should invite her for dinner," Mom said, going back to her sauce and that would be simple enough... If I could even get Adeline to agree to a first date.

"Uh," I huffed as my phone rang again. I silenced the unknown number and set it back down. "Well..."

"Well?" She lowered her voice.

"I haven't exactly taken her out on a date yet?" I confessed and the laughter that exploded from Dad turned my cheeks pink. "I'm trying okay, Dad you don't have to mock me. I'm not exactly smooth, and she's..." I blew out some air and smiled, "she's everything."

"Malachi," Mom used my full name and I knew I was in trouble. She set the spoon down and turned the stove lower without taking her eyes off me.

"I'm working on it," I said with a small groan as I slid into the chair next to Dad's. Mom was about to rip into me when Dad intervened. "I gave her my number, told her to call me... I've been trying to get her to go on a date but it's like she enjoys saying no."

"You're sure she's interested?" Mom asked, raising her eyebrow.

"Very," I hummed. "She's flirting and it's fun but that's as far as I get with her. It's infuriating," I laughed softly.

"You make it sound like she's homework, that's no way to get a woman," Dad scoffed, pushing his glasses down on his nose.

"I'm sorry '*man who knocked up his girlfriend at sixteen*'. It's frowned upon now to trap a woman in a marriage," I joked with him and he glared at me.

"I was in love with your father long before he gave me you," Mom added to the conversation, "accident or not."

"It wasn't an accident, I knew what I was doing." Dad feigned his intentions with a smile.

"Sure Dad," I laughed at him. "She's too smart for me," I confessed. "Everything I say she has a better response, quicker, more intelligent. It drives me nuts."

"That's a crush kid," Dad snorted.

"She's stubborn, and funny too. Every time I think I have her figured out she flips the script on me." I fidget with the soda can.

Mom turned with a smile on her face and leaned across the counter.

"What?" I asked her when she just stared at me.

"The home run," Mom noted, "that was for her?" Of course Mom was watching, even when she couldn't be there, it was always up on her laptop or coming out of the radio.

"*That* was because I could." I looked up with a smug grin on my face.

"And the bunt last week?" Dad grumbled under his breath.

"Alright that one *was* for her," I admitted.

"Is she pretty?" Mom asked me finally.

"I can't stop thinking about her," I said a little quieter as the confidence rushed out of me at the thought of her sharp smile and beautiful hazel eyes.

"You know your father had no game either," Mom teased and Dad scowled.

"Yes I did," he argued. He ran his hands through his hair and puffed his chest. "You were smitten."

"No you didn't," she shook her head. "And I tried to maim you with a hammer more than once." She winked at him. "But he showed up when I needed him. For all my intelligence I've never been able to figure out a power tool and if he hadn't been insistent on helping me with the estate, it would have never become the Roost."

"I Stockholm-ed her," Dad joked.

"I don't know if that's the term you're looking for, Honey." Mom shook her head.

"Drove you crazy until you loved me back?" Dad said it like it was the obvious definition of the word.

"Okay maybe?" She agreed.

"You were conceived in the bones of the very first Roost." Dad said, with a wink.

"Right on the floor where the lounge is now, very awkwardly... so much saw dust..." She scowled and I shook my head.

"You're both being disgusting and you change the story of how I came into the world every time you tell it. Last time it was in the back of Dad's Toyota. So, focus," I said to them both as they spiraled into their little love bubble of nonsense. "Pot is bubbling over." I pointed to the stove and Mom turned to pay closer attention to it.

"Intelligent women like to feel seen," Dad whispered, leaning closer to me so Mom couldn't hear him. "They seem complicated but they're not. Just take your time and show her that you see her."

I looked over at Dad and he winked, I barely understood what he meant but I saw Adeline, or at least I thought I did. Maybe I just needed to work harder. I thought about it the entire time we ate dinner, floating through the conversation until we moved to the living room. I crawled under a terribly knitted blanket my father made while he and Mom argued about what movie to watch.

Eventually he let her win and she put on Jurassic Park. The two of them went back to their puzzle and I pulled my phone out of my pocket. The last messages from Adeline were about her favorite food. Every answer she gave was like playing Russian roulette. I never knew if she was giving me an answer just to see my reaction or if she was being serious.

> **Rodeo food**

> **Do we even have Rodeos in Rhode Island?**

She had left me to guess what the hell she meant and I could only assume that it was fried food on sticks and cotton candy. It only made me like her more, infuriatingly so.

> **So the first date is the boardwalk?**

I typed and deleted it. That was stupid, she didn't want to be told where to go. She enjoyed surprises, that was apparent enough. I could try to cook for her but that would end in disaster. Between my mom and Mrs. Cody, I'd never quite gotten the hang of it. I burned toast at the Nest so often that the guys had started to assume that's how I liked to eat it.

Shit. Okay. Don't let her see me sweat.

> **Favorite Movie?**

I asked, looking up at the TV that hung above the massive fireplace. I didn't expect her to answer right away but my phone vibrated like she had been waiting on my message.

> **Speed**

> **Sandra Bullock?**

> **Keanu Reeves in a tactical vest should be studied.**

I laughed at my phone and my mom looked over at me suspiciously, her glasses on the edge of her nose.

> **Lake House Keanu and Sandra are superior.**

> **Did you just rom-com me?**

> **It's just the simple truth.**

More often than not my Mom's insane collection of movies came in handy. I grew up in front of the T.V. It was our favorite pastime. Girls never saw it coming, the idea that a cocky baseball player has extensive knowledge of romance movies. It's a golden goose. Mom would kill me if she knew I was weaponizing our quality time but it was for a good cause.

> **Cotton candy and Keanu Reeves it is.**

> **You'd spend our first date with another man, wow.**

> **You can come if you want? Tomorrow at 7**

> **Looks like it'll just be you and Keanu. I bet he uses tongue.**

> **Rain check?**

> **Maybe.**

I was going to go insane. I would ask her out a hundred times, it wasn't about that. I could handle the avoidance, the flirting, the teasing. What infuriated me was missing a girl I had never even touched. My brain had started to fantasize all the trouble we could get into and it was twisting down into my consciousness. I couldn't shake Adeline. I shoved my phone back into my pocket and slid down into the chair falling asleep before the movie was even over. Mom shook me awake at some point with a smile on her face.

"You're getting a little big to be carried to bed," she teased.

"You could have least tried," I groaned sarcastically and pushed from the chair. She laughed, patting me on the cheek before starting back to her room. "Hey Mom," I called out quietly to her. "I think I really like this girl."

She turned back to look at me and I knew what she was thinking, *silly little boy*. It was written all over her face, she had never been one for pulling her punches. Especially when it came to me being an idiot.

"You think?" She challenged and wandered back toward me. "Your father tells the story of the first time we met a little differently than I do every single time we tell it but do you want to know the truth?"

"Yeah," I said without hesitation.

"The most attractive thing about your father is he *knew*," she said. "Be certain about her, don't waffle on your decision. She'll see it."

JENSEN

"Take me to tonight's Hillcats game," I bombarded Van in the locker room.

"Good morning to you too, Jenny. How was breakfast, you look particularly fit today, new workout routine?" He angled his massive frame in my direction with a scowl on his face as he stripped from his damp practice gear.

"What?" Mine scrunched up in confusion.

"Making a conversation with a teammate before demanding shit from them is a social norm you dickhead." He laughed and shoved me back playfully with one hand. "This about that girl, isn't it?" He asked, slipping into a clean shirt.

Yes. "Maybe," I said, stepping back as he turned around to face me fully. "Has anyone ever told you how handsome and tall you are?"

Van shook his head with a laugh, "yeah Zoey all the time. You don't have to suck up," he said, clapping a massive hand on my shoulder.

"I don't?" I gave him a confused smile.

"I was going anyway, it'll be nice to have some company. We'll leave the Nest in thirty. And wear a hat." He grabbed his bag and left the locker room without another word.

"Wear a hat..." I mumbled to myself, what the fuck was that supposed to mean? I shoved all my shit in my bag so I could run up the hill to the Nest and get clean clothes. Van would absolutely leave me behind if I wasn't fast enough and I *needed* to see her.

I had never moved up the hill so fast. I slid into a pair of jeans and tossed a t-shirt on before swiping a hat from the dresser. Van was waiting on the steps outside when I finally made it back down the stairs. He looked me over with a scowl.

"You have to keep your hat on, Cosy's rule." He pointed to it.

"Why?" I asked, pulling it down over my head.

"Because, *pretty boy*," he mused, slapping my cheek. "You'll take away from the game and that's rude. If you come, you keep your head down and your mouth shut."

"I can do that," I said, just trying to keep my tone even so he didn't pick up on how excited I was to see Adeline. He stopped just before his truck and turned back to me.

"I'm not your wing man here," he warned me.

"I don't need a wingman, Mitchell." I laughed.

"You're cocky for a man that can't get a date," he joked.

"What about me makes you think I can't get a date?" I looked down, chewing the gum in my mouth with my back teeth, my arms wide covered in dark ink and looked back up at Van. "I'm a single, well educated, tattooed, semi-professional baseball player."

"What's the problem then?" He challenged.

I laughed and tugged the door open, staring at him with a grin on my face, "I'm *picky*."

Van stared at me for a moment, no doubt trying to figure out a jab but he gave up after a moment and said, "you forgot *arrogant idiot*. Try to behave," he added, "and no gum in my truck."

"You keep adding to the rules, how am I supposed to remember them all?" I teased, spitting the gum out and climbing in.

"You're well educated, you'll figure it out," Van chuckled and pulled from the driveway and out onto the street. The drive to the pitch wasn't long and I knew because of the game I wasn't going to get a response out of her, but I checked my phone a hundred times anyways.

The stadium for the Hillcats was a shared space where they played opposite days of the soccer team and alternate weekends with the Lacrosse teams. What I wasn't expecting was how packed the arena was when we arrived.

"People really like rugby..." I said following Van up the steps to the back of the bleachers.

"How have you never been to a game?" Van grumbled, tucking his head down as a group of college girls found seats in front of us.

"Between practice, games, drinking and school?" I shrugged. One of the girls looked back at us, her blue eyes looking me over slowly from top to bottom. I gave her a wink and she melted into a puddle of giggles as she turned back to her friend.

"What didn't you understand about keeping your head down and mouth shut?" Van nudged me.

"I didn't say shit," I said with a weak laugh, smirking at him and leaning against the concrete behind my back. "Who are they playing?"

"The Gators," Van said, handing me his phone. The roster meant nothing to me but my eyes dragged down until I found her name. Adeline Sarah - Number Seven - Winger.

I had no idea what it meant but at least now I knew her number. When the girls came onto the field, I sat up straighter and Van laughed at me but it was easy to ignore his mocking when she stepped onto the field. Her hair was braided back in two thick cords that rested over the shoulders of her navy jersey and I could see the smile on her face from where we were sitting.

"Fuck," I swore with a sharp inhale of air as she spun on the field. The shorts she was wearing rode up on her strong thighs and hugged tightly to every single curve. "Please never leave me behind again," I said to Van, swallowing tightly at the sight of her.

He patted me on the back and leaned forward to come shoulder to shoulder with me. "You have no idea, Jenny," he laughed.

It didn't take long for me to figure out what he was talking about. Once the game started, so did the competitiveness. They were fast, *really* fast. I'd never seen the kind of speed some of them produced. It was clear that they relied heavily on Kaia Keegan, Sunday Black and Adeline. The three of them were unstoppable in the pockets. If one managed to sneak by, the other two were quick to produce a line behind them as they pushed down the field.

It was rough Every time one of them took a hit my whole body tensed as I waited for them to rise. The game itself moved quickly, there was barely a whistle blown and all of the preconceived notions of how rugby is played went out the window. Van cheered his sister on with every person she wrapped up and put down into the dirt. It was impressive to see players of their size flying around that quickly. The endurance involved was practically witchcraft. I spent the entire game in awe of them.

I flinched forward as Adeline was tossed into the dirt, her body contorting backward to present the ball to Sunday who was giving Cosy the space to wrestle with the opposing teams player in the pile up. The play moved on and it took Adeline a moment longer to push from the turf and orient herself on the field. A streak of blood poured from her eyebrow down to her jaw line but she didn't stop moving. Her legs carried her with precision down the field, darting around other players until she was able to back up Sunday.

The ball transferred hands quicker than a blink and Adeline goose-stepped out of danger to her left and into the scoring zone. Darting around to the middle of the posts to press the ball to the ground.

"Breathe," Van slapped my knee and I inhaled. "They're tougher than any of us, that hit probably tickled."

He could have been right but it didn't mean that my heart wasn't in my throat just watching her get knocked around like that by players twice her size.

"Shit," I winced as the action instantly started again. There wasn't a moment to breathe between the plays and the ball bounced out of bounds. Adeline stood on the line, watching her teammates position parallel to her in a line of four. Rhea Drake, the back of the line was quite possibly the biggest woman I'd ever laid eyes on. Pure muscle, she had to be close to six-two and she lifted Sunday off the ground like she weighed nothing. Pushing her into the air to snag the ball as Adeline reached for the pass over her head into the field toward them.

She slipped back into play and within seconds her and Kaia were racing down the field side by side just trying to avoid hits from the opposing team.

"Are you serious about her?" Van asked a moment later. The loud buzzer that ended the game echoed around the arena and the Hillcats came together in celebration of their hard fought win. Covered in grass stains and freshly blossomed bruises, they had more than earned it.

Adeline tilted her chin to the sky, her hands hanging loose at her sides. Her jersey was rumpled and dirty, her face covered in mud and dirt, and she looked like an angel. The light from the arena bathed her flushed skin in luster as she took in the win. I'd never been so impressed.

"Yeah." I turned to look at Van.

"Good because chasing after that one is a death wish," he said and I wanted to ask what he meant but he was smiling so it couldn't have been that bad... Van stood from his spot as the arena started to empty.

Chasing. I had never been so desperate for something. I felt like an idiot when my heart rate picked up at the thought of her and *fuck, all I did was think about her.* That day at the stadium, her hair moving around in the wind, hazel eyes highlighted by the setting sun and lips parted as she giggled with her friends. It was like that moment in time was frozen in the forefront of my mind and it burned brighter than any memory before.

Screwed the moment I saw her, and willing to upend everything just to keep that feeling.

The problem was, I was homesick for Adeline.

Homesick for a girl who refused to give me the time of day.

Mother fucker.

I was turning into a fucking simp.

"Stay here," he warned as I went to follow him down the bleachers.

"Will you tell her I'm here?" I asked him as he jogged down the steps and he turned back but only to give me the middle finger before he disappeared out of sight.

"Cool," I huffed and sat back against the concrete. I tossed my hat off and ran my hands through my hair. It had been too long since that first game, I needed Adeline back in my gravity so badly I was starting to feel pathetic.

I pulled my phone out, opened my messages from her and typed out at least four messages before I gave up trying to sound like a total flirt. I leaned forward on my knees and watched as the arena emptied and the staff started to clean and prep for whatever was next.

I pulled up her name on Instagram and scrolled through her feed. She posted one of three things, food, rugby and the most insane photos of herself. Ones that made my mouth dry and feel like I was looking at something private. There was a mirror in her room that showed off the softer tones of her style with pastel comforters and tons of pillows.

The majority of the photos were her body from the shoulders down. Her lengthy form made of tight luscious curves begging to be grabbed and kissed, I shifted on the bench to get comfortable. I wanted to map every inch of her with my lips and teeth. Baggy t-shirts, underwear pulled over her broad hips, her soft stomach demanding attention resting against the band on display more often than not.

My favorite of them all was one of her in her rugby jersey and a pair of small shorts, her hand pressed against her stomach, lifting the jersey just enough to give view of her ass in the mirror. I wanted *her* hands in my hair and her ass in my *hands*. I shifted again, it had been a long time since a girl had made my dick hard with pictures. It was like I had side stepped back through puberty and couldn't control the thoughts that were pumping the blood around in my body.

Fuck.

I zoned out thinking about Adeline pulling my hair and suddenly I needed a cold shower.

"Earth to loverboy," Van called up to me from the bottom of the bleachers. I jumped from my position and cracked my shins against the row of seats in front of me. Van barked out a loud laugh. "Cosy wants dinner, you coming?"

"Just Cosy…" I shook out the pain and took the steps down toward him.

"Take it or walk home," Van said plainly and I shrugged.

"I am kind of hungry," I said and he threw his arm around me.

We waited for her by the truck and she appeared from the arena with a few girls on her tail. Cosy was a girl version of Van, funny, friendly. She was like the big sister none of us asked for but she had always been around. Her burgundy hair was pulled up into a bun and there was a nasty bruise forming on the inside of her arm.

She turned to say goodbye and that's when Adeline stepped out into the light of the parking lot. I straightened out against the truck and Van followed my eyeline to where she talked to his sister quietly. Her hair was damp and loose, covering the bandage over her eyebrow but her smile filled my chest with unbearable warmth.

"You're like a cat in heat, relax," Van started to laugh and slapped my chest.

Adeline swung a busy, heavy looking keychain in her hand and waved bye to Cosy, her eyes scanning over the lot until she found Van first and waved. I held my breath as she spotted me. Her smile turned into a soft smirk, and her cheeks turned a pretty shade of pink.

She stopped in her tracks, staring me down and even though every muscle and nerve in my body was screaming at me to go over to her. I forced myself to play it cool, shrugging one of my shoulders and turning my attention to Cosy as she approached us.

Adeline stood in the corner of my eye line for a moment longer before she shook her head and wandered through the lot to her car.

"Shotgun," Cosy said, pushing me out of the way and climbing into the front of the truck. Usually I'd fight her on it but I didn't care today. I waited another couple of seconds watching Adeline get into her car before I slid across the back seat of the truck.

SARAH

"I don't think you'll need another surgery." Silas Shore dug his fingers into my quad above my knee and I fought to hide the wince as he did. "Stop pretending that doesn't hurt, I'm being rough on purpose," he said, not looking up from my knee in his hands.

Silas was handsome, in that *'wow if I had a thing for an older man'* kind of way. His brown hair was sprinkled with grey here and there and his voice was lower, huskier than most of the other guys around campus.

The Hillcats had lucked out that he was willing to take on more clients. He was a busy guy, anytime I saw him outside the stadium he was rushing around, never having enough time to talk to anyone. But when we sat down in his office he became a different person. Softer, attentive and careful with his clients.

It was clear that his favorite place to be was here.

He was funny too, funnier than he had the right to be.

"Is there pain when you're playing?" He asked, finally looking up as he pushed back from the table and into his chair. He turned to his computer and plugged something in before giving me his attention again.

"It's a contact sport, Doc," I laughed a little, shifting on the edge of the bed as he eyed me knowingly. "A little, but that's par for the course. I can't take a hit without pain."

"I'm more concerned about pain when you're running," he scowled, his eyes darting down the small scar that already sliced my skin from the first surgery.

"Not that I can tell, but usually my adrenaline is so high..." I tugged my bottom lip between my teeth.

"Right," he ran his hand over his face and nodded, clearly trying to come up with a solution. "We're going to start doing cardio during our meeting, here at the stadium. I want to stress test the muscle, I'd rather something go wrong here than out on the field. The staff is good but—" he turned back to the computer to type some more.

"Not snapped muscles good," I joked and he sighed. "Sorry, not funny."

"Remind me of your schedule for the week?" He said with a small stretch of his shoulders to work out the tiny yawn that fell from his lips.

"Wednesday, Friday are games. Practices in between, I work most days until four but I can come by after on Thursday? I can just tell Coach why I'm missing practice... Or Sunday." I offered.

"Sunday doesn't work for me, but Thursday will have to. I'll move some things around and we'll get you in here," he said without looking over at me.

"Thursday works," I said.

"Do you need a note to get out of practice?" He asked me, adjusting in his seat to look at me. I gave him a head shake and a smile. "Alright." He stood from his chair and helped me from the bed, my knee a little sore from his inspection of it. "Careful," he warned, not letting go of my hand until I showed him that it was fine with a tiny hop.

"Do me a favor?" He asked as I collected my bag, I turned to look at him and waited. "Listen to your body," he said, "you've got a massive career ahead of you and I don't want you in the news because you ignored the pain."

"Yes Doc," I said with a phony salute that made him roll his eyes.

"Get out of my office," he groaned and I closed the door behind me.

It was warm out so I took advantage and walked across campus to the Athletics gym housed on the third floor of the main building. I let myself in with my entry card and one quick look around the massive space told me it was pretty quiet inside as I changed into my sneakers. The bulking sweater I wore hung against my thighs just above where my bike shorts cut off around them. I took my time and stretched out all my muscles until I was warm enough to start my circuit.

After the abuse on my knee that morning, I knew it was better to do something that took off the stress but my heart called out for a leg day. Silas echoed in my head and I groaned in annoyance as I slipped my earbuds into my ear and let the music relax my shoulders. I started to jump around on the mat and dance to the beat. I turned around and grabbed a few free weights, tricking my body into wanting to do arms and back instead. The weight felt good in my hands as I curled them close to my chest and tried not to sing the song rushing through my ears.

Working out cleared my head but now every song that played over my earbuds reminded me of Jensen. When I saw him standing there outside the game the urge to text him about it was feral. So I turned off my phone and spent the night working on projects that didn't need my attention. It was the only way to get him out of my head.

I set the weights down after my set leaving them on the mat to move onto the next round. The beauty of an empty gym was that I could wait to clean up after myself until after I was completely finished.

I rotated around a few of the standing machines, working out my shoulders and back until the muscles were begging for a rest. Out of the corner of my eye I saw movement as I wandered back to the mat. I turned to look over my shoulder and shook my head in disbelief.

Jensen was running at a grueling pace on the treadmill against the back wall, his head down and his focus tight. The tattoos he regularly showed off during ball games extended well past his shoulders and over his chest. The swirling ink shone with sweat as his stomach clenched with each step. His dark hair was damp and his chest was heaving and glistening under the bright white gym lights. He had been here for a while and my stupid ass had completely missed the show.

I tripped over the weights I left on the ground, barely catching myself before stumbling across the mat. My skin turned bright red as I turned away from him and back to the long mirror. I sank to the ground, "workout over," I grumbled in shame and kept my head down.

I knelt over on the mat, stretching out my shoulders. I crawled my fingers across the fabric and sank down on my knees until I could feel the stretch in my lower back. I shifted my head to the side peeking over to where he ran.

I reached out and pulled my bag closer, digging out my phone and texted him.

> **What are you doing?**

Part of me didn't expect a response, usually when I was in the gym I left my phone off but I couldn't resist knowing. All of the information that I was able to dig up on Jensen pointed to him being a fuckboy. Cosy had said he was quiet and polite but everyone was able to behave in someone else's house. With family, in front of strangers. That wasn't the Jensen I saw at the ball game and it certainly wasn't the one I was drooling over.

The naked jogging session was going to take over as the wet dream of the week. I woke twice last week in a pile of sweat dreaming about his ass in baseball pants *and* his ass out of baseball pants. I was starting to think Kaia was right and I needed to get laid. I hated when she was right, she'd never let me live it down when she found out I was dreaming about being rough housed by Jensen.

Fuck.

I took another peek to see if he had seen my text and when I looked over he was staring down at his phone with a smile on his face. His pace had slowed to a lazy jog and all his muscles were tight from the exertion. I pressed deeper into the mat in a pathetic attempt to quell the tingling buzz between hips and the rampant butterflies in my stomach.

My phone vibrated and I moved embarrassedly fast to flip it over.

> **Cardio. Alone.**

> **Alone?**

I responded with questionable speed. I needed to relax before I invited him to come fuck me in the middle of the gym like some frat boy without self control. I tapped the mat with my finger, at least he hadn't seen me yet.

> **Alone. The cardio I want to be doing is across the gym stretching out her shoulders and staring.**

Fuck, fuck, fuck.

I looked over at him and he was staring at me with a smug smile on his face. Pieces of his hair stuck to his forehead and he leaned back making the already impressive expanse of his shoulders broader. I turned my head away quickly, typing up *'please tell me that every inch of you is that impressive.'* Before deleting it with a frustrated groan, changing it to something more dismissive in a pathetic attempt to seem less desperate.

> **I plead the fifth.**

> **Not sure that works in this instance. Is it at least a good show?**

I could say no, I could string him along and destroy his ego with one foul blow. But I was caught, red handed. Ass up in the air, face down stretching on a mat in tight shorts. I looked like I was asking to be mounted. There was no chance I was getting away with teasing him.

> **Very entertaining**

The sound of him stumbling echoed over the music in my headphones. I giggled and pressed my head into the mat just to keep myself from looking at him again. I needed him to go the hell away so I could concentrate. I was ready to count the beads of sweat on the mat just to clear my head. My phone buzzed again.

> **You're running yourself into debt here, Adeline. Texts, flirting… free shows. Soon enough I'm coming to collect.**

He recovered quickly. I would give him that.

> **Is that a threat?**

> **Depends on how rough you want me to be.**

My cheeks turned a new shade of red and I rolled over on my back to stare at the ceiling. I waited like that until I could breath again and when I sat up on my elbows the treadmill had been vacated and Jensen was gone.

SARAH

"Hey Bright! Can I get a cinnamon whiskey and cranberry?" I leaned over the bar to get his attention. He looked over at me and nodded as he flipped a few cups over onto the bar. It was busy tonight but it was the only place my brother would eat in Harbor. So I snuck in early with my laptop and commandeered a table in the back before the dinner crowd flooded in to watch the games.

The Hollow was popular with the first responders and a few of the semi-professional sports teams. Sunday's brothers, Brighton and Boone Black, owned it. Twins that couldn't be more different in personality seemed to flawlessly run the bar so smoothly that they had won more than one award for being the place to spend your Fridays in Harbor.

Brighton mixed up the drink, slid out from behind the bar and walked it over to my table. A few tattoos picked out from under the short sleeves of his loose black shirt as he handed it to me and tipped his chin up to look at the TV I was staring at.

"You think they'll win the series this year?" I asked him.

Brighton was that kind of handsome that if you looked at him for too long you'd find things wrong with his face. A pronounced jaw, combined with high cheekbones and narrowed, judgmental dark blue eyes all highlighted by thick dark waves of hair that regularly fell against his forehead while he worked. The Black family were all like that, painfully beautiful. Boone was tall like his twin brother, drenched in tattoos, but for all of Brighton's serious nature, Boone was a goofball. He was the life of the Hollow. Him and Sunday were always dancing on the bar and starting shot trains when left alone for more than two minutes.

"They have a decent shot, but that Tucker kid is struggling to keep them together." Brighton shrugged and looked back at me. "Do you want me to put your dinner order in?" He asked me.

"Sure, Zane and Taylor should be here soon, throw theirs on too?" I asked and he tapped the table with his fingers. "Hey," I called to him, "will you turn it up?" I pointed to the TV and he nodded before slipping behind the bar again. With the volume up I could hear what they were talking about just barely over the sound of the bar crowd. They were discussing the Hornets' ability to work as a team. The upcoming series against their biggest rivals in Lorette was going to be tough but in order to get to the finals, they needed to beat them.

They panned across the field showing the team warming up for the game and my heart fluttered funny in my chest when they showed Jensen stretching and laughing with a few other players. Since the day at the gym he had been quiet, too quiet. I missed his texts and that was dangerous. I had so many regrets and they were only amplified when I told Kaia what happened over the phone on the walk home.

She yelled at me for nearly an hour for the "the cardio I want to do" line and how I should have capitalized that instance. And for what it was worth, she was right because every time I thought about him, sweaty, naked and...

"Addy." Taylor wrapped around the table and pressed a kiss to the top of my head knocking me from my thoughts. He sat at the table as I closed my laptop and squeezed my thighs together in protest to the growing heat at the inappropriate daydream I was having.

Taylor was my oldest brother, and he mirrored my awkward smile back at me. It was a running joke that my fathers genes were too strong because all three of us looked exactly the same just a few years apart. Zane gave a wave to Brighton before slumping down onto the stool next to me with an exhausted groan.

"What's up your ass?" I asked him, with a gentle kick to his foot under the table. He loosened the tie around his neck as Brighton dropped two beers on the table and left.

"Case today was rough," he said, downing the first beer and then the second much to Taylor's annoyance. "I hate when the kids are involved in divorce."

"Hits too close to home," Taylor mused, entertaining Zane's small melt down.

"You talk to Mom today?" He asked me and I nodded. We usually took turns babysitting our parents feelings and expectations. I was nine when they divorced, Dad was military and moved to Japan with the Navy leaving Mom to manage three kids on her own. She did her best and we spent summers overseas but nothing had ever really been normal after that.

"She's fine, she's going on a cruise with her new boyfriend so most of our conversation was her talking to her suitcase while I stared at her forehead." I took a sip of my drink and Taylor laughed.

"Dad's coming to visit at the end of the month," Zane said and I choked on the tart cocktail, the cinnamon whiskey hitting the back of my throat in surprise.

"What?" Taylor scowled and waved down a passing waitress for a new beer. "Why?"

"He talked in circles, you know Dad..." Zane shrugged.

"You're the only one that gets confused when he explains simple details, you jackass, where is he staying? How long is he here for?" Taylor pushed and his oldest sibling nature slipped out in the middle of the Hollow.

"I didn't ask him any of that," Zane said with a shitty smirk on his face. "I honestly don't give a shit, we all know he's not getting on that plane. He never does."

Zane had a point.

"He's not wrong. When was the last time he actually followed through? The day before an excuse will come up and we'll be off the hook," I said, cleaning up around my glass.

"You better hope so because he's not staying at my house," Taylor warned.

"That's right he still doesn't know you're married," Zane teased, "that would be awkward."

Taylor growled at Zane from across the table but my focus was pulled upward to the start of the game while they argued to themselves about our father. I didn't particularly care either way. Me and dad had never been close, I was the youngest and required the least attention from him when everything started to fall apart. Taylor was two years from graduating and Zane was so brilliant at such a young age my parents had been arguing over how they were going to pay to put him through law school.

I had been an afterthought of a child.

Independent, self-sufficient. I was invisible in my own family dynamic. My brothers did their best to pick up the slack but monthly dinners where they argued about our parents wasn't exactly what I had pictured when they suggested we started them.

Their argument faded out as the pitcher took the mound and started to silently communicate with Jensen behind home plate. I could see the worry on his brow as he slapped the cage down over his face and prepared for the opening pitch of the game. It was clear that the game was a stressor, the times before everything had been so light and fun. The urge to win was always present but the Jensen on the TV screen was a different animal and it stirred something around in the pit of my stomach.

My hand flexed around my cup as the ball was thrown, it looked like it was going to hit leather but instead the bat caught it and it was rocketed right back at Logan on the mound. It bounced off the ground and spun through the air toward the shortstop. He pocketed it like it was nothing and rifled the ball across the infield to Tucker on first. I didn't even realize I was holding my breath until the play was called dead.

When I turned back to the table both my brothers were eying me.

"What?" A nervous chuckle left my lips.

"Since when do you like baseball?" Taylor asked, his voice as judgmental as his harsh stare. He leaned over the table and tilted his head to the side to really drive his question home.

"It's sports…I like sports," I said trying to recover and looked to Zane for help. Usually he was down to team up on Taylor but I was being hung out to dry.

"Sure, you like a lot of sports," Zane laughed, and I knew I had stepped in it. "But you've never found *that* much interest in baseball."

"It's the playoffs, I'm just supporting the hometown team," I brushed him off, pressing my lips to my glass to find the drink empty. I looked around for a waitress in a pathetic attempt to get out of the conversation, without luck I rose from the stool.

"Sit," Taylor said, narrowing his eyes on me.

"I need a refill." I whined and Taylor shook his head.

"You're hiding something," Zane accused, finally catching on.

"This is bullying, just so you know. You're bullying me," I said in a tight, nervous ramble as my throat grew dry. I didn't want to tell them why I was obsessively watching the game, it was new and not serious. And definitely not older brother worthy.

"You're turning red!" Zane pushed my shoulder and I snapped at him with my teeth. "She's turning red..."

"There's a guy." Taylor lowered his voice as a waitress dropped our plates on the table.

"There's a fucking guy!" Zane yelled and turned up to the TV with an excited gasp.

"You're both overgrown toddlers, shut the fuck up," I growled and tugged on Zane's dress shirt to keep him in his chair.

"Who is it?" Taylor asked.

"It's none of your business," I said, knowing that the pushback for my short attitude would be worse.

"The pitcher?" Zane asked, watching the game and then searching for my reaction. "Nope," he said looking back. "The shortstop!"

"She hates blondes," Taylor grumbled but I could see him starting to get into the game and I hated it. Zane was intelligent, quick and very observant. It's what made him a good lawyer but Taylor had always caught on quicker. He was good with formulas, theories... he enjoyed knowing what made things tick. Once he started to pay attention it would take him seconds to figure it out. "It's the catcher," he said, turning slowly from the TV to look at me with a smug look on his face. "Isn't it, Addy?"

"How do you know?" Zane asked and started to pick at his french fries.

"Tattoos, dark hair, he looks tall..." Taylor listed, and dropped his tone again. "Tell me I'm wrong and I'll drop it."

"I hate you," I said, getting in his face with a frustrated grin.

"Omission!" Zane snapped his fingers at me. "What's his name?"

"Jensen." I spun my fork nervously into my pasta, and kept my eyes down. I didn't come into the Hollow without ordering the Caper Lemon linguine. It was my comfort food and I was really glad I had a massive plate of it to lose my feelings in.

"That's the name on the back of his jersey," Taylor said, picking up his burger. "What's his first name?"

"I don't know, he goes by Jensen." I shrugged.

"So you're sitting here all worked up over a college baseball player and you don't even know his first name?" Taylor questioned. "Adeline."

"Don't do the mom voice, I hate that voice, it makes me feel like I'm in trouble." I scowled and shoved some food between my lips.

"You barely know the guy, you *are* in trouble," Taylor scolded.

"Drop the snarly big brother routine," I said to him, "I've been texting him for a bit now, he's nice and I like him."

"You've been texting him and you don't even know his name?" Zane laughed and both Taylor and I shot him a death glare. "I just don't believe you're actually talking to him, that's all!"

"I'm not in junior high you idiot, I can talk to boys without your approval," I said to him and he stuck his tongue out at me.

"Prove it," Zane said, throwing some more food in his mouth. "Prove that you're talking to that guy and I'll drop it."

The chances of him dropping it were low. I flipped my phone over on the table, trying to shove it in my pocket before he got his hands on it but he was too fast and it was in his grip and lifted away from my reach.

"I'll fucking put your ass on the ground, give me my phone back," I warned through gritted teeth.

"You might be strong, but I can still kick your ass Addy," Zane laughed and moved a little further away from me.

"That's laughable!" I growled and slipped from my stool.

"You two are embarrassing," Taylor said, sipping on his beer as we fought for dominance. "You're going to get us kicked out," he added when Brighton slapped the top of the bar with a hockey stick that he kept around to keep people from getting too rowdy.

"Sorry, Bright!" I was tempted to sucker punch Zane just because I could.

"Whatever the fuck that is, it isn't talking!" Zane gasped at the messages he was reading and tossed my phone at me.

"What is it?" Taylor's face contorted in worry.

"I want to wash my eyes out with acetone," Zane whined.

"That's what you get, asshole!" I punched him in the shoulder.

"No little sister should ever act like that," he said, pushing his food away. "I've lost my appetite."

"I'm a grown woman Zane," I argued and shoved my phone into my pocket. "You're such a baby."

"That was disgusting!"

"I'm going to fuck him and it's going to be great!" I argued back and Zane looked like he wanted to puke.

"Enough, both of you." Taylor used his big brother voice before he looked directly at me. "Just be careful," he said, ignoring the obnoxious gagging sounds that Zane was making beside me. "And for fuck sakes, figure out his first name before he turns out to be a serial killer or something."

"Great," I rolled my eyes, "good talk guys."

JENSEN

The card that Van held up read *maul* but I couldn't for the life of me remember what the fuck that meant. "That one messes with my head, I just think of bears." I said, leaning back on the couch.

Cosy snorted as she set the bowl of chips on the table and lowered to the floor across from Van. "You're on the right track," she said. "A maul is sort of like a ruck..."

"When a player gets downed and the ball is on the ground?" I tried to remember the term, but there were so many that at times I couldn't keep them all straight.

"Right, but with a maul the ball is being held up, trapped by three players," she explained.

"So the ball is being mauled..." I groaned, feeling stupid for not catching on faster.

"There you go," Cosy encouraged and smiled at me. In those moments I could really see the sibling similarities. She had the same goofy smile and soft brown eyes, but she wasn't as lanky as Van or scrawny in the face. I'd never met their oldest sibling but I assumed they were just another carbon copy of the Mitchell face.

"There's so many weird terms in Rugby, it's like a drunk person was in charge of naming them," I said with a shake of my head. "Like who calls a player a *hooker?*"

"Kaia is incredibly proud of that term, you should be careful what you say," Cosy laughed. "Her main job in a scrum is to hook the ball and push it backward to our team."

"Very literal of the drunk person..." I rolled my eyes. "Do another," I said to Van who was watching quietly and shoving chips in his mouth. He rubbed his greasy hands on his jeans and held up another card that said *conversion*.

"Extra points the team can gain after a try is scored," I said confidently.

"That's our boy!" Cosy clapped. "You know it's really cute that you're trying for her."

"It's nothing." I dismissed the praise.

"Cosy's standards for men are in hell so take the compliment, it's the only one she'll ever give you," Van said with a mouth full of chips.

"It's true," she agreed with him. "But I see you trying."

"I've never felt so lost with a girl, usually it's a smile and a wink, a peek of the tattoos and they're puddy. Adeline just doesn't give a shit, or at least she's damn good at hiding it if she does. I flirt my ass off and she's just better at it." I slumped down into the chair with a loud sigh of defeat.

"Don't take it personally," Cosy said, leaning back on her hands. "Addy has only ever had one dream, playing professional rugby. And the Hillcats are fucking good, but it's not where she belongs. There are teams popping up all over the states, professional teams that want to push rugby into the forefront of mainstream sports media. Addy belongs on one of those teams. She knows it, we know it. She's just determined."

I could understand it. I had always been that kid that just did the thing. No matter what, my parents always supported it and I was kind of just always good at whatever it was. I finished my masters almost a year ago but didn't want to stop playing ball so I picked up classes that would keep me enrolled at Harbor. Just because I could.

"I get it."

"You don't," Cosy stopped me, "You're smart though so you can understand that being determined isn't a single definition, not to a woman like Addy. It means all her focus is on rugby, all the time. She doesn't have time for men or games. If you want her attention you have to take it."

Take it.

Cosy wasn't saying force her, or blur the lines of consent. She was telling me to stop being a pussy and win the game once and for all.

"Addy is the best of us," she said to me, her tone serious and hostile, "and if you break her heart, I'll have Rhea and Kaia break your legs in ways that Silas will never be able to repair."

Dread filled my chest at her threat but I nodded in understanding before looking at Van for rescue but he was just as scared of his older sister as I was.

"Good, now back to the pop quiz," she said, pointing to the cards in Van's lap.

> **UNKNOWN:**
> Do you take dick as good as you suck it?

> **UNKNOWN:**
> How many dates before I can get in your pants?

> **UNKNOWN:**
> Are you into threesomes?

I laid in my bed at the Nest staring at the ceiling, deleting all the random messages after we had gotten home from Cosy's. Every once and a while it was nice to go there for dinner. She was a terrible cook and we always ate out but I enjoyed the change in conversation. If I had gone to my parents, Mom would have grilled me about Adeline again before we fell asleep watching movies. I'd needed a chance. I wanted to be proactive about my intentions with Adeline.

Learning rugby terms was Van's idea and I had been on board without hesitation which only made me feel more shame because the look on Van's face said it all.

I was wrapped around Adeline's finger.

Might as well go all in, I'd never been one for doing something half assed and I wasn't about to start now.

> **What are you doing?**
>
> **Just got home from training.**
>
> **Without me? Must have been lonely.**
>
> **It was peaceful.**

I laughed at the texts and thought about her face that day. I'm not usually the kind of guy that stripped off his shirt in the middle of a public gym but the second she paraded in there I knew I had to do something to get her attention. And shameful as it was, it worked.

> **Peaceful is just a fancy word for boring.**

She asked me what I was doing in return, completely bypassing my flirting and I groaned loudly, frustrated that I wasn't getting anywhere before I answered that I had been with Cosy and Van.

> **So now I can quiz you on rugby positions?**
>
> **Only if you promise hands on corrections for the moves I can't name.**
>
> **I don't think you're ready to rough house.**

She had no idea how ready I was. I shifted in bed until I was sitting up against the headboard and looked over at Todd, snoring in his sleep. I really needed to get my own place but the Nest was home. Unfortunately, it wasn't conducive to having a relationship unless you had your own room.

> **I've been ready since you lost that bet.**
>
> **You poor boy.**

There was something in her message that made her voice sound giggly in my head and I was going to go fucking insane. Todd sounded like he was going to choke in his sleep so I pushed back the comforter, dragging it with me and left the room. Padding down the hallway to the stairs and finding a comfortable spot in the sitting room at the back of the house.

> I can take it, promise.

> **You look like you bruise easily.**

I got comfortable on the couch and pulled the blanket over me, as I tried to come up with a response that didn't scream desperate but all I could think about was her, exhausted and sweaty after training standing in front of that mirror from all her pictures. My mind spiraled into dangerous dreams.

> Like a peach. I'd wear the ones you give me with pride. I don't look like it but I'm a quick study and a good listener. Real submissive when I need to be.

So much for playing it cool.

> **Jensen.**

> Yes Adeline?

> **Cut it out.**

Hook, line and sinker.

> Because you're uncomfortable or because you like it?

Silence. A whole five minutes of it.

> **Because I like it.**

I exhaled and set my phone on my chest. Even the thought of her bossing me around had my dick so hard between my legs it was unbearable. I shifted and tried to ignore the heat. I needed Adeline in my bed, under my body and in my fucking hands as soon as yesterday. The next text would either get me in a lot of trouble or delay my impatience until she was good and ready for me.

> **Do you have any of those mirror photos? Ones you don't post for everyone else?**

I held my breath. "Come on Adeline, play the game. Just give me an inch and I'll run a fucking mile for you," I whispered to the stupid three dots dancing across the bottom of my screen. "Fuck."

The picture that comes through my phone is enough to make my entire body tense into the scratchy fabric of the couch. It's her and that damn mirror that haunts my dreams. Wet dark hair hung around her jaw and even though I couldn't see her eyes, the smile on her lips gave away just how much she was enjoying the attention.

Her body is damp and red in spots from the heat of her shower, and the white t-shirt she's wearing is bunched up with her arm under her breasts. The way the dark red, lacy underwear stretched and curved over the round of her ass was the star of the show. Her olive skin was marked with bruises in all kinds of sizes and I hated how easily her pain softened my thoughts in the middle of wanting to get my hands on her.

> **Did you just take that for me?**

> **Would you tease me if I said yes?**

> **No, I'd ask for more.**

If she took that just for me, I was going to spontaneously combust.

> **Insatiable.**

> **Starving, Adeline. I'm fucking starving.**

Pathetic, maybe? But she needed to know just how badly I wanted it. I could feel her getting nervous about the picture and she needed to understand just how grateful I was that she sent it to me.

> **How did you know it was new?**

> **Those bruises are new.**

I finally answered her after agonizing over the photo for a few more minutes. There were six of them painting her thighs and one larger one that was partially hidden beneath her fingertips around her ribcage.

> **I can't tell if that's creepy or endearing that you know that.**

> **Let's go with endearing.**

> **Okay.**

The mood had shifted by accident and I knew there was little chance of getting it back to how flirty we had been moments ago but I wasn't ready to say goodnight to her just yet.

> **It's harder to watch you play than I expected.**

> **Sorry I don't live up to your rugby star standards lol.**

> **I meant that the game is rough. It's rare that I walk away from a baseball game with bruises. You do it every night, it's intense.**

She was quiet for a little while and I wasn't sure if she had fallen asleep or had gone back to ignoring me. Both were very real possibilities with Adeline but my phone buzzed again after a few minutes.

> **Wait, you've been stalking my Instagram?**

I leaned back against the couch laughing hard at her sudden realization. I scrolled up in our conversation and saved the photo before she decided to take it away from me in a fit of rage.

> Do you need me to define the term - starving, Adeline?

> **Which one is your favorite?**

I hadn't been expecting that question but my immediate answer was *all of them*. I smiled down at my phone mentally flipping through all the photos I had been staring at for days but settled on one after a short moment.

> Mine.

> **Good answer.**

SARAH

I was juggling a bag of snacks and my Dungeons and Dragons books when my phone vibrated in my pocket. *Shit*. It had become a dangerous habit to look almost instantly in anticipation for Jensen. I hated it but in the kind of way that every time it was him there was a stupid grin on my face and a swarm of rabid butterflies in my chest.

> **You gotta stop wearing that jersey to games.**

> Why?

> **My number is on the back of it, Adeline! Thirteen calls just today asking about my sexual preferences, thirteen.**

> Sounds like you'll be busy for a while.

I marched up the walkway to the apartment building, and shifted the bag in my arm as I stepped into the elevator and checked my phone again.

> **Not too busy for you. We could go get dinner tonight, I just finished practice.**

> Sorry, D&D with the girls

> **Dungeons and Dragons?**

> Yeah

> **You're full of surprises, what about after?**

> It's gonna be a long night.

I giggled at his panic and shoved my phone back into my pocket. We were doing D&D at Sunday's apartment this week and while she was really good at making drinks thanks to her brothers and the bar...she was terrible at feeding us.

I kicked the heavy door with my foot and it swung open almost immediately to a smiley Rhea. Her hair was pulled back into space buns at the top of her head and she was wearing the cutest pair of black overalls with a cropped black tee.

"Are you expecting company?" I teased her as she went full grabby hands for the bag. I tickled her bare ribcage as I followed her into the kitchen where everyone else was. Kaia was sitting on top, sipping out of a cup and picking at Cosy's dice bag with a distant expression on her face.

"Hey Minty," Sunday cooed as she shut the door of the fridge with a slam way too loud to come from her tiny body. "You need to break the tie," she said holding up a blender of pale green slush, "daiquiris or margaritas?"

"Both?" I smiled at her, "I thought we were getting drunk?"

"Someone's sexually frustrated and snippy today," Kaia teased without looking up from the bag.

"I hope all those dice are cursed," I said to her and Cosy gave me a dirty look.

"Take it back," she said with a serious look.

"Fine, I hope whatever dice that Kaia picks out to use today are *cursed*." I winked at Cosy who took that as enough of an apology for bringing her into the middle of it.

"Have you fucked him yet?" Kaia looked up at me through her long lashes, her dark hair spilling over her shoulder.

"No," I said.

"Why not?" Kaia pushed.

"I'm busy," I responded and leaned against the counter next to Rhea who was digging through the bag with her head down.

"We could have cancelled tonig—" Sunday started but I shot her a silencing glare and she fired up the blender in awkward response.

"You're stalling," Kaia said the second the blender was turned off.

"No I'm not," I said, Sunday handed me a drink and it smelled like citrus and rum. I took a sip and nearly choked to death. "You have to add juice," I laughed at her.

"There's juice in that!" She feigned innocence but the bottom of white rum on the counter was practically empty and the drink tasted like antifreeze in a pretty glass. "You said you wanted to get drunk."

Kaia was still giving me a judgmental glare when I relaxed against the counter and drank more of my drink with a sour look.

"What are you scared of?" Rhea asked.

"Don't gang up on me, not tonight..." I whined and slumped over sideways.

"Answer the question, slut." Kaia poked me with her foot. "And if it has anything to do with being too busy, too tired, unbothered or anxious about commitment..."

She added when I opened my mouth to say I just didn't care enough to chase.

"Mmhm," she laughed. "You posted two extra thirst traps this week and I know they weren't for us! We get to see that ass for free every day," she teased.

I groaned but it came out more of an exhausted squeal that gave away just how nervous I was about everything.

"He asked me for one," I confessed and all four of them stopped what they were doing.

"Asked for one what?" Cosy sounded confused.

"A picture," I said.

"Like a nude?" Kaia giggled.

"No like he—" I sighed, unable to probably explain what happened. "He asked for a photo that I hadn't posted yet. Like one just for him."

"Just for him?" Sunday yelped like a feral animal.

"Which one did you send him?" Kaia asked, completely un-phased. I pulled my phone out and showed them. "Holy shit, Addy."

"Have you heard from him since, was there proof of life afterwards?" Rhea laughed, her eyes trained on the screen. "Minty, was there proof of life?"

She reached out to scroll down and I realized she was asking if Jensen had replied with a nude. "Oh god, no, Rhea!" I snatched the phone back and shoved it in my pocket.

"What? We have to know all the facts to assess the situation," she argued playfully.

"His dick is not being submitted to the court for evidence!" I crossed my arms over my body and Rhea pouted.

"You're going to edge that poor idiot to death," Cosy laughed.

"He's not the only one suffering," I said, "I feel completely out of control every time he opens his mouth."

"So we're avoiding, it's not a stalling tactic or scheduling conflicts. It's a crush." Kaia declared, snapping her fingers.

"That makes me feel fifteen," I complained.

"I'm just calling it how I see it," she said, finishing her drink. "The guy is obsessed and you're tiptoeing around the situation like he already broke your heart."

"I haven't... I haven't had sex in a while."

"We know!" All of them said in unison.

I held out my empty glass on Sunday as I turned red from embarrassment.

"What about a booty call, hook up with a random person," Sunday suggested. "You could always fuck Boone," she added as she took my glass to refill it. "He's always had a crush on you... just spare me the details."

"Boone will fuck anything that moves," Kaia said. "I've seen it."

Kaia and Sunday had been friends since elementary school and with that came her twin brothers. It wasn't until junior high when Kaia knocked him out cold during a game of flag football that the two became inseparable. Everyone knew they were in love except for the two of them. Boone kept his space when Christian came into the picture but it was heartbreaking to watch Kaia get treated like that when Boone was right there willing to take the mantle. It was endearing and concerning all at the same time.

I shook my head, "thank you for the offer...I think?"

Rhea leaned over on the marble countertop and laughed at Sunday, "what is wrong with you?"

"I'm sick of family dinners where Brighton yells at Boone in front of my niece about his promiscuous lifestyle. Daisy and I have heard way too much. She's thirteen and she can name more STDs than she can name states." Sunday poured the drink and handed it back to me. "It wouldn't really surprise me at this point if he started in on the Hillcats, he's gone through half the Hogs on his own team."

I giggled and Sunday shook her head, "what? They called themselves the Harbor Hogs, it's hilarious."

"She's not wrong, they could have been anything. Harbormen, Hawks, Helicopters..." Rhea added.

"Hammerheads...Hamsters..." I carried on. "We sound stupid lumped up with them, the Hillcats and the Hogs."

"You're distracting her," Kaia said with a snippy tone. "Stop dancing around it, Addy. Fuck the boy!"

Sunday broke out into the Little Mermaid song under her breath and found space between Kaia's legs handing her a full cup too.

"We have three days off next week because Coach is at that conference," Cosy suggested. "I know it's not worth a lot but he's pretty much willing to do anything at this point to impress you. He spent six hours going over cards with Van during dinner the other night. Van was ready to kill him by the end of it because he made him cancel on Zoey for it."

"He didn't tell me it was that long," I sighed. Every stupid thing Jensen did made it harder not to melt into a puddle.

"Jensen is down bad," Sunday sang and wiggled her hips.

"Can we just play now, I can't handle this interrogation any more. And the idea of falling in love makes me want to vomit." I held up both hands before downing my drink with a breathless pant and a twisted face. "More juice next time," I whined as the rum hit my belly and warmed my chest.

Cosy and Rhea set up the table while I put out all of the snacks. Kaia stayed close to me and wrapped her hands around my face the first second she got.

"I love you and I mean this in the nicest possible way but you need to stop being afraid to be loved." She stared me in the eyes and I could feel every single conversation her and I had ever had flowing through me at once.

I was terrified of getting attached. Of being dependent on someone else to respect my feelings and prioritize them. The reality was I saw my brothers once a month and I saw my parents even less. I had always been the forgotten one and it was preventing me from taking a chance on a guy that might make me feel special because I was scared that what could be given and felt, could be taken away.

"Okay," I whispered to her and she pressed her forehead against mine. When Kaia got drunk, she got pushy and affectionate.

"Promise?" She asked.

"Promise." I said, she backed away from me and grabbed the blender instead of her glass and chugged down more of the frozen drink before crying out from the brain freeze.

SARAH

The music pumping in my headphones made it hard to focus on anything else in the gym, but it was quiet for the first time in a week and I couldn't help but let out all the stress by dancing around between my sets. I'd been taking it easy on my knee but Silas had given the okay to start working more leg days to strengthen the muscles now that it was healing better.

Although I was dancing more than I was working out.

I was avoiding the squat machine because I was afraid to blow out my knee but I knew I had to get back on it eventually. I watched Jensen come through the front doors like clockwork. I had been coming earlier so that I could get most of my workout done before allowing myself to get distracted by him. He consistently forgot to bring a shirt.

I couldn't tell if he was actively trying to cause chaos or if he was genuinely just that unaware of how attractive he was but it was impossible to keep him out of my head when he walked around like that. His gym shorts hung low on his hips, every ounce of his tattooed skin on display under the harsh lights of the gym.

You're staring.

I shook loose of the daze and tried to hype myself up for something a little more simple. I turned myself sideways on the mat and started my lunges as Jensen wandered around the gym landing on the deadlift platform. He had a hat low on his brows today and was already so sweaty from the heat outside that I could see the droplets running down his skin. I cleared my throat and continued to do my lunges, focusing on the mat in front of me so I didn't lose my balance and embarrass myself again.

My knee stung a little in the deeper lunges and it took a second to warm up to the movement but eventually the pain dulled and the muscle loosened. My step stumbled a bit in the planting but it felt better than it had all season. I could feel Jensen's eyes on me and it pushed me to stay upright as I worked across the gym in slow uncomfortable lunges. He set himself up on the opposite end, getting set up on the deadlift platform as I switched legs and moved at a grueling pace back across toward him.

I watched him load the weight on the bars, genuinely impressed as he totaled close to three fifty. He looked up at me as he wrapped his lifting belt around his taut stomach and stepped back to the bar. I positioned myself behind a long bench, grabbing some weights but never taking my eyes off of him as he readied for his first set.

Far gone past the shame of sharing, I started my step ups. The least I could do was look busy as my mouth went dry and my temperature rose higher. Jensen's shoulders rounded out, the muscles in his arms flexing tight as he lifted the weight from the ground to his hips. His chest heaved as he worked to keep his breathing steady, his focus entirely on the bar between his hands.

His abs flexed under the strain, and a thick corded vein twisted around his forearms up into his biceps with every lift.

All I could do was count my own steps, almost missing the bench more than once. I felt like I was sweating through the thin fabric of my sports bra and the oversized t-shirt I was wearing over my bike shorts.

I chuckled, setting down the weights the second my set was finished before I stepped back from the bench in full view of Jensen. I grabbed the hem of the shirt, lifting it over my head and chucking it into my bag before continuing on with my next set of lunges.

Alternating the two workouts helped keep my knee moving in different ways, never placing too much stress on the same muscle. The lack of shirt had stolen Jensen's attention from his own set and the bar crashing to the platform noisily. I turned over my shoulder to look at him as he snapped the clip on his belt and dropped it to the ground. He glared at me, his chest rising sharply as his head shook gently back and forth in amused disbelief.

I gave him a little shrug and kept doing my lunges well within his eyesight with more skin on display than before. Two could play the game he started, and I knew I could play it better. I giggled as he huffed something under his breath, his lips moving as he ran a hand through his hair, knocking his hat to the ground. He tugged on the fabric of his shorts and it exposed the hardened sweaty lines of his hip bones just enough for my head to get a little dizzy from the sight of it.

Fuck this man.

I wanted to tell him to leave, to give me some space to breathe but even the thought of telling him to go away made me lonely and sad. If what I felt was a crush, I didn't want to feel it anymore because I was going insane.

How is it possible to be this horny?

I wandered back in a straight line, my lunges getting wobbly as my thighs started to become overworked. Taking a break I downed some water, my head tilting to the side as Jensen went back to his deadlifts. He hadn't fixed the band of his pants and I was two minutes and one more piece of skin from finding out exactly what tattoo he had that high on his thigh with my tongue.

For research of course... I wet my bottom lip and tried to focus on anything but his sweaty, tanned hips for two minutes but nothing cut the edge and my eyes were back on him within seconds.

He pushed his set harder the second time around and I couldn't tell if he was doing it because I was watching but it was going to cut my workout short if I was forced to spend twenty minutes in the shower with my hand between my legs. All in some pathetic attempt to be able to concentrate at work after.

I gave up on the step ups, my focus was too foggy to ensure I didn't fall and break my ankle so I switched to the squat bar in hopes that I could round out my workout. Was the squat bar in front of the deadlift platform? Yes. Did I *need* to do the squat bar today? No.

I loaded it up to my max, wandering around and watching his eyes on mine as he snapped the belt off his body with shaky hands. He walked toward his bag, squatting down to grab his water, we were locked in a quiet, brutal game of who would cave first out of the eye-fucking. I had never been so grateful for an empty gym.

It was a mistake, and it was quickly realized because as I pushed through my first set, aiming for a failure so I could up my personal best next time around, I realized that my knee was still too weak for the weight.

It buckled slightly, my face scrunching up in pain as I pushed through the next explosion of strength. Jensen rose slowly, watching carefully as he approached. My focus faltered for a moment, my fingers flexing around the bar tensely just trying to keep control. I exhaled sharply and lowered again with the bar. I was pushing my luck but I needed to know just how weak my knee had become. He didn't say a word as he rounded behind me in the mirror and hovered his hands beneath the bar.

"Is this alright?" He asked and all I could do was nod, I just wanted to get through this set without feeling weak. "You can do it," he encouraged. "Slow," he whispered, "control the movement."

The next squat was better, the confidence slowly returning with him there to catch the bar. He left a decent amount of space between us but I could still feel the heat vibrating off his chest as he lowered himself with me.

"I like this," his voice was low, barely a whisper as his fingers ghosted over the grouping of thin straps holding my sports bra up. I tried to focus on the workout, I was almost tapped out on my set. The bar was heavy across my shoulders as I pushed backup to full extension, a tiny smirk forming on my lips at the sight of him mesmerized in the mirror.

"If you wanted more one-on-one training, you could have just asked." His breath fanned over my neck as I pushed through the squat.

"I can do one more," I said in a half-pained grunt that was definitely not sexy but I couldn't concentrate on how he was making everything warmer from his attention. I shoved through the next squat, shaking too hard to get it to the top.

"All the way, Adeline," he instructed, his tongue brushing over his bottom lip with his eyes on my legs in the mirror. "Atta girl," he murmured low as soon as I hit the top.

I nearly whimpered from the praise and cursed the betrayal of my body trembling. He moved in close behind me, his chest against my back as I dropped the bar into the hooks and took a breather. His eyes were fixated on mine in the mirror as his hand ghosted over my hip. His fingers flexed tightly but he never touched, he just leaned in a little closer.

"Think you can handle a bit more?" He teased, his voice low and full of implications.

"Funny, I was just about to ask you if that was all you had?" I teased back and stepped away from him. Jensen rested his arms across the bar that separated us and smirked.

He stepped around the bar, closing the space between us again. "I can't show you just how much I have," he raised an eyebrow at me, "at least not here."

"That's a shame." I smiled at him, "maybe next time."

"Mm," he hummed watching my body move as I backed away from him and lowered to the ground to stretch. His jaw tightened uncomfortably as his eyes flickered to the strap sliding off my shoulder. I stifled the amused laughter that bubbled up as he shifted on his feet, clearly doing everything he could to adjust himself without being obvious.

If he only knew how badly I wanted to find out if I could handle more.

Fuck.

"How about we get dinner tonight?" He asked, squatting on the mat across from me with his hands resting on his knees.

I almost caved in the moment and said yes to him but I knew that I could hold out just a little while longer. I just needed to make sure that my future was in order before I gave into something so simple and fun like Jensen. I had to make sure all he wanted was a physical connection before I allowed myself to get tangled up between the sheets with him. I needed hard evidence that he was just the fuckboy everyone made him out to be. No strings.

"Help me stretch?" I asked him, pushing my luck and ignoring his question. If he was as determined as he made himself seem, it wouldn't bother him.

He smirked, looking away from me and swallowing down the rejection before he dropped to his knees and shifted over on the mat toward me. I laid back against it and pressed my hands into the material to keep steady as he grabbed my ankle gently in his hand. I inhaled beneath my teeth at the sudden warmth that wrapped around me as he shifted closer, lining his hips up with mine and rested my ankle on his shoulder.

"How's that?" He asked, his fingers pressing into my calf as he worked a deeper stretch into my hamstring.

I winced at the heat that flooded my sore muscles but nodded. "Good yeah," I said, trying to ignore the sudden shift in temperature and tension that was building between us. I cursed myself for biting off more than I could chew, inviting him to help me. I could feel him against my ass through his pants and all I could do was dig my fingers into the mat to keep from falling apart completely.

Jensen watched me carefully, no doubt noticing the blush that flooded my cheeks under that feeling of his bat calloused hands. My breath hitched as he pushed further my shorts riding up over my thigh as he took what was supposed to be an innocent stretching session into dangerous territory.

His fingers dug softly into my hamstring, unknowingly making my inner thighs tighten under his touch. My head rolled back as his fingers worked the tight muscle loose and my legs fell open, slack and relaxed.

"Mrnm," I practically moan, melting into the mat beneath me.

Jensen's fingers brushed against the inside of my shorts as he reached the top of my hamstring and he paused, his breathing shallow. "Adeline, you have to stop making those noises," the request was strangled as he looked up at me from the base of my body.

"Or what?" I mistakenly challenged him in the lusty haze of my intense relaxation.

"Or I might do something stupid," he growled, lowering himself until his shoulders brushed against my thighs, "like put my mouth somewhere it doesn't belong in public."

A fire bloomed in the pit of my stomach and it took what felt like an eternity for me to calm down enough to be reasonable. I wanted to tell him to prove it, that maybe I was sick of waiting and didn't give a shit if he ate me out on the gym floor.

But I couldn't.

A low, frustrated growl bubbled up.

I pushed my foot against his shoulder, digging the toe of my sneaker into this bare skin as I slid upward on the mat out of his reach. I hid the immense void I felt from the lack of his touch and exhaled quietly before speaking.

"I have to get back to work," I smiled, rolling to my feet. "Thanks for the stretch."

"You're welcome," he said, his voice still husky from the tension between us. He stood after me, adjusting his gym shorts to hide any evidence that he enjoyed himself. He shook his head and I watched as he wandered back over to his gym bag in the mirror. He grumbled something under his breath before grabbing his shirt from the bag and roughly threw it over his shoulders.

I knelt down by my bag, smiling to myself and pulled on my t-shirt before digging around for my phone only to find a tiny cloth bag I definitely did not put in there. I picked it up and shook it gently before pulling on the ribbon that was keeping it closed to find a set of D&D dice inside that I'd never seen before. I looked over my shoulder at Jensen, knowing that they had to be from him and it made my heart squeeze with affection in my chest.

How was it possible that he was Harbor's most feral fuckboy while simultaneously being its softest, most obsessive loverboy. I dropped them back into my bag and stood up to text that I was on the way back to work when I felt a rush of heat at my back.

"Next time you make those noises, make sure we're somewhere I can do something about them," he warned, his shoulder pressed against my back and his voice a dark whisper. I kept my head down to hide the blush and my satisfied smile as he left me standing in the gym alone staring at the present he left me.

JENSEN

Nothing at the gym made my heart race the way Adeline did and she hadn't shown up today. After the session we had on the mat, I figured I'd scared her off for good and was cursing myself for pushing too far. Or at least I'd given up hope that she was going to when the front entrance opened and she paraded in. I perked up instantly only to be cock blocked by the sight of Kaia Keegan and Sunday Black. Not that they weren't welcome, but it would make it a hell of a lot harder to get under Adeline's skin if she had a buffer.

I knew the second she smiled at me that she had done it on purpose.

I dropped the dumbbell in my left hand to the ground noisily and grinned at her, my smile lopsided with admiration. She was always one step ahead of me and I couldn't tell if it pissed me off or turned me on. But she bent over in those tiny bike shorts and my dick hardened with the answer. Loud and clear, *it turned me the fuck on.*

Every giggle broke my concentration and I could hear Kaia losing her mind about something as they started an intense arm circuit. Half way through both Kaia and Sunday had slowed, whining that Adeline was pushing them too hard. She had worn some tight black and dark green sports bra that hugged her ribcage and showed off her stomach and paired with her dark green workout shorts that showed off her perfect ass. Her hair was pulled up into a half bun and chunks of touchable hair fell out around her face.

I could stare at her for hours even if she was doing her best to ignore me.

I watched from my seat on the bench, digging out my phone to antagonize her a little just to see her cheeks turn red in front of her friends.

> **Can you ask Kaia what she thinks of my form?**

I set my phone down and lifted the weights back up to finish my set of curls before moving on to the rows. I watched as Adeline glared over her shoulder at me, her phone in her hand before she chucked it at Kaia who was balancing on a stack of jump mats.

Kaia broke out in laughter and tossed the phone to Sunday on the floor. I turned the music off in my headphones and had to keep from laughing at Sunday's gasp. Pushing up onto her elbows she looked over at me, her blonde hair falling down her back and her eyes wide in shock.

"Smash!" Kaia cupped her face and yelled across the gym.

Adeline nearly tripped over her own feet trying to get her to shut up. Her whole body is tense while she texts and it's hard not to laugh at how quickly she got riled up.

> **Don't be too flattered, Kaia's bar for standards is six feet under.**

> Ouch

> **Don't flirt with my friends.**

> Are you jealous, Adeline?

I didn't get a text back. She threw her phone into her duffle bag and started to boss around her friends. Both Sunday and Kaia laughed through the entire grueling workout. I curled around and eventually ended up closer to them on a machine that took very little focus.

"Am I attracted to arrogant men or is he the exception?" Sunday asked with a giggle.

"That man is the exception," Kaia confirmed. They were unknowingly stroking my ego and it was increasingly hard to pretend that they weren't.

"He can probably hear you, you know," Adeline huffed, walking toward them out of breath.

"Good," Kaia said quickly, "I hope he hears every slutty thing we say about him, he deserves it…"

"I need you to find out if those tattoos are *everywhere*," Sunday purred and tied her long blonde hair back into a ponytail.

Adeline snuck a small glance at me through the hair that had fallen out of her bun and rolled her eyes. "Pretty sure he got them for attention," she grumbled.

"Well they have my attention," Sunday giggled.

"Are you two going to work out with me or metaphorically suck his dick all morning?" Adeline snapped and pushed a medicine ball around with her foot.

"You're a human chastity belt," Kaia whined.

"I don't know, I think the whole playing hard to get thing is working..." Sunday's eyes flickered over to me, a smiling curling on her lips.

"Don't stare at him," Adeline hissed and threw the medicine ball at Sunday.

"It's so hard not too..." she took the ball into her arms with a grunt.

"Honestly, him working out without a shirt on is such an attractive red flag," Kaia added and I tried not to smile. *You aren't supposed to be able to hear them, idiot.*

"What exactly makes up an *attractive* red flag?" Adeline asked.

"That," Sunday swooned, her chin tilted toward me, nearly dropping the ball that time. I chuckled, tossing her a wink and watched as she turned beet red. The sound she made was something between a gasp and moan as she clumsily handed off the ball to Kaia and walked away to get some water.

Adeline looked pissed as Kaia threw the ball to her and she slammed it to the ground before spinning on the mat and coming straight toward me working on my flies.

"Cut it out," she kicked the metal of the bench and vibrated the entire thing beneath me.

I let go of the machine and pulled out an earbud as I looked up at her. "What?" I pretended not to hear her without missing a beat.

"You're distracting them," she scowled, the wrinkles between her eyebrows were the cutest thing I'd seen yet.

"I'm just working out," I feigned innocence.

"You're peacocking!" Adeline snipped and I couldn't help but laugh.

"Did you just refer to me as a bird?" I chuckled again, leaning forward on the bench to get closer to her. I wanted the warm, spicy smell of her perfume in my nose and her soft olive skin beneath my fingertips.

"I did, because you're parading around the gym like an animal," she said, her tone was tight and vicious.

"I parade around for you all the time," I clipped smoothly back to her.

"That's— you're infuriating," she huffed. *'That's different'* almost rolled off her lips and it lit a fire in the pit of my stomach. It might as well have been a *'just for me'* because of the way my body reacted. "Behave, and put a shirt on!"

"Unfortunately, both of those things are out of character for me, so I'll be doing neither," I smirked at her. "It was cute that you thought they'd act as a buffer," I said to her quietly, my tone low to hide how needy I was.

"They asked to come," she lied, I could tell because her fingers flexed at her side.

"No," I whispered and slid forward on the bench some more until I had to tilt my chin all the way up at her and I could feel the heat pouring off her skin through her clothes. It took everything in me not to hook my finger into the damp elastic of her shorts to force her even closer. "They're here because you thought it would keep me at a distance," I whispered only for her to hear. It wasn't about embarrassing her, it was about reminding her who's turn it was in the game we were playing. "But you should know something," I said, and did it anyway. She hissed as my finger hooked into the band and pulled her hips toward my chest.

"What's that?" The next breath she took was shaky and it gave away how nervous she was.

"I see you," I said, daring to explore how far she'd let me go. I ghosted my thumb over the small bit of exposed skin at her hip. *Fuck, I loved that little piece of her. So soft...* I swallowed, trying to keep myself together, I moved my hand downward and let it fall tracing two fingers against her inner thigh just to feel her tremble, "and no amount of buffer will keep me away."

I looked around her at Sunday and Kaia who were laying across machines with wide eyes.

"No matter how *cute* a buffer," I smiled at them and they both scrambled to pretend they weren't listening with their mouths wide open.

She covered her face with her hands to compose herself and backed away from the bench. "And Adeline?" I called out, before slipping my earbud back in. My breath caught in my throat as she turned back to look at me, I still hadn't gotten used to her stealing it with such ease. "You're the prettiest Hillcat," I smiled at her and watched her cheeks turn red.

I heard Kaia whine, *"you're the prettiest hellcat."* And Adeline playfully pushed her over on the mat before scooping up the medicine ball and forcing them back to their workout.

JENSEN

> **Are you coming today?**

> **Maybe, work is sort of insane right now.**

I wasn't exactly used to feeling disappointment but for some reason the idea that Adeline wasn't going to be here today ate at me. My only accomplishment that week was that I had only dreamed of her twice a night... every night.

I had started looking at apartments because waking up to Todd snoring with my dick hard was going to be the reason I snapped. On the team, in class... It wouldn't matter. I just needed a release and Adeline was making sure I worked for it.

> **How am I supposed to win without you?**

> **Show off for all the other girls.**

> **I only wanna show off for you.**

I sighed, trying to scrub my thoughts of her and focus on the game ahead of us. Winning was the goal, everyone was fighting hard to prove to the entire college circuit that we didn't need Arlo King to win but it was harder than any of us expected.

We needed this series to stay in the playoffs and it was one of the hardest we had played in a long time, the first *six* games went into extras. Both of our teams played the best defense of our lives and every game clocked out with low scores and one win for each of us. Tonight was the tie breaker. It was now or never.

> **Maybe later, one thing at a time.**

That maybe later was like a rocket had popped off in my chest. I could hear the way her voice hummed it in the back of my head and it made my mouth dry. We would win today's game and I would get Adeline Sarah back beneath me if it killed me.

"Are you planning on doing anything stupid today?" Van double-knotted his shoes and looked up at me with a glare.

"Define stupid?" I flashed him a smile and buttoned up the bottom of my jersey before shoving it in my loose pants. I did up the belt, turning to find him still staring at me with disapproval tight across his usually goofy face.

"You," Van said, standing up to his full height and towering over me. "You're the definition."

"One more outburst and Coach is going to have a stroke," Josh said from my left.

"That would mean, no more two-a-days for a while," I offered and both of them shook their heads at me.

"Just behave for one game," Van warned, holding up a finger, "earn some brownie points with Dean, maybe he'll take you off the laundry early," he teased.

The bunt had gotten me on eternal service. I'd been doing laundry since that game and I didn't see the ending in sight but it was worth it. I'd clean every single piece of clothing in the Nest if it meant giving Adeline my number that day.

"There's no way I'm letting him off laundry," Dean grunted in passing, "I got yelled at by Coach for an hour after that game."

I tried to hide the smile on my face as I brushed my hair under a hat, "I have nothing to lose," I said to Van who was evidently very sick of my shit but very much interested in finding out what I'd do next.

I stopped him before everyone flooded from the locker room, "hey thanks for suggesting that shop."

Van had brought me down to his favorite comic shop on the weekend and I had spent way too much on dice. I knew less about Dungeons and Dragons than I did about convincing Adeline to go on date with me, but once I started picking out sets... I couldn't stop. The top drawer of my dresser at the nest made noise when I opened it and I had enough dice to give her a set once a week until our children put us in a retirement home.

"Yeah man," he said with a smile, "did she love them?"

"I think so?" I shrugged. She hadn't said anything, but I watched her confusion when she found the bag with a smile on my face. She seemed excited but if I knew her, she'd wait to bring it up at a time when she could use it against me. And oddly, I was okay with that, as long as she was using it against *me*.

We packed into the concrete hallway shoulder to shoulder and Dean stood in the center of the team staring around at all of us. "There's no option today but a win. Tonight we prove to Harbor and the rest of the country that we will never be reduced to the skill set of a single player. We're a team, we're a family. Now let's show them what the fuck that means to us."

Everyone cheered and hollered, shoving wildly against each other until our hearts were racing and our blood was pumping through our veins. Dean gently tapped Josh against the jaw, who was standing clear of the physical contact against the wall, but still offered a few hearty cheers. With our adrenaline high and our eyes clear on the goal, we all took our spots in the lineup. Our cleats created a rumble of noise as we all stomped our feet and the stadium above us became a thunderous boom of applause.

"Put it together for your Harbor Hornets!"

The lights in the stadium had already been flickered on for the late game and they buzzed in excitement alongside the crowd. Everyone was ready for a fight.

Philly's team was already fully immersed in their warm ups, and I could feel the animosity rolling off Dean as we took them in.

"Focus," Coach barked, a loud clap from his clipboard against the side of the dugout brought us all back from the edge. "No fights today, I don't give a shit if they say the most heinous crap you've ever heard. Beat them on the scoreboard and send them home for good."

"Can we kick their asses in the parking lot *after* the game?" Cael asked, perched over the banister of the dugout with a shit eating grin on his face.

"Win the game and you can do whatever the fuck you want, kid." Coach stared him down. "But you don't do it on my field. Understand me?"

"Understood, Coach." The team erupted.

"Go stretch, you've got fifteen." He snapped and we all jolted into action. Van came up behind me and leaned over against the banister until I could see his face equipped with a goofy, mischievous smile.

"What?" I asked, tightening the straps around my calf.

"Your girl." His eyes drifted up past the dugout to the seats behind the backstop. She was facing Cosy with a bright smile on her face, in my fucking jersey looking prettier than I'd ever seen her. Her dark hair was down around her face in massive, messy waves and all I wanted to do was find out what sound she made when I pulled it.

Focus, Jensen. I said to myself, *focus on the game, not the girl.*

But *the* girl... my heart skipped a beat.

The goddamn girl.

"Field," Dean snapped. "No funny business," Dean warned, tugging on my collar.

"Yes, Cap," I said mindlessly, my eyes still on her.

I hated how quickly my concentration on the game disappeared and how quickly my determination to have Adeline appeared. Cosy's words rattled around in the empty space. *Take it.*

"He's going to do something stupid, isn't he?" Dean's concern was palpable as I walked out of the dugout to my spot. I carried my cage in my hand, tucking it under my arm as I looked at Adeline in the stands.

The smug look on her face made my dick hard.

"Van," the desperation was thick as I turned to him and he jogged up behind me, "warm up with Logan for a minute?" I asked.

"Remember when we all said multiple times to behave?" Van said.

"Stall for five minutes and then I'll take over," I all but begged him. "Five minutes!"

"You're taking the heat once Coach and Dean see what's happening." Van shrugged and turned, getting Josh's attention to warm up.

I looked back to the stands, inhaling slowly, trying to push down the immense sexual frustration and decided that today was the day I was going to take it.

I hooked my finger at her and she pointed to herself like there was a chance I was talking to anyone else. I nodded, my jaw tight as she shook her head no and her smile grew.

Brat.

"Come here," I said loudly, "*please?*"

Cosy choked on her pop and looked over at Adeline like I had just confessed my feelings instead of asking her to simply come over and talk to me. Cosy nudged Adeline who never broke eye contact urging her to go.

"You're going to get in trouble again," she said, leaning forward in her seat.

"It's important, come here," I said again, that time she rose from her spot and moved toward the backstop. She leaned against the cage, "I need you to take the jersey off."

"What?" She laughed.

"I'll get you a new one but you have to take it off now, it's not funny anymore," I said quietly enough that she moved closer just to hear me and she looped her fingers into the cage. "Bingo," I whispered under my breath. I wrapped my fingers over hers and felt her tense, trying to move away. "What time am I picking you up for our date tomorrow?" I asked her loudly.

The grumble that left her was adorable. "Let me go Jensen," she warned.

"What time," I said with more force. Commotion came from the dugout as Arlo yelled to Josh questioning why the hell he was warming up with Van.

"You have a game to play, stop it," she laughed and tried to wiggle away more.

"It's just stretching, it's fine, I'm already warm," I said, and shook my head at her. "I'm sorry, I can't do anything until she agrees to it," I yelled over my shoulder at Coach and Arlo who both had the look of death on their faces.

"Jensen!" She hissed but the smile on her face was wild with excitement. "You're being insane, let me go."

"Answer the question, Adeline. Everyone is waiting on you, we have a playoff game to win." I teased her but my voice was demanding, I needed her to tell me when. I had waited long enough.

"You'd delay the entire game over a date?" She scoffed, shaking her head in disbelief as she tried to get her fingers free.

"The game hasn't started so it's entirely up to you," I said, lying. There's very few boundaries I didn't cross on a day to day basis, but letting down the guys was never one of them. If she really wanted to push that far, I'd let her have my surrender but I had to bluff for just a few minutes longer.

"Jensen, I will bench you!" Coach snapped, I could hear the threat on his lips as his clipboard slapped against the concrete.

"It's not my fault Coach!" I called back, "blame the girl! Listen I can hear Dean Tucker stomping down the foul line to kick my ass so if you don't agree to a time tomorrow I might be in the hospital..." I laughed wildly when her head snapped to first base.

"He looks mad..." she whispered.

"I like the bones in my body, Adeline. I promise you will too," I teased and she blushed. "Come on, just save me from the wrath of Hulking and say a time," I begged her.

"Addy!" Cosy yelled, standing up in her seat. "Just give him a time."

"Jensen!" Our names were being yelled from every direction as the announcer boomed through the stadium taking note of the commotion happening. *Looks like we have a little pre-game Hornets shenanigans happening on home plate!*

"Adeline," I said again.

"Jensen," she huffed back. "You're embarrassing yourself."

"No, you're embarrassing *us*," I teased her over the sound of everyone screaming. A few of the Philly players had started to loosen up and join in on the yelling. "We're going to forfeit our only shot at the playoffs because you're too scared to go on a date with me!"

That scared her enough. I could feel it coursing through her. Luckily she knew as much about baseball as I did rugby. Adeline looked around at the chaos, fans were screaming, Coach was hurling threats, Dean was getting closer.

"You're in control here," I told her. "It's all up to you."

She stared me down and I could tell her heart was racing as fast as mine because her throat bobbed and her fingers tightened around the cage.

"Saturday, I'm free all day."

I instantly let go of her hands, allowing her to step back against her seat almost losing her balance.

"Saturday," I repeated with a shit eating grin before shoving the cage over my face and turning to the field. "Let's win a fucking ball game," I called out with more pride and excitement than I'd ever felt in my entire life and started warmups with Josh.

SARAH

"This one?" I asked the girls. They were lazily strewn across my bed and couch as I rifled through my collection of clothing.

"No," Cosy said in disapproval at the baby blue cropped t-shirt. "It's too…"

"Sunday," Rhea said, rolling her head to the side.

"Pretty sure that *is* mine," Sunday said, shoving bits of croissant into her mouth from her spot on the couch. "I agree though, you need something that screams—"

"I need to be fucked disrespectfully," Kaia cut her off and crawled over the bed to my closet. She smacked my ass and shooed me away with her hand as she started to rifle away inside. "This," she handed me one of the sheer button ups that I keep in the back of the closet for nights out to the Hollow.

"Kaia." I took it from her nervously, "this feels too fancy for an afternoon."

"It's not an afternoon." She turned on me with her dark eyes narrowed and a pair of leather shorts in her clutch. "This is nearly two months of eye fucking one of the hottest players on the Hornets every time he's in your sights. This is your chance."

"You making it sound like life or death is only making it worse you know?" I said to her and pulled off the blue crop top, throwing it on the bed and replacing it with the sheer black button up.

"Good, maybe if it's dire you'll take me seriously," Kaia grumbled and got down on her knees to dig through my shoes and boots. "These." She handed me a pair of chunky black boots that had always fit snug to my calves. I shuffled out of my jeans and into the leather shorts.

"He's going to fall over dead," Rhea said, her eyes raking up my legs as I buttoned a few of the middle buttons on the shirt, leaving the rest open. The dark bralette I was wearing hugged tightly to my body and made me feel feminine in the sexiest way possible.

"That or he'll get down on one knee." Sunday propped her head up in her hand and sighed. "You're so pretty, Addy," she cooed.

"Oh you are too, Sunny," I walked toward her and flicked her chin with my finger before sitting down on the couch and tugging on the boots quickly. My phone vibrated on the table and I grabbed it seconds before Kaia had the chance. I shot her a glare and opened it.

> **Have you decided what we're doing today?**

> It's a surprise.

I could tell my answer made him nervous because the three dots appeared and disappeared a second later.

"You guys need to get out of here." I set my phone down, "he'll be here soon and I don't need him thinking that this was a group project."

Cosy laughed, the sound light and amused, "he knows Minty."

"Get out!" I scoffed and started to push Rhea to her feet.

They all gathered their shit and filed out of the apartment but Kaia held onto the doorframe and smiled at me, "don't do anything I wouldn't do."

"That's a short list," I said and returned her smile.

"And look how happy I am all the time," she teased. I chucked a pillow at her and she disappeared out of the front door closing it just before it hit her. I turned back to the mirror and fluffed the messy loose curls in my hair before I fixed my lips and inhaled a sharp, nervous breath. I wiggled around my nose ring and double checked my makeup again, my toes fidgeting in my boots.

Why the hell was I so nervous?

We had been flirting for weeks, it's not like I didn't know exactly what I was getting myself into. But today it would just be us, one on one for hours. I could feel my heart beating out of my chest, so noisily that I almost missed the soft knock at the door.

I stared at it for a second over my shoulder in the mirror. I could bail on him, tell him that I just couldn't do it today. Hide. If I hid, it meant not getting my heartbroken down the road, it meant being safe from all the negative feelings that came with having a crush.

I hadn't stopped long enough in the last few weeks to think about getting attached, flirty texts and avoiding deals were easy. There was no guarantee of what today might bring and it was the lack of control that made my heart race.

A second knock made me turn that time and I shook away the what ifs. I could enjoy today without worry about tomorrow, without catastrophizing my entire future over a single date. I couldn't let them get to me, I just needed to have fun and whatever happened next, I'd have to trust that it was for a reason. My phone buzzed in my hand and I looked down with a smile.

> **Open the door, Adeline.**

On any other day I would respond quickly and with unmatched sarcasm but today I just inhaled once more, shoving my phone into the back pocket of my shorts and opened the door. He was standing on the other side in a dark fitted tank top that hugged tight to his sculpted chest and a pair of blue jeans with a striped button down t-shirt that he'd left open.

"What no baseball hat today?" I teased, the words almost catching in my throat.

"Nope. Looks like neither of us needed our buffer today," he looked around my empty apartment. "A heads up would have been nice though, your downstairs neighbor might call the cops for a wellness check after Rhea and Kaia's speech."

"Seriously?" I could feel myself turning red.

"I'm kidding, they were perfect angels," Jensen said, pushing his hand through his messy hair with a rough swallow. "Well, Rhea was but the chances of survival are low if I insult your best friend."

I shook my head gently and tried my hardest not to show how insufferably warm I was by his gentle flirting. Almost worse than when he was out right telling me how he wanted it. I looked back up at him and he was still watching me with bright, attentive brown eyes.

"So where are we going, Adeline?" He asked.

"I want to get tattoos," I said, mustering up some long lost confidence. I allowed the feeling to take over and guide the conversation because if embarrassing, no game Adeline had her way, she'd shut the door in his face.

"Tattoos on a first date?" He asked, for a second he almost looked nervous and it fed the little monster inside of me. Like a spark to a flame.

"Are you scared, Jensen?" I asked him.

"No, but we're going to have to stop for snacks and gas," he mused without skipping a beat and stepped back to let me out of my apartment. "Ready?"

I eyed him for a second, drinking in the boyish grin on his face as he extended one arm down the hall, the impatience vibrating from him in waves. I couldn't tell if he was nervous like me, or excited but either way it was bringing a soft pink color to his cheeks as he wet his bottom lip, his mouth no doubt going dry as I stepped forward. I locked the door quickly behind me and turned back to him.

"Why do we need snacks for tattoos?" I asked him.

"Those are for the road trip, if you want tattoos, fine," he agreed with a small laugh, "but we're going to my guy and he's two hours west of here."

Snacks and gas.

I should have been infuriated that he wasn't even remotely upset by the spontaneous want to do something insane for our first date. Kaia had told me to keep it simple, dinner at the Hollow, or at home. Rhea and Cosy, voted for a movie and a make out, where Sunday said I should let him pay to take me to the Zoo. Nothing screamed at me though until I saw Jensen, standing there in front of me ready for anything I threw at him.

I didn't even have a single tattoo on my body and compared to his ink saturated skin I could have seen him questioning the idea. Instead he came up with a plan to make it happen, on the spot and without a single complaint.

"What exactly did Kaia say to you?" I asked him as we took the stairs to the bottom floor, he held open the front door for me and a laugh rolled from him. "She gave you the *'you'll have to re-learn how to walk'* speech, didn't she?" I stared at him as we wandered across the parking lot to his car.

"I got the *'you'll have to re-learn how to get hard'* speech. Which is horrifying because I didn't even know you could break your penis until Rhea showed me the google results," he said with his brows furrowed tightly and his hand on the handle of the passenger side door.

Mental note to kill her later. "Well, don't screw up," I warned quietly as I stepped up to the open door separating us. He didn't say anything but the smile on his face and the gesture of him tapping two fingers to his chest seemed to quell the nerves that bubbled up inside. I had zero idea what it meant but I trusted it as I slipped into the seat.

He pulled from the parking lot and it dawned on me that he was driving an old man's car... "Is this your dads?" I asked him, laughing at the clean car smell. It barely looked used and it definitely didn't scream college kid.

"It's mine," he said, turning onto the road out of town, "Why?" he looked over at me confused.

"It's just..." I ran my hand over the dashboard and laughed. "Boring?"

"Practical..." Jensen scoffed, "good on gas, low maintenance and easy to clean."

"Are you sure it's not your dads?" I teased him and he just shook his head.

"Not every guy drives fast cars Adeline, this isn't a movie..." he joked.

"But we agree it would be hotter if they did?" I laughed and he echoed the sound. When we reached the edge of town he pulled into the gas station and filled the car. My phone buzzed and I pulled it out to a text from Kaia.

> **KAIA:**
> **Why are you stopped, are you already naked?**

I cursed myself for not turning off my location before I left the house, I should have known that the first thing she'd do was check it.

> He's getting gas.

> **As in— you're pumping his gas?**

I shoved my phone away as he got back into the car and handed me two bags of cola bottles and a bottle of water. I looked down at them and then back up at him, a chocolate bar hanging out of his teeth as he did up his belt with one hand.

"Who's the snitch?" I asked, holding up the bags.

"You eat two bags a game, three if you're nervous," he said, dropping the chocolate bar into the cup holder. I looked down at the bag, hiding the flicker of appreciation that crossed my face at the thought that he had just *noticed*.

"I don't get nervous at your games," I scoffed, at least I didn't think I did but when I thought more on it, stress eating cola bottles was a subconscious trait that most of the time I didn't even realize I was doing until the bag was gone.

"Figured you'd need one for the drive, one for the tattoo," he brushed me off, ignoring the denial.

"I'm not nervous to get a tattoo," I argued, letting the bags rest between my legs on the seat.

"Do you have any others?" He asked, pulling onto the highway finally. I shook my head no. "Not even ones I haven't found yet?" His smile twisted and I felt the heat rise on the back of my neck.

"Not a single one," I confessed.

"Save one of the bags," Jensen laughed gently and looked over at me.

"Are you implying that I can't handle tattoo pain?" I turned in my seat, sliding my knee across the seat so I could really look at him. His jaw tightened with amusement and his eyes flickered off the road to watch me shift.

"Being nervous and being scared are two different things," Jensen teased. It drove me insane how relaxed he was, like he couldn't be bothered to be anxious about today, about our date. The sun soaked him in warm light and made his olive skin glow, and highlighted the few freckles that danced around on his cheeks and nose.

My body shivered as his tongue pressed out over his bottom lip.

"I'm not scared of a tattoo gun," I said after a second, confident and sure of myself for the first time today. It wasn't necessarily a lie, because I was a little scared but it wasn't over a little pain...

Jensen looked at me and the sun illuminated the golden undertones of his brown eyes. My heart tripped over the feelings that the look gave me, little did he know I was already facing my fears.

JENSEN

I could smell the warmth of her perfume and spent the entire drive trying to keep my eyes on the road and my hands on the wheel. Adeline made it increasingly difficult as she chewed on her gummies in a particular way that made my mouth dry. She hung them between her lips, chewing nervously on each one as we drove down through the thick tree lines.

She said she wasn't anxious but there was something bothering her. I just couldn't put my finger on it and Adeline was a steel trap of emotions. Even if I thought I'd figured out what was going on in her head, the chances of her admitting I was right were low.

I'd asked her about her favorite movies and I shouldn't have been surprised when most of them involved fast cars. She could tease my car all she wanted, I didn't need anything fancy to drive back and forth from the stadium to the Nest. Half the week it sat untouched in the driveway because I walked or hopped in with another player.

It was only when someone pointed it out that I was reminded how strange my habits were. I had grown up on both sides of wealth, watching my parents struggle to make ends meet. To own over two hundred hotels across the world. I spoke four languages conversationally from summers spent on location while mom oversaw construction. I was homeschooled for most of my life but I had always been taught that wealth didn't equal need or want. Even though my parents could live anywhere, they had found a comfortable home in Harbor to be close to me. They went on one vacation a year and it was usually to visit family in Canada.

I wasn't raised on money even when we had it.

I guess that surprised a lot of people but it just seemed normal to me to be well adjusted in my generational wealth. Adeline hadn't meant anything by it when she teased me, all of the guys at the Nest had nice cars. But to them owning a car was a big deal, it made them feel successful and it was a worthy reason, they had all worked hard for those cars. I just didn't share those feelings, at least not when I was just driving around Harbor. There was a time and a place for a fast car, the feeling under your feet and speed in your bloodstream.

"Alright," I said, pulling onto Main Street. "Favorite TV show, and I want something you secretly watch and don't tell anyone."

Adeline laughed as I found a parking space close to the tattoo shop and cut the engine.

"You'll never get that one out of me," she giggled and I nearly melted to the seat as she clicked herself free and climbed out. I smiled when she took the bag of cola gummies with her and led her down the street to the shop resisting the urge to take her hand.

"In you go," I said, holding the door open for her.

I inhaled as she passed, letting that spicy, citrus shampoo drown me before following her in. The shop was bright and every inch of the walls was covered with art, skulls and taxidermist animals. I snuck past her as she stopped to admire a giant painting at the front of the shop, her eyes widening in amazement.

"Hey, is Harry in?" I tapped the counter and Jo looked up at me. They were heavily pierced, shaggy bleached hair and always a little quiet. They pointed me to the back of the shop. "Thanks, Jo. Adeline," I said to her and she turned to follow. Harry's room was at the back of the shop, it was just lucky that today was normally his walk in day and he owed me more than one favor.

"Knock, knock," I banged on the open door and Harry looked up from his iPad with a scowl on his face. "What's up grumpy."

"I see you haven't learned manners since the last time you were here." In his leather jacket and heavy boots, his long dark hair was tugged into a bun at the back of his head and if it weren't for the goofy British accent I might have been intimated. Harry stood, setting his tablet down and stepped forward like he was going to throw a punch.

"I told you, I'll learn manners when you start taking more than one shower a month," I teased and he laughed, wrapping me up in a tight hug.

"Who's the blank canvas?" He said, pulling back and giving Adeline a glare.

"Adeline," I said, extending my hand to her so she would come a little closer. "This is Harry," I introduced them, "he's done at least eighty percent of the art on my body," I laughed, "at least."

"He cried getting his underarms done," Harry said, his lips curling upward as he took Adeline's hand to shake it. "My God you are a pretty thing," he added and I tossed him a dirty look that tugged a small laugh from Adeline.

"Addy," she corrected me. I crossed my arms over my chest to keep from being glaringly jealous about the interaction.

"And you came here with this skud?" Harry scoffed. "There's got to be a good reason," he said, letting go of her finally and stepping back.

"First date," Adeline said, her smile bright and her cheeks slightly red. *Harry wasn't wrong,* I thought, just admiring her. I had forgotten how charming he could be and I was already annoyed that he was flirting with her, and that she was playing into it. Whether to bother me or not, I was instantly over it.

"Adeline wanted to get a tattoo," I said.

"I wanted *us* to get tattoos," she corrected me but all I was thinking about was putting my hands through her hair

"Alright, what do you want to get?" Harry asked, grabbing his iPad and getting comfy again. Adeline sat up on the bed, her legs swinging over as I rested against it next to her. I just wanted to be close, to smell her, to feel her. I didn't want to be in public or around other people. I craved the solitude and her laugh.

"He can pick," she said looking over at me and I raised my eyebrow at her. "You pick mine, I'll pick yours." She poked my side, "unless you're *scared*."

I knew that word would come back to bite me in the ass.

"Fine, but when you have a property of Jensen tramp stamp, you'll have to start wearing low cut jeans," I teased, "really show it off."

"Very funny," she said, "brave for a man who is begging for an *insert here* tattoo."

Harry barked a loud laugh, "You two bicker like you're married."

"Are you really going to let me pick?" I asked Adeline.

"Promise to do something that fits me?" The question was softer than I was expecting out of her usually sassy mouth. I nodded, tempted to push back the rogue lazy wave that hung down in front of her face. "You go first!" She was quick to say, the bold smile returning quickly to her features.

I conceded to her excitement and shrugged out of my shirt leaving me in the fitted tank I'd stolen from Cael's closet that morning. I felt my temperature rise as Adeline's eyes raked over me. No matter how many times she did it, her gaze managed to stir up fireworks in the pit of my stomach.

"Do you even have space left?" Adeline stepped forward into my space and my fingers balled into the fabric of the shirt at my side.

"There's some on my legs," I said looking down at the minimal space separating our bodies.

"Would you get one here?" She circled me and when her finger ghosted over the skin of my neck behind my ear I shivered, unwillingly and I know she felt it cause a tiny laugh slipped from her. I looked down at her standing by my shoulder and stared into her eyes for a moment, wanting to tell her I'd get her name on my ass if she asked me nicely... hell, I'd do it if she asked me rudely.

"Yeah," I said, shrugging off the moment of sporadic boyish idiocy that was my feelings. "No dicks." I pointed at Harry specifically, "Even if he begs you, please don't put a dick there."

"No dicks," Adeline giggled, shuffling closer to Harry to look at his iPad with her hands in the air. The two of them whispered for a few moments before seemingly deciding something that had Adeline turn a new shade of red and sporting a new, unbridled look of excitement on her adorable face.

I sat in the chair and Harry pressed the transfer to my skin, changing the placement twice before Adeline gave him a nod of approval. She said in a chair with her arms over the back staring at me as Harry worked. The needle seemed to vibrate every bone and nerve in my head, I closed my eyes as it dragged in tiny, precise lines.

"Does it hurt?" Adeline asked quietly, her eyes watching my every move.

"It's just loud," I said, and I wasn't lying. The buzzing was incessant and right at the base of my skull as Harry worked.

When I opened my eyes Adeline was staring at me with more worry than amusement, her brows furrowed and her lips were pressed together in a tight line.

"Adeline I'm covered in tattoos." I tried to sooth her concern, giving her a soft smile in return. "It doesn't hurt." I winked but my jaw tightened as Harry ran over a practically sensitive spot of bone.

When Harry was finally finished he cleaned up the skin and let me stand up, "I think you're right Addy, I think that cock and balls suits him perfectly," Harry said, clapping me on the shoulder as I turned to the mirror terrified to find a tattoo my mother would absolutely disown me for.

Behind my ear in loose, light handwriting was the word *lover*. I looked over my shoulder and Adeline who looked proud of herself and I couldn't help but love it. It was clear that she had written it in handwriting and I should have been worried about her adding such a personal touch to it but I shamefully liked the idea of her marking her territory.

"You're lucky, I had the perfect tramp stamp planned but I think now I'll be nice," I said, before singing Harry's praise. No matter the subject matter he never failed to impress.

"I think it's cute," Adeline said with a smile, "all the girls will love it."

"Do *you* love it?" I asked her as I turned and Harry covered it with a little saniderm to protect it. She leaned against the wall watching him work when her eyes met mine, a little mischievous glint in them as she nodded.

"Good," I said, dropping my tone and stepping away from Harry. "Your turn," I said, stepping closer to her and dropping my eye line to match hers, "or are you chickening out?" I asked in a quiet tone. Harry excused himself, asking Adeline if she needed anything before leaving the room and us alone again.

Adeline looked up at me and shook her head, finally answering my question, "*never*. Pick a place." She straightened out with a smile and put her arms out at her side ready for me.

I ghosted my fingers along the underside of her arm, never touching her but I could feel the warmth of her skin. It was intoxicating enough that I almost forgot what I was doing as I circled around her and brushed a knuckle down the side of her throat.

"Are you going to pick, or just touch?" She asked me and when she turned her head our noses nearly touched. I admired the shape of her bottom lip as it curled into a serious expression.

"Well if I have a choice," I huffed and a smirk formed on my lips. Adeline shook her head but her smile dropped as my fingers splayed out over her stomach. The shirt she'd chosen to wear showed off all the toned muscles of her arms and the lacy bra beneath left nothing to imagination but the urge to get rid of everything between us was loud. Too loud. I needed to breathe, to take a step back before I did something stupid.

"Your thigh, visible at the gym but you can hide it if you want," I said, our faces still close together and her expression unchanged.

"Okay," she conceded. "Nothing vulgar."

"Awe, I was thinking *Daddy's Girl* or *Brat*," I teased.

"Don't you dare," she warned in a low voice but the corner of her lip lifted into a smile.

When Harry returned I talked to him about what I wanted and where we should put it. Harry drew up the stencil quickly, printing out two different sizes before he handed me the smaller of the two.

"Make sure it's straight," he said, eyeing me with a smile before handing me the stencil and backed away to get his table clean and set up for the next tattoo.

It wasn't like I hadn't done it before, Harry and I had been doing this for a while and sometimes he just couldn't be bothered after a long night. It was a trust thing and now he was handing that trust off to me. I was quietly glad. I would have lost my mind watching him touch her like that, especially when I hadn't even had the chance to do so. I trusted Harry with a lot... creative design, permanently scaring my body with ink but I did not trust him around a pretty girl. Worse, around *my* pretty girl.

Adeline was still standing, nervously waiting with her arms crossed over her chest and her eyes scanning the art on the wall. I placed the stencil on the table next to her face down, and watched her expression shift as I knelt before her.

"What are you doing?" She asked me, looking over at Harry who was spraying down his station.

"Trust me?" I responded, tilting my chin up to meet her concerned gaze as I tentatively reached out to touch her hip. The little nervous nod was all I needed to slip my hand under her shirt and brush my hand against the skin above her shorts, guiding her forward until she was standing straight. "Don't move," I whispered, my eyes trailing back down her body, stopping briefly to admire how her stomach fluttered with breath at my touch.

She stayed perfect still, her eyes watching my every move as I brushed my knuckle over her thigh and cleaned the spot on her inner thigh with the cold pad of alcohol. The adorable gasp that fell from her caused my grip to momentarily tighten on her hip and steady myself.

We could do better than that, I thought. Needing more.

"This will be cold," I whispered, applying a little of the primer with the pad of my finger across her inner thigh. I felt her stiffen at the contact, and her fingers reached out to balance herself with my shoulder. Her skin was so warm it was like standing in the sun on the first day after the longest winter.

I carefully pressed the thin paper to her skin, smoothing it out with my fingers slowly. I was taking my time because I wasn't sure how close I'd be for a while and if this was the only contact I received, I was going to make the best of it. My eyes flickered over her skin, taking in every scar and freckle, frowning at the amount of bruises she had. New and old they were all a part of her sport but they looked sore and uncomfortable.

I swallowed down the urge to brush my fingers over a particularly nasty newer one on her calf and looked back up at her. Those hazel eyes were still watching my every move like a hawk. Her long lashes and pretty dark eyeliner highlighted every green and golden fleck within them. She was smiling, it was small and nervous but the slight curl of her lip was intoxicating as my finger brushed the innermost corner of her thigh.

"Almost done," I whispered, watching her swallow down whatever she was going to say.

I begrudgingly took my eyes off her and started to peel back the paper to reveal the blue ink staining her freckled, olive skin perfectly straight and curved to her thigh like it belonged there. I shifted my grip on her hip, and wrapped my left hand around the back of her thigh to keep her from moving before leaning forward and blew on the skin gently to help it dry.

The feeling of cool air on her warm thigh dragged the prettiest of throaty whines from her lips that was so gentle and quiet, I almost missed it. Her fingers left my shoulder and found the back of my head, raking into my hair and my entire body shivered at her sudden, bold touch. I was embarrassed to admit how much I liked the feeling of her nails against my scalp as she fought to regain control of herself.

The air was thick around us and for a second I forgot that we were in public as I stood releasing her thigh from under my fingertips and taking a moment to press my lips to her hip as I moved my hand away. Her fingers tightened around my hair at the feeling and a throaty chuckle left me at the surprising tug of pain. Her skin was velvet under my lips and my breath hitched in my chest as her hand carefully retreated from my hair and I pulled away, pushing to my full height and coming face to face with her.

I put my hand back on her hip to keep her balanced but mostly because I wasn't ready to put space between us just yet. Her cheeks were flushed with color and her chest was rising and falling slowly under the sheer black shirt.

"Does it look okay?" She asked me, her eyes fluttering open as she tried to disguise her sexual frustration faster than I could spot.

"It's perfect," I said with a smirk, the tattoo, *you*. Everything was perfect.

"Lay down for me." Harry cleared his throat and pointed to the bed.

It took her another moment to collect herself, but Adeline listened, pulling away from my touch and pretending like the entire interaction hadn't happened as she slid back on it and laid down with her thigh exposed to the bright light above the bed.

She looked nervous but she'd never admit to it. Harry asked her twice if she was ready before she finally answered him and the sound of the machine buzzing made her flinch. I pulled my chair up next to the bed, reaching out to grab the bag of cola gummies and tearing them open with my teeth. I rested my elbow on the bed next to her shoulder and dug into the bag, tossing one between my lips as Harry started on the first line.

Adeline had her eyes closed but at the first whiff of candy her head lulled toward me and she popped one eye open while her face scrunched up into a bundle of cute, pain filled lines.

"Do you want one?" I asked her, taking another out of the bag. I was just trying to focus on her because Harry's face was between her legs and I was going to lose my mind if I thought about it for too long.

"Saying yes would be admitting defeat," she said, her words coming out in tiny stutters.

"I won't tell anyone if you don't," I whispered to her and leaned closer with the cola bottle in between my finger and thumb. She eyed me for a second longer before parting her lips and letting me slide it between her teeth. Adeline popped it into her mouth and I retracted my hand, but not without brushing my thumb against her pouty bottom lip.

It took everything in me not to react to how soft her skin was as I pulled back, seemingly unaffected and grabbed another piece of candy. Harry took longer to finish with Adeline, he worked slowly and after about an hour of her soft, stifled whimpers he finally finished and let her sit up to admire her first piece of ink.

"So?" I asked her. I refused to move from my spot, my body was stiff from leaning on the table to feed her candy but it was worth it when her shoulders eventually relaxed and she started to figure out how to manage the intrusion of pain.

"*Belle âme?* What does it mean?" She asked me. The script we had picked wasn't mine, but I wasn't about to maim her body with my thirteen-year-old chicken scratch. The one chosen was soft and loopy. I stood to look at it, my fingers creeping over her thigh just below it. I felt her tense under my touch, her eyes never leaving mine, waiting for an answer I wasn't prepared to give her.

"Better hope it's not French for something gross," I said with a smile, my fingers flexing on her thigh once before releasing her to let Harry clean and cover it.

"You wouldn't," she said back.

"I might," I said, wetting my bottom lip to keep control of how badly I wanted to kiss the attitude out of her body.

"It's pretty," she purred, looking down at it as Harry finished. "Thank you."

SARAH

Jensen wouldn't let me help pay for the tattoos and sent me up to the lobby while he did. I looked down at my thigh, fingers brushing over the thin covering that wrinkled around my skin and smiled.

It would be awhile before I forgot the hot, overwhelming need that flooded my body when Jensen had been that close. Any hesitation I had been feeling seemed to rush out as the sexual frustration receded and all that was left was the want and need to have more.

His hair was soft and his touches were purposeful, strong and burning my skin with an invisible branding that I could still feel as I busied myself with the art on the walls. I heard Jensen laughing and turned to see him saying goodbye and slipping back into his button down.

"You hungry?" He asked without skipping a beat.

Butterflies erupted across my chest at how natural it felt to be around him like that and I couldn't even remember why I was so worried this morning about today. It was like Jensen had always been a permanent fixture in my life and I was only noticing him now.

"Starving," I said, as he whipped the front door open.

He took my hand without asking as his confidence blossomed and I was quietly dying inside at the feeling of his fingers linked into mine. He glanced at me for a second and his smile softened around the edges.

"What?" I asked, looking over myself for anything that might be making him laugh.

"Nothing," Jensen chuckled and slowed his pace, "you're just going to have to get used to me staring at you just because I want to."

Alright. I could feel the blush crawling up my neck and I narrowed my eyes on him. "Some girls might find that creepy, you know?" I challenged him.

"If it made you uncomfortable, I wouldn't do it," he said back, his tone dropping as he wet his bottom lip and stepped in front of me to stop me. Our chests brushed and his eyes flickered to my lips as his smirk grew. "But it doesn't, you like it. So when you're done arguing with me…"

"I thought arguing was our thing?" I asked and pressed up on my toes to get eye level with him. "If you're sick of it already, I'm sure Harry wouldn't mind picking up the slack," I said, spinning on my heel to go back to the parlor.

Jensen's hand tightened around mine and pulled me back, tucking me against his chest and holding me tight with his arm around my lower back. His annoyed huff was hot as it fanned over my cheek and down my neck.

Kiss me.

I begged silently as his eyes looked down at my lips again. He could just as easily reach out with his own and give us both what we've been wanting. His fingers pressed into the skin of my lower back and I hadn't even noticed they'd crept beneath the fabric of my shirt until I was fighting for my life trying not to melt into a puddle from the way he was staring at me.

"That's fine, Adeline. Be a brat all you want but just know I'm keeping tabs and the day will come when you learn exactly how I deal with your attitude," he practically growled it, his voice darkening as people walked by us on the street. I held my breath, my thighs clenching together at his threat while my heart raced under my thin shirt.

He loosened his grip and tightened his hand on mine again, "I would like to show you my after tattoo tradition."

I finally inhaled once he stepped back and started to walk beside me again. I aimed for the car but he gently tugged on my hand to pull me in the other direction. We walked down the street for a while until we came to a restaurant with a busy patio out front and smelled like heaven.

"My second favorite thing in the entire world is chicken wings," he said to me, letting go of my hand and opening the door for me. "And you will never eat another one as good as these guys make them."

"Chicken wings?" I chuckled and walked inside with him at my back. The restaurant was nice, it wasn't as busy inside but there were booths set up in rows and a massive marquee bar against the back wall. The waitress seated us in a quiet back booth and as I slid into it against the burgundy leather it dawned on me, "what's your favorite thing? You said, chicken wings were your second favorite thing in the entire world, what's the first?"

"Ask me later," he huffed, his eyes bright and focused. He ordered us a bunch of food and a beer for himself, leaving me to order what I wanted to drink.

"You know chicken wings on a first date is a bold move," I said to him as the waitress handed me my gin and seven-up.

"I couldn't take you to some stuffy steak restaurant," he scoffed, pausing to scowl at me. "It might have been impressive but it didn't feel like something you'd enjoy."

It vibrated through me like a flash of lightning that he had so easily read me like that. I couldn't remember the last time I sat in a fancy restaurant and enjoyed it. Environments like this, close quarters, loud laughing, stiff drinks... my head was spinning with the amount of care he had taken with me even in the midst of my spontaneity.

"Is this like a mukbang fetish I wasn't aware of?" I mocked him, brushing off the rush of intense feelings I had gotten just then.

"Oh now, Adeline I know you aren't afraid to get a little messy," Jensen said, pressing the bottle to his lips as they curled into a devilish smirk. "Or did I make the wrong call?"

"Out of the two of us, I can confidently say that I get dirtier than you on a regular basis," I argued, "have you ever had to get grass stains out of your underwear?" I laughed gently and he joined in with a surrendering nod.

I watched him interact with the waitress as she returned and despite her actively trying to flirt with him, his focus wasn't on her even for a second. It was strange to be in a public setting with him in such a way, everyone knew his name or his face. With most of the towns around Harbor being so small, every male sport team was treated like they were famous.

But the majority of our interactions had been private, give or take a few. Most of our conversations took place over the phone and I had almost expected him to be a much bigger flirt with other women than he was turning out to be. He excused himself from the table to use the bathroom and I pulled my phone out of my pocket to text Kaia.

> I don't think he's fling material

KAIA:
Is it going bad?

Do you need us to come get you?

I can tell Rhea to get the bat!

> No

It was actually comical how fast she answered and even more how quickly she had decided that violence was the first and best option.

Then what?

> He's just… really nice and I don't know.

I might actually like him?

The dots appeared and disappeared more than once and I was starting to sweat that he'd return before Kaia gave me advice on how to proceed.

There is not a world that exists where you don't fuck that man.

> Kaia. That's not helpful.

Just try not thinking so hard about it. Are you having fun?

> Yeah

> **Then have fun and put your phone away, that's so rude on a date.**

I scoffed and tucked it away as Jensen came around the corner, "calling for an emergency evacuation already?" He asked, his eyes drifting down to my lap as he slid into the booth across from me.

"No," I said, "she was just checking to make sure you didn't murder me."

"If I was going to murder you I wouldn't have taken you to get identifying markers on your skin." Jensen's voice was low, his intelligence almost frightening.

"That's terrifying," I said with a laugh. "Is that why you got all those tattoos so no one can murder you?"

"No I got them because they make me look cool," he mused as the waitress set two massive trays of wings between us. "Can we get some more drinks?" He asked her quickly before she wandered away.

"This is a lot of food," I said, looking over all the different types of wings he ordered. There had to be at least twelve sets of eight wings each.

"Trust me once you start, it won't be enough and you have to try a little of everything or this date would be a bust," Jensen promised, grabbing his first wing. I looked at the table and rolled up the sleeves of my shirt before I started from the other end of the flight. The wing I chose was sweet, garlicky and it melted over my tongue.

"Holy shit," I mumbled with my mouth still a little full and a bright smile spread across his face.

"Told you," he beamed, clearly very proud of himself. "Try that one," he said, as I cleaned the chicken wing and set the bones into the discard bowl she had left for us.

"Do you guys have a code?" He asked after a few minutes of us eating in silence. He wasn't wrong, these were the best wings I'd ever eaten, and I definitely hadn't realized just how hungry I was until I had that first bite.

"A code?" I asked, taking a different flavor He lifted his bottle with two of his only clean fingers and took a sip.

"You know," he paused, setting the bottle down, "like if you don't like a guy, or if you're in trouble?" He asked. "Cael had a sentence, it was something we knew he'd never say…"

"What was it?" I laughed.

"I love my dad," Jensen chuckled and even though I didn't fully understand it was kinda ridiculous.

"Okay, what's your sentence then? If this date goes badly—"

"Do you think it's going badly?" He cut me off and I shook my head.

"But if it did, what's your out?" I asked him. He took another drink and thought about it for a moment.

He leaned on his elbows toward me across the table, "I don't have one, I never have."

"Wow, *cocky*," I smirked, finishing my drink.

"Optimistic," Jensen corrected. I giggled and Jensen raised his eyebrow at me, "what?"

"Optimistic, makes you sound like a man whore," I teased him.

"Man whore is harsh, I like to think of it as I'm not a quitter." He called the waitress over for another beer and ordered me another drink.

I pressed another wing between my teeth and smiled at him. I wanted to see how far I could push him, "so what if I told you that I don't wear deodorant?" I asked.

"I like the way your sweat smells," he whispered without a lick of hesitation.

"And if I told you I snore in my sleep?" I asked.

"I go to bed every night with a little white noise," he countered. I waited as the waitress cleared our empties before starting up again.

"Okay," I said, thinking on the next question a little harder, "if you come over for a booty call and when you get there I make you watch all ten Fast and Furious movies instead…"

"Are you a popcorn girl or nachos?" Jensen said without skipping a beat and my heart stuttered a little at his response. "Nevermind, I'd bring both."

"You'd do all of that to get some ass?" I asked him, nervously chewing on another wing.

"What about any of the things I've done or said over the last weeks gave you the idea that I'm only in this for sex?" He asked me and I almost choked on my wing from his response.

Shit. I hadn't prepared for him to be so quick and responsive with his answers, hell I wasn't even ready for this date to go as well as it had. The Jensen leading up to it had been smooth, and charming.

"The texts, pushing for a date, the flirting," I listed all of his efforts.

He huffed, setting down his beer and sliding out from the booth.

"I thought you weren't a quitter?" I looked up at him and he scoffed.

"Enough," his tone was low, demanding and silenced whatever argument that was about to leave my mouth next. "Move over," he said, sliding into the same side as me. He leaned over the back with his arm and braced on the table, effectively trapping me in with his body. "I know this is hard to believe but there can be duality to a man, Adeline. I can take you on dates, treat you right, feed you, make you laugh... keep you happy," his voice changed again as he leaned in closer. "I like doing all those things..." He breathed out and I could feel it across my throat and chest as his fingers curled into the cushioned booth behind my head.

I could feel the heat rising on my cheeks again, a ferocious mixture of gin and Jensen's cologne flooded my senses and made it hard to think about anything other than kissing him.

"But that's just one side of me," Jensen said, his hand coming up and pressing against my cheek, his fingers long enough to curl against the back of my jaw and pull me closer to his lips. "I want to be the one that fucks every bratty thought from your head until I'm the only thing on your mind."

I swallowed, pressing my hand flat to the table close to his while his gaze stayed intently connected to mine.

"Do you understand now?" He asked me as we shared a single breath. "Answer me, Adeline," he whispered with a smirk. I was going to die in the booth of a chicken wing bar in the arms of a fuckboy baseball player and I'd never been more ready for my last moments.

"I understand," I finally forced off my lips.

"Good," he said, turning back in the booth like he hadn't just completely violated every resolve I had left about fucking him.

We continued to eat and drink, the conversation lulling into something softer and more connected than it had been before. I was starting to understand what he meant when he said he could be both. Sweet and attentive when he wanted to be but in those quick moments he was a completely different animal.

"You're going to protest and before you say no, I have a plan," Jensen said, finishing another beer. "I'm not driving back to Harbor, and neither are you," he laughed, leaning closer and pointing to the four empty gin glasses.

"You want to stay here? In town?" I said, my voice clearly a little nervous.

"Hey, just to sleep it off. I'll even get us two beds," he said, "scout's honor," he said tapping his chest again.

"That's suspicious," I scowled.

"If I'm going to be inside you, I'm going to remember every goddamn second of it," he added without flinching and hailed down the waitress for the bill.

"Let me," I asked, reaching for it.

"Pretty sure, *feed you*, was on that list," he said, plucking the bill away before I could take it.

JENSEN

I grabbed my gym bag from the trunk of the car and we walked three blocks to the closest hotel. Adeline was giddy, her laugh infectious as we walked and I was alright, definitely a little tipsy, and I wasn't chancing putting her in a car and driving the two hours home. It was nice to be away from everything in Harbor. There wasn't anything on my mind, it was just Adeline and me having fun in a random town where no one knew who we were and we could laugh as loud as we wanted.

"Two beds," I said to the receptionist, handing him my card and ID as we entered the hotel and walked up to the main desk. I didn't mention to Adeline that it fell under the umbrella of my mother's company, but that wasn't something she really needed to know.

"Sure," he said, he couldn't have been more than eighteen and he stared at me for a second, checking my ID and then checking my credit card against it. "Mr. Jensen," he handed me the card back.

"You know I never asked what your first name was," Adeline said, her arm pressed into the crook of my elbow as I took the keycard from the kid.

"You didn't tell me yours when I asked," I scoffed, leading her to the elevator, "why should I tell you mine?"

"Aren't we past that little game?" She narrowed her glossy eyes on me and I leaned close, scrunching up my nose at her.

"About as over it as you are compliant," I teased and she rolled her eyes at me.

"Well it's not on the roster card," she said as the elevator took us to the fifth floor.

"Yeah it is, my first initial is there," I reminded her.

I found amusement in how unsteady she became in her footsteps with a little booze in her system. It wasn't that she was drunk by any means, but she had started to relax a little and she was so focused on asking me questions that she wasn't paying attention to how she was leaning into me for support, or how her smile turned wide and playful on her rosy cheeks.

"This one," I laughed and stopped her from walking.

"Well, what's your first initial?" She let go of me and leaned against the wall beside the door.

"Check next game," I said, flicking her chin with the card before swiping it and popping the lock open.

"You're cheating," she gasped in disbelief, sliding into the room before me. She stopped in the small entryway before looking back at me. "If you wanted to cuddle, you could have just asked."

"What did I do?" I dropped my duffle and locked the bolt behind me. I moved through the room around her, flicking on the light to illuminate the one king-size bed. "You were standing right there when I asked for two," I said, trying not to laugh at the delicious misfortune. "I'll sleep on the floor," I offered.

She stayed quiet for a moment before inhaling and exhaling one big breath, "You have to keep your hands to yourself..." she said, "mostly."

"*Mostly?*" I surged forward like she had called me like a dog, "what does mostly mean?" I asked, dipping my head to meet her gaze and reaching my hands out to her sides but not touching her as she backed toward the bed.

Her giggle only made controlling myself harder, when her thighs hit the bed she fell back on it and stared up at me with a smile.

"Adeline," her name rolled off my lips from the bottom of my throat. "*What does that mean?*" I asked her again.

"If you tell anyone, I'll sick Kaia on you," she stuck her hand in the air, trying to be serious and I paused my slow approach. "I'm scared of the dark and I wouldn't be opposed to some cuddling," she uttered words like it pained her to say them and I couldn't help but smile at her. "No laughing!"

"I'm not laughing," I said, raising my hands and lowering to my knees between her legs. "That's probably the most endearing thing I've ever heard out of your mouth."

"Don't tease me," she snapped. "It's not sexy and I'm a little tipsy so..."

"It's incredibly sexy that you're scared of the dark," I dropped my tone for her and spread my hands out over the bed beside her hips until our noses almost touched and our chests met. "I guess you could say I'm a hero," I joked, "I couldn't bear the thought of you sleeping alone in that big bed in the dark."

She laughed finally and her shoulders relaxed a little.

"Feel better?" I asked her, desperate to kiss her but restraining until she asked me for one. "There's some extra t-shirts in my duffle." I told her after a beat of silence, her glassy eyes flickering back and forth watching mine. Despite what Adeline believed I hadn't gone into the date expecting sex. I had truly just wanted so desperately to spend the day with her that I wouldn't have cared if we sat on the floor in her apartment and just stared at each other.

It had only been about hanging out with her at a distance that I could touch her and hear her laugh. "Go change, I'll find us a movie or something," I said to her pushing up off the bed and wandering around the room to look for the remote.

She picked up my duffle from the floor and locked herself in the bathroom giving me a few seconds to collect my thoughts as I flipped through the pay-per-view rentals. I could hear her shuffling around on the other side of the door as I pulled off my shirt and laid across the bed in my jeans. I laughed seeing the first Fast and Furious movie as an option and hovered over it knowing that it would rile her up to see it playing. "Thirteen dollars?" I scoffed and hit enter, starting just as the door clicked open.

I tried to keep my eyes in my head but Adeline sauntered across the room in nothing more than one of my navy Hornets gym shirts. It hung around her thighs and I thought for a second I might die right there and then when I realized she had taken off her shorts.

"You're making it impossible to *mostly* keep my hands to myself," I whispered to her and she smiled, looking down at herself with a feeble shrug before she crawled across the top of the bed toward the pillows. The hem of the shirt lifted, falling over the curve of her perfect ass and gave view to the small pair of black underwear she was wearing beneath. I shifted uncomfortably on the bed to hide how hard the sight of her made me.

"Is this—"

"Fast and Furious," I rolled over onto my back to look at her from the end of the bed. My eyes roamed up her bare legs and my mouth went dry at the sight of her completely unarmored and relaxed in the dim light of the lamp.

"What are the chances?" She giggled, sinking down into the mountain of pillows. I watched her wiggle beneath the comforter and get comfy. "I was joking, but I really do love these movies." Her eyes broke from the screen for a quick second to smile at me.

"I'll be right back," I said, as I climbed from bed and found my spare shorts, before retreating to the bathroom to calm down. I wasn't going to last much longer that close to her without saying something stupid and ruining her confidence in me to behave.

I splashed some cold water on my face in a weak attempt to wash the image of her toned skin from my mind but the peek of her black underwear as she climbed across the bed was burned into the back of my eyelids and every time I shut them my stupid dick got hard.

Shuffling out of my jeans and boxers, I threw on the shorts and tied them up around my hips loosely. I gave myself one more pep talk in the mirror before returning to a sleepy Adeline curled into the bed smiling lazily up at the movie.

She looked like an angel. Her messy, thick hair consumed the pillow in dark waves and I almost didn't want to disturb her but I couldn't stand being that far away for much longer. I walked around the bed, and her eyes broke from the TV to follow my path. She kept to her side as I pulled back the sheets and crawled in next to her.

"I love this movie," she hummed as I wrapped my arm around one of the pillows, angling my head to look at the screen but still keeping her in my peripherals.

Today had been nice, I couldn't have dreamt up a better first date if I tried. I truly hadn't meant for us to end up in the same bed but I'd be lying to myself and her if I didn't like having her so damn close. She smelled so good and looked so comfortable.

"Thank you for today," she said, exhaling a deep breath. "And for behaving," her laughter was like honey, "I know it can't be easy when you have a half-naked girl in your bed."

My eyes flickered downward to her fingers playing with the hem of the shirt and chuckled softly. "Well, I'd like to think that I have some self-control," I said, hiding how little of a grip I actually had on that control with her just out of reach. "Besides, ravishing you on the first date might scare you off."

"Is that what you planned on doing? Ravishing me?" She teased me, looking over at me with a smile on her face. "Who even uses that word anymore," she giggled and I shrugged. I smirked up at her, shifting on the bed so I was closer, "I won't lie, the thought did cross my mind. But I figured I should at least try to be a gentleman first. I'm trying to make a good impression here," I said back.

In reality there were too many clothes, too many sheets and not enough pretty noises dripping from her. It was driving me nuts. I curled my hand into the sheets to keep from touching her but she was right there, so close I could feel the heat radiating off her.

"And after the good impression?" She turned her face downward, sliding into the pillows more and inching toward me. "What would you do?" She asked me in a tone that turned my resolve into steam, it rolled off my body and I couldn't help but brush my hand over her bare thigh.

Her eyes darkened at the touch but she didn't move away. "After? I'd kiss you senseless, explore every inch of you with my hands and my tongue. Leave you so desperate you beg me for more." I whispered and watched her throat bob. I could get off from the sight of her like that, flushed cheeks, parted lips, her eyes wide and hazy.

I was getting hard from the thought of what that pretty mouth could do given the chance, all of the control I thought I had was slipping.

"A woman never begs," she said, rolling her eyes at me made her lashes flutter and when she looked back at me it was a heavy lidded lusty gaze that pushed all of the blood between my legs.

A low, husky laugh left my lips at her declaration, "Sure. Well, it'll be fun proving you wrong and I'm not someone who backs away from a challenge."

"Right, *you're not a quitter*," she mocked me.

My hand crept up her thigh, the touch light and teasing as I said, "At the very least, I bet I could make you say please."

"Is please considered begging?" She teased.

"Semantics," I hummed as my fingers found the hem of her shirt, "I'm thinking more whimpering, clinging to me, demanding more..."

"Is that how you see this going?" Adeline smiled at me and caught my hand in hers. "You sure have some ego on you," she whispered, her perfect lips falling open at the end making it excruciatingly hard not to kiss her.

"Can you blame me?" I grinned at her, not bothered by her jabs about my ego. It wasn't going anywhere. "When the girl in my bed looks like an angel and talks back every chance she gets... it's hard not to feel a little cocky." I wove my fingers into hers and squeezed gently.

"Always so smooth," she whispered. "You haven't even kissed me yet and you're leading with whimpering and clinging?" I could tell she was trying to keep control of the conversation but her resolve was slipping faster than mine.

"Adeline, if my words alone make your cheeks that red, god forbid I actually touch you the way I intend to. You'd probably explode," I said, the smirk on my face growing as I watched her reaction. I loved watching her blush, every text at the gym was just to see what color I could elicit from her that day. "It's alright, there won't be any of that tonight, you have nine more Fast and Furious movies to watch before we even get to the make-out stage," I teased and she laughed, squeezing my hand tighter as I turned my attention off her to the TV dramatically.

"You can't be serious?" Out of the corner of my eye I could see her pouting.

"Sorry, I don't make the rules," I said, trying not to laugh as I shrugged off her frustrated growl. But I underestimated the way she was playing the game and before I could stop her she was crawling out of the sheets and over my lap, pressing my back against the headboard as she straddled my hips with her perfect legs.

"Kiss me," she demanded.

My eyes widened in surprise as I took her in and a smug, satisfied smirk spread across my face. The problem with us was that neither would back down from the challenge, and Adeline had just thrown down the gauntlet.

"Bossy," I murmured, secretly loving the way her body reacted to being called it. "I thought you didn't beg?" I asked, pushing the hem of her shirt up to expose her more and resting my hands lightly on her hips, I couldn't help myself. I needed to touch her.

"I'm not begging, I'm demanding," she argued, "there's a difference." There was a huge difference. Bossy Adeline had every nerve in my body screaming.

I threw my head back in laughter, extremely amused and turned on by her defiance. "There you go with semantics again," I teased, my grip tightening. "Either way I see it, I win," I said, drinking in every inch of her.

"How's that?" she asked.

"You're sitting in my lap, issuing orders and it's turning me on," I hummed.

She stared at me for a long moment, no doubt trying to decide her next move. The longer she sat there the more relaxed she became and soon it would be hard to hide just how turned on I was.

"So submissive," she whispered.

"I did warn you." I lowered my voice and tilted my head up more.

"Are you going to kiss me or not?" She pushed on my chest with her hand, her bottom lip jutting out. I caught her hand in mine, bringing it to my lips to kiss her palm before intertwining her fingers.

"I'm considering it," I laughed under my breath, she was determined. I'd give her that. I smiled up at her, her face so serious about it all and I knew that I wouldn't be able to say no for much longer. Adeline was like a breath of fresh air.

"Consider faster," she demanded.

"And what if I don't?" I teased, my thumb doing a small circle on her thigh as it dropped down from her hip. "What if I deny that pretty little mouth?"

"Then you can sleep on the floor," she lowered her voice and it only made me more inclined to give her what she wanted. I knew she was serious, only because she had proved time and time again that she was of her word. I wet my bottom lip and let go of her thigh and her hand to cup her face in my hands as I shifted straighter in the bed.

"Just *one*," I whispered, "Put this desperate man out of his misery," I said to her, hands in her curly hair and eyes locked on her pouty bottom lip. *Just one kiss.*

Adeline nodded, waiting for me to make the move.

My lips hovered over hers, our breath mingling and then slowly, *deliberately*, I closed the distance. We collided with a soft explosion of heat as our lips tangled together gently at first and then she melted against my chest. I did my best to keep it teasing and tender as my hand wrapped around the back of her neck.

She refused to be the first to pull away, her ability to hold her breath contingent on how long she could stretch her one kiss. When I pulled back the most adorable and equally sexy noise rumbled from the base of her throat in protest.

"Happy now?" I asked her, trying to hide just how dizzy the kiss had made me. I closed my eyes trying to rein in the desire that nipped at my fingertips. When I opened them again hers were staring back at me, warm with affection and something else, something deeper.

She was debating asking for another.

"Just one," I murmured, shaking my head.

"Stingy," she growled, searching my face for any point of weakness that she could prey on to get more.

It was killing me trying to be a gentleman, I wasn't going to have sex with her. Not tonight, not when she was still slightly tipsy and couldn't feel every single thing I wanted to do to her. But I couldn't deny the sad, frustrated lines that formed between her eyebrows. I leaned back in, pressing a second, quicker kiss to her lips.

"Now it's two," I said proudly, pulling back before she could follow me and drag it out. I enjoyed watching a hundred sassy remarks flicker behind her hazel eyes as she pulled her bottom lip between her teeth.

My lips burned with her aftertaste and I was going to break all of my plans if she didn't stop staring at me like that.

"You're just being a tease," she grumbled.

"Maybe," I said, a low, breathy laugh leaving my chest, "But I'm a tease with a conscience. I'm not going to rush this, Adeline." I brushed my nose against her jaw just for some extra contact and felt her lean into it with a muffled moan. "I want to do it right and that doesn't include a hotel, cheap movies and both of us smelling like chicken wings." The words came out rougher than I expected, but I was serious and I couldn't stress that enough to her. No matter how badly she wanted to push further, I would keep stopping her.

"How dare you call this movie cheap," she teased, as she stared me down, a mischievous glint in her eyes. I swore that grin was begging for trouble and I nearly broke from the sight of it. Adeline knew exactly what she was doing to me and she loved every second of it. She leaned forward, still resting against my hips and pressed that grin to the underside of my jaw.

Fuck.

My hips twitched beneath her and it fueled her behavior like gas to fire as she worked down over my throat in small warm circles with her mouth.

My breath hitched as her lips made contact over and over, my hands finding her hips again to steady myself. I tilted my head to the side slightly, allowing her better access to the skin, my voice strained as my body reacted like a touch starved idiot to her lips. "Adeline," I growled, it was a warning but it was weak and she didn't even flinch at the sound.

"Jensen," she hummed back, her teeth grazing over my collarbone as her hands splayed out over my ribcage on either side.

"Fuck, you aren't playing fair," I panted, as my head fell back against the headboard. My fingers dug into her hips as I tried to maintain my self control but her lips on my neck were making it increasingly difficult. I could feel all of my muscles tightening with arousal as the control in me began to crumble.

"One more kiss and I'll stop," she tried to bargain.

I swallowed hard, torn between my gentlemanly resolve and the infectious torment of her lips on my throat. I knew I couldn't win, I was so far gone that she could have asked me for anything and I would have moved heaven and earth to make sure she got it. With a low growl, I surged forward and captured her lips in a searing kiss that demanded surrender.

"Greedy little *brat*," I huffed against her mouth, completely undone by her touch and shamelessly breathless from a high school make out. I flipped her on the bed until she was trapped beneath me, the soft flickers of the movie still playing in the background as her feet twisted into the sheets to steady her trembling thighs.

It drove me to the brink of madness knowing that they were mine, marked clearly now with words I chose for her. I had picked her left thigh on purpose, it was the closest to me when she sat in the passenger seat of my car. I wanted to make sure I could get my hands on it whenever the fuck I wanted. The desperation for her was sickening, I barely recognized myself anymore.

She dug her nails into my chest and I groaned against her lips at the tiny explosion of pain. The combination of the love bites she had left over my neck and the sting of her nails was almost too much to bear. I deepened the kiss, my tongue sweeping into her mouth claiming every inch. My hand pushed up her shirt, just needing to feel more skin as it splayed out across her stomach. Two fingers brushed the hem of her thin panties and I felt her hips lift from the bed. My head was too hazy, too incessant on taking everything too far.

"We need to slow down," I begged her, I needed her to be the one to stop it because I had lost all control of my rational thought with her writhing beneath me on the bed.

"Okay," she whispered as I pulled away, her chin tilting upward to follow my lips for just a little more. "Okay…"

A defeated laugh left me, the sound muffled against her mouth as I gave into the silent request. The kiss turned deeper instantly, my hand exploring upward to the underside of her impossibly soft breasts. *Fuck, fuck, fuck.* My thoughts were possessive for her, my touch gentle but the urgency I felt to claim every inch of her inside and out was building faster than I could stop it.

I broke the kiss again, resting my forehead against her as I tried to catch my breath, "one more?"

"One more?" Adeline giggled breathlessly.

"One more." I repeated with finality, closed my eyes and savored the feeling of her fingers as they brushed into the hair at the base of my neck. It did the trick to slow my racing heart and when the room stopped spinning I opened my eyes again, my gaze on her, full of tender admiration. I couldn't help but lean in for one last kiss, slower, softer… almost reverent in nature.

In that moment it was like Adeline had always meant to be there, kissing me. The world slowed down a little just to give us a moment in time that was all our own. I pulled back slightly, my eyes never leaving hers as I brushed a stray strand of hair away from her face, tucking it behind her ear. "You know," I said quietly, still slightly out of breath, "I've imagined kissing you a hundred times, but none of them compared to the real thing."

Adeline laughed quietly, "you've been having wet dreams about me?"

I shook a small bark of laughter from my lips, the sound deep and filled with a love for her ability to make every moment feel natural. "Yes," I said, not embarrassed in the slightest that she had been consuming my every thought. "Every night, I'm surprised my sheets aren't permanently damp." I smiled at her and kissed her nose.

"You're really giving away all your secrets here," she said quietly.

"Hey, if a gorgeous woman asks, I'm not going to lie, and maybe..." I leaned in closer, lowering my voice, "I want you to know just how thoroughly you've gotten under my skin."

The statement was serious and it made my chest warm with excitement as her lips parted. I could practically hear her asking for more when her phone buzzed under her pillow on the bed. I glanced up at it, trying to hide the flicker of disappointment that tossed my mind as the moment was interrupted.

I rolled to the side, giving her the space to grab it as I propped myself up on one elbow to watch her reaction. "Someone important?" I asked, trying to keep my tone light and free of the surge of jealousy I felt.

Adeline raised an eyebrow at me, but she snuggled closer against my chest and hooked her leg around my waist, stealing what little breath I had collected with her touch. "Not unless you're worried Kaia is the love of my life," she giggled, "you sound jealous."

I wrapped my arm around her waist possessively, pulling her closer, "am not," I muttered, pretending not to be offended. "Is it her then?" I asked, attempting to sound casual as I glanced at her phone. "Kaia seems like the type to steal my girl from right under my nose. She's sexting you isn't she?" I teased.

"Worse," Adeline laughed and showed me a string of worried texts, the last one asking rudely if *Jensen has a nice dick*. "She's going to be so sad when she finds out that she was the world's biggest cock block tonight."

My cheeks went red as I read the text as my eyes narrowed in amusement and I buried my face into her neck, my shoulders shaking with laughter. "She's insane."

"I'll tell her it's below average and maybe she'll leave us alone," Adeline teased.

I immediately lifted my head feigning insult, "below average? Fuck that," I said dramatically making her laugh some more. "I'll have you know it's very... above national average."

"Oh yeah?" She turned her face to look at me, "do you guys have... like a database?"

"Yeah totally... uh," I stumbled through the joke, "penisdatabase.com," I replied, "look me up sometime, my stats are impressive." I winked at her trying to keep the mood light and flirty again.

Adeline lost it laughing at my defense tactics. Her mood was so playful and sweet, a stark contrast to how it felt to kiss her. She texted Kaia back that she was safe, tucking her phone away with a small yawn as she rolled back against the bed under the sheets with her back to me.

I used the distraction to wrap myself around her properly, pulling her against my chest and resting my chin on her shoulder. "Tired?" I asked her and she nodded curling deeper against me. I squeezed her gently, my arm tightening just a touch, "we should get some sleep." I said, unable to resist the urge to kiss the back of her neck before nuzzling deeper, "for the record," I dropped my tone into a low, husky murmur, "it's actually quite a bit bigger than average."

I couldn't help but laugh, my body relaxing around hers. I wanted her to tease me in that sleepy innocent voice forever, it was so different from the sassy, mocking one she used when she was fully awake.

"Oh we know," she giggled, "those light grey sweatpants you wear in the gym..." she trailed off in a sleepy voice. She turned in my arms and pressed her lips against my temple before whispering, *"Hide nothing."*

SARAH

Rhea knocked me into the dirt onto my back and all the air rushed out of my body as I hit the ground hard. "Sorry Minty," she said, crawling off me as the drill ended.

"Where's your head at?" Cosy came up beside us, her cheeks flushed and her dark red hair braided back off her face. "You've been out of it all damn day and you're going to get someone hurt!"

"Simmer Mom," Kaia was quick to defend her as she caught a ball a few feet from us. "She left all her conscious thoughts on some hotel floor with her favorite pair of underwear," Kaia snorted.

"The underwear stayed on my body all night I'll have you know!" I argued back and Kaia let out a long, exaggerated boo.

"You're playing like shit because of a boy?" Cosy scoffed, "that's something I never thought I'd hear. Adeline Sarah, star winger...distracted by dick."

"Yeah, yeah laugh it up," I said, almost embarrassed that I had been that easily rattled by Jensen. But since that date I couldn't keep my thoughts off him. What was once, rugby, rugby, work and more rugby was now. Jensen, his hands, his lips, his laugh...

"Oh she's six feet under," Rhea laughed, putting her hand on her hip. "We've lost her to the dark side."

"My head is spinning a thousand different directions right now," I admitted and slumped back to the ground. "Give me five minutes," I begged and Coach called for water.

"Spill," Rhea said, tumbling into the grass beside me as Sunday and Kaia came closer. I told them everything, not sparing a single detail of the day turning sleepover and when I got to the make-out, all four of them were completely enamored.

"Show us the tattoo," Cosy demanded.

I rolled up my rugby shorts and pulled the compression shorts beneath out of the way of the tattoo. It was healing and the skin had taken the ink so well. The lettering was smooth and stood out on my inner thigh.

Rhea practically climbed into my lap, her fingers brushing over it as she swooned. "Belle âme?" she asked, "What does it mean?"

I hadn't actually ever looked it up.

"She didn't look," Kaia called my bluff with a nasty grin on her face.

"It means beautiful soul," Sunday said without skipping a beat and we all looked at her. "Brighton spent two years of deployment in France, and Boone went to school there..." she said in defense of our confused stares. "You learn fast when you're dragging around your seven year old niece in the middle of Paris trying to find your idiot brother."

"I feel like every time you open your mouth out tumbles sensitive matters of national security," Rhea said to her and Sunday just smiled.

"Back to the fact that the fuckboy *picked*, beautiful soul to mark our girl with on a first date," Kaia sounded as impressed as she was pissed off. Her voice dipping into swooning territory just as quick as it rebounded into possessive.

"He could have picked his name," Cosy shrugged, pulling my leg toward her so she could get a better look. "And it looks well done."

"It's extremely hot," Rhea agreed, "if I had a man chasing me around calling me pretty French pet names, I'd probably submit to anything—"

"Anything?" Kaia perked up.

"Okay, not *that*," Rhea said, looking scared. There was clearly a story there that neither of them wanted to share. I'd ask about it later because the look on Rhea's face was pure, unbridled disgust mixed with terror.

"So you didn't even have sex?" Sunday asked, her brows dipping together a little confused.

"He was a perfect gentleman and refused because I had too much gin," I pouted.

"How the hell did you manage to screw up a booty call with a fuckboy?" Kaia asked, her dark hair blowing around in a messy ponytail.

"That's just it, he's not... well he is but he's also..." I trailed off trying to explain.

"An absolute simp?" Sunday asked with a smile.

"Who taught you that term?" Rhea scowled at Sunday, who hilariously was about half her person and the complete opposite in every way.

"Daisy sends me Tik Toks," Sunday laughed.

"That is it though, I expected to be fighting for my life to keep my clothes on and instead..." I shrugged. "He wanted to do things right and I'm not complaining but there's so much going on that I don't think getting involved with someone who's life is so tied into the soil of Harbor is smart."

"You're so fucked," Kaia started to laugh but her eyes softened.

"This was supposed to be a fling and now it doesn't feel like one," I almost whined the words because of the frustration building. "This is your fault!"

"How do you know he doesn't just want to build a connection?" Sunday asked innocently.

"A connection still feels like attachment," I said. "Love is stupid. This is stupid! He was just supposed to help me relax and fuck my brains out and now I'm laying on the ground in the middle of rugby practice contemplating my entire fucking life. What the hell happened?" I started to panic and felt like at a moment's notice I might start to cry.

"Get up." Cosy demanded.

"What?" I sighed, my entire body reacting.

"Get off your ass," she said, standing up and throwing the ball at me.

"Cosy," Kaia tried to interject and got tossed a dirty look.

"Run it again." Cosy dropped into stance when Coach blew the whistle and Rhea stood back, letting her take position as my partner. I stared at her for help but she just shrugged her shoulders.

I was in for it.

Cosy surged forward and I protected the ball as she pushed me into the hard ground without remorse. I rolled the ball out to Sunday who gave me a whimper of sympathy.

"Do it again, don't get caught this time," Cosy grumbled and pulled me off the ground.

"We're running ground drill, Cosy not—"

My excuses were silenced by her glare.

Coach blew the whistle again and I stumbled over my own two feet before Cosy caught my hip, wrapping me up and pushing me back until I was in the dirt again. I slammed the ball down and rose to my feet as she yelled at me to do it again.

I understood her motives. Out here all that mattered was our dedication to each other.

My chest was pounding with short breaths as the whistle blew. I was more prepared that time, shifting off my left foot and narrowly avoiding her grasp while pushing forward out of her reach. I laughed hard, expelling all the pent up energy out of my body with a funny little scream.

"Feel better?" Cosy asked out of breath and I nodded.

"I'm good at rugby, that's not the problem," I grumbled.

"Balance, Minty. You just gotta find balance." She smiled, "now everyone off your asses, get back to practice," she snapped and everyone groaned as they moved into position.

An hour later Sunday laid in my lap as we watched the Hogs practice, "Boone's hungover," she said. "I can always tell." He was moving like his feet were casted in cement and the slower he moved the more pissed off Judd Loveday became.

"Helps that he's always hungover..." Rhea laughed quietly, well she texted on her phone.

"Bets on Lovey throwing the first punch?" Kaia asked, squinting into the sun as it peaked out from the heavy clouds that hung over our heads.

"He won't, Loveday is a pussy," Cosy grumbled, her attention on the drills they were running at the other end of the field.

"You hate that guy for absolutely no reason," Kaia snipped, "his accent alone is enough to make me wet," she said loud enough that a few players looked up at her from the field and Cosy almost pushed her from the bleachers for disturbing the peace.

"He's also a cop, an egotistical piece of shit, and he thinks he's god's gift to rugby," she added with disdain. At six-two and one of the most fit members of the Harbor Hogs, the last part of her statement wasn't a lie but he sort of had a right to act that way. "I have to get to the shelter, enjoy watching the sausage fest."

"She's not wrong though, if anyone is going to throw a punch it'll be Bright for even looking at Boone funny," I said as Brighton Black marched across the field in the smallest shorts he could possibly wear. "He's like a feral cat caught in a bag."

"His temper should be studied for science. Here we go," Sunday groaned, "they say women are too emotional but not a single one of us have ever fought each other on the field. Boone and Loveday go at it once a practice."

"It's crazy to think they even get along off the field." Rhea said. "I don't think I could be friends like that, it would give me heartburn."

"The constant mud wrestling is the only thing that makes these practices worth watching," I said.

"That and Bright's thighs," Kaia moaned, chewing on her lip and earning a gagging sound from Sunday in my lap. "Shut up, you offer up Boone like a mail order slut on a regular basis."

"He *is* a mail order slut," Sunday giggled and turned her head back to the field.

Boone and Judd were nose to nose, pretty similar in size and ready to get violent. They were in a screaming match at center when the rain started to fall and everyone spectating started to clear out.

"Take it off!" Kaia yelled as the rain came down hard and began flooding the field. "'I'll pay good money to see you get dirty!" She hollered.

"We could film it and upload it to the Dirt Ruckers site, and make a pretty buck." Rhea said, nudging Kaia with a smile. There was a popular site that was basically rugby porn in its lowest form. Hard hits, nasty breaks, big fights. On hard days we'd pile into the same bed and send horrible videos back and forth as we laughed so hard we inevitably ended up in tears.

"Boones on there enough," Sunday said, sitting up and grabbing her bag, "it's over-saturated with his ugly face," she grumbled. "I'm going over to the bar, someone needs to open up, you coming?" She asked Kaia who shrugged and collected her shit.

"At least the rain held out until we were done, I'll catch you later Minty," Rhea kissed my cheek and left me sitting in the rain. Sometimes it was just nice to have the cold water to clean away all the thoughts that were plaguing me.

Coach Welton was standing in the doorway of the massive athletics building that sat off the rugby pitches and I carried myself over to her. She was watching the men practice, her focus the same as Cosy's as I approached.

"Have you heard anything from California?" I asked her, shaking out my hair as I walked through the door into the building. It was a moment longer before she turned to address my question.

"There's a scout coming in a few weeks," she said, crossing her arms. As if she could feel my apprehension she spoke again, "All you need to do is play your best."

"In front of the man that has my future in his hands," I added.

"Play like he's not here, show him the player that they make highlight reels of and he'll have no choice but to sign you," Coach encouraged. "This is a big deal but you can't let it muck up your brain, that's what makes you a good player."

"Easier said than done." I smiled and adjusted my bag on my shoulder.

"Go home, relax. The next little while you're going to have to train harder, we need to be ready," Coach said, patting me on the shoulder before she disappeared down the hallway.

I shook out the feelings of dread, picking up food on the way back to my apartment knowing that once I crawled into bed I wouldn't be getting out of it. My body was sore from the abuse it suffered at practice. I could feel a few over tightened muscles and could pinpoint the location that the bruises would appear in the morning.

"Ms. Sarah?" My name was called when I walked through the front doors. The building I lived in had a sweet younger girl that worked less as a doorman and more of a guard dog but occasionally she would collect oversized packages or food deliveries to keep the lobby clean.

"Hey Tina," I said, wandering over to her.

"Someone dropped this off for you earlier but he didn't wanna leave it outside your door so I stashed it for you," she smiled at me with a mouth full of braces that made her look way younger than she actually was.

"Thanks," I grabbed the small purple gift bag from her and wandered toward the elevator. Instead I dug in the bag and found two jars of cream that looked like someone had filled themselves as well as a note. The door dinged open and the second I was inside of my apartment with everything tossed on the counter I pulled the note from the bag, laying it on the counter as I opened one of the jars.

I got Silas to mix up some arnica cream with something that smells like you. He says it will help with bruising. If you need any help rubbing it on, text me but until then heal up, so I can leave marks of my own.

I lifted the jar to my nose and it smelled like citrus and arnica but it was less harsh than usual... I couldn't help but smile at the note resisting the urge to feign idiocy just to see his face.

> **Very obsessive loverboy of you**

I texted before taking a little cream between my fingers and rubbing it on a faded bruise on my arm gently. He had gone out of his way to leave me this and it was going to fuck with my head.

> **Duality.**

JENSEN

Adeline opened the door in a pair of tight jean shorts and a knitted crop top that showed off her stomach, it made my mouth dry. I leaned against the door frame, gripping the top frame in my fingers to keep from grabbing her and locking her inside for the next week where only I could see her.

"I'm not changing," she said, reading my expression.

"I don't want you to change," I said, wetting my bottom lip as my eyes traced the script around her thigh. "Unless you want to skip our date and get naked?" I suggested and she rolled pretty eyes at me.

"Going out was your idea and it took me an hour to fix my hair. I'm leaving the house," she snapped, pushing on my chest with her hand but I didn't budge. "I have to lock the door, tough guy," she said as I inhaled her.

"Pay the toll," I teased with a stupid, lovesick smile.

"What are you, thirteen?" She laughed. "Move."

"It's been nearly a week, Adeline, I'm not moving unless you make me," I threatened. I felt cocky and free. The energy that she gave off surged through me like electricity and I wanted to feel like that every single day of my life.

"You know I can make you right?" She smiled at me and the world slipped off its axis.

"Excessive force turns me on," I whispered as she pushed forward until our shoes met and tilted her chin up to me, obliging in the demand like she hated it but the second our lips met it was clear she had missed me too.

She pulled away too quickly and I grabbed her chin, tugging her gently back to me for another one, "one more?" I mumbled against her mouth, sliding my tongue against her bottom lip as she leaned into me.

"One more." She kissed me again with a tiny hum that vibrated from the base of her throat. I could feel her smile against my lips and allowed me one more quick peck before pushing me backward out of the way.

I choked on my own spit as she turned, the back of her shorts cut higher than the front and showed off the sweet under-curve of her ass. "You're going to be the death of me," I grumbled under my breath. "Don't mumble. If you're going to compliment me," she sounded annoyed as she turned to me with a smug look. "Say it with your chest, Jensen."

"I said, *you're going to be the death of me,*" I lowered my tone and leaned into her space but she didn't even flinch.

"You sound ungrateful," she said, fluttering her eyelashes at me.

"Wouldn't want it any other way," I hummed, leaning closer but she was quicker and moved clear of the kiss.

"You never told me where we were going in your text," she said to me as we stepped onto the elevator, I couldn't help but link my hand into hers just needing her touch.

"It's a surprise," I said to her.

"I hate surprises," she groaned as we made our way to the car.

"No you don't," I argued, "you hate not having control *of* the surprise."

Adeline eyed me as I reluctantly let go of her hand and opened the door for her. She had left her hair down again and it was even curlier than the last time, messy and bouncy in the wind. Always begging to be touched. She didn't say anything else as she slipped into the passenger seat.

We'd been in the car for all of five minutes but I couldn't stand it anymore, my hand slipped over the center, finding the tender skin of her thigh. My fingers tickled across the raised ink and she parted her legs just enough for my hand to lay comfortably before she closed them again and trapped my fingers against her.

I looked over at her, expecting her to be pissed off at my brazen touch but she leaned back against the seat watching the trees pass by completely at peace. She liked my hand there. I smiled to myself and turned back to the road. We only had to go to Lorette for the evening and it was worth it when I pulled into the parking lot of Kojo's just from the look on her face.

"You did not," Adeline scoffed and looked over at me like I was insane, her entire body going tense with annoyance.

Kojo's was the only bar in decent distance that played good country music and I could see the panic setting in on her face as I climbed from the car and opened her door for her.

"Argue and walk," I said to her when her lips parted to say something. She grumbled at me but climbed from the car.

"Jensen I can't dance," she whined and my eyebrow raised at her. "Me dancing around to loud music at the gym is not line dancing," she argued with my silence.

"Who said anything about dancing?" I smirked, my eyes crinkling at the corners. I placed my hand on the small of her back and steered her inside. The bar was small and packed with people dancing around to the music that blasted from the speakers.

"Everything about this place screams we're about to dance." Adeline swallowed tightly and looked up at me with a nervous expression I had never seen before.

"Relax." I tried to soothe her concern, witnessing the tension in her shoulders grow. "I'm not going to make you dance," I said.

"Yes you are, it's written all over that stupid, handsome face," she argued as we wandered toward the bar. I ordered her a drink and watched her down it in one go. I laughed and took the empty glass from her.

"You *think* I'm handsome?" I leaned over on the bar into her gravity and asked.

"I *know* you're stupid," she said with a bite. She was getting feisty because she was nervous and I wasn't going to lie and say that I didn't enjoy every second of it. I wrapped my arm around her waist and started walking us backward toward the crowded dance floor. Adeline had a smile on her face but I could sense how uneasy she was about it all as she tried to play annoying.

Her footsteps were heavy as she dug her heels into the ground trying to slow our approach but the sneakers she wore slipped against the dancefloor and she couldn't find a proper grip. I laughed at her subtle outrage.

"Adeline, you play one of the toughest sports in Harbor with more grace than I've ever seen on anyone and you're telling me that you're scared to dance?" I smirked at her, amused by her scowl.

"It's a different kind of coordination Jensen, and you know it!" She tried to wriggle free from my grasp but I was determined to get her on the floor and dug my fingers into her lower back, pulling her hips against mine.

"Prove it then," I raised my voice over the music, knowing that no matter how intense her fear in the moment, her competitiveness would always get the better of her.

"That's not going to work," she warned me. Her eyes alight with the challenge.

I leaned in closer and Adeline paused, waiting for me to say something but I just smiled at her before spinning her around so her back was pressed against my chest. "It's already working," I said, pressing my lips close to her ear as I wrapped my arms around her waist and rested my hands on her stomach.

"I can't line dance," she said again, tilting her head up.

I ignored her protest and slid my hands up her sides as I started to sway us to the music in a subtle attempt to teach her the steps without her realizing. "You can follow, can't you?" I asked her, my voice muffled in her hair.

Adeline nodded.

"First step, right foot back," I said, before slowly guiding her arms and legs into the correct position, nudging her with the toe of my shoe. I tried to be encouraging but she was so stiff that it was hard not to laugh, "second step, left foot to the side."

"There should never be this many instructions to a dance," she grumbled but she was slowly starting to get it as the music picked up.

"It's not about the dance," I said, guiding her through the motions again but faster that time.

"Then why are we *dancing*?" She asked, her voice a little less argumentative as she stumbled over a step, groaned and restarted the count.

"Because," I sighed, kissing the space behind her ear, "it's a public activity where it's socially acceptable to have my hands all over you."

"You could have done that in my apartment," Adeline said in a grumpy, frustrated voice but her feet were moving and her heart was racing. I smiled, straightening out against her back and not answering her.

After the hotel I wanted nothing more than to keep her locked up tightly where only I could get at her but… there was something different about Adeline that made me wanna try harder. It wasn't just about getting in her pants, if I wanted that she'd give it to me, that much was obvious.

I'd never complain either. But I liked taking her out because it forced us to talk, to get to know each other in other ways than physically. And I liked to show her off, I wanted everyone to know that a girl like Adeline gave me the time of day. That she was happy with me. Granted maybe that was a little self-conceited but it was also pretty clear that she enjoyed the attention.

"Without an audience?" I teased, hiding the fact that I was desperately trying to hold on to the casual nature of our relationship, my fingers slipping a little more each time I saw her. "Where's the fun in that?"

"Sounds like a *lot* more fun than this." She pushed back, and I groaned as her ass ground against me on purpose. "I'm starting to think you can't line dance either and that this was all a ploy to get me in shorts," she teased.

I inhaled her once more, just trying to settle the heat in the pit of my stomach from her teasing as a smile tugged on my lips. She was relaxing, her hips started to move to the music more and she was focusing less on her steps and more on the music.

"My mom's side is Canadian," I said to her smoothly, ignoring her accusation because she was half right, it was a ploy to get her in shorts. "My grandmother and Aunt live on the east coast and I spent formative summers of my life growing up sneaking into crowded, backwater bars that only played country music."

I hooked my finger into the front left pocket of her jeans and spun her out from me, grabbing her wrist at the last second and guiding her back against the railing that partially outlined the dance floor.

"Now listen," I said to her over the music, "this is going to make you want to sleep with me and I'm going to need you to control yourself."

"Cocky," Adeline mouthed but a smile curled on her lips as she leaned back against the barrier.

I stepped back, grinning as I shook out my shoulders. As the music shifted I looked over my shoulder at her and winked, "watch and learn, rookie," I yelled with a bout of laughter before taking off across the floor and fell into step with the already forming line of bodies.

Adeline watched intently with a soft smile on her face as my feet moved effortlessly in time with the rest of the crowd. My muscles relaxed as my focus slipped the more I lost myself in the music, a smile spreading across my face as the two guys on either side of me joined into the unbridled fun.

Confidence flooded me and the enjoyment of those around me was infectious. I moved fluidly with the music, following my newfound friends in the fun as they added in their own touches on the dance. When we turned back to the other side of the bar, I found Adeline quickly. Her laughter was loud and unbridled with joy as she watched us dancing around like idiots. The music swelled and I kept my eyes on her, my heart on fire beneath my chest. I had never been that happy in my entire life and it was almost terrifying to know that she had something to do with it.

As the music died and was swallowed by the sound of another I shook the hands of the guys around me and wandered back through the crowd toward Adeline.

"Alright, that was impressive," she smiled at me.

I stepped up to her with a satisfied grin playing across my lips as I tried to catch my breath in a smooth way. I placed my hands on the railing on either side of her, trapping her in, "told you," I said, leaning in so no one else could hear.

Adeline froze as I closed the gap between us, her smile mirroring mine with a tiny laugh.

"Something funny?" I asked her, our faces inches apart. The heat radiated between us and mingled in the air creating a warm bubble of intimacy right there in the middle of the bar.

"No," she said. Her eyes flickered up, raking down over me and stopping at my lips. "I hate being wrong," she whispered.

I raised an eyebrow at her, curious about what she could have possibly been wrong about. "Happens to the best of us," I said with a smug grin.

"It's going to be an issue," she hummed.

"What?" I asked her, still sucked into her gravity and itching to kiss her.

"I think you might be even more attractive than you were before," she started to laugh, sweet like honey and I wanted to steal the sound from her lips.

I laughed gently at her statement, my eyes never leaving hers. The compliment had dug its way beneath my skin and I felt a warmth spread through me that had nothing to do with the dance or the attention. I leaned in further, our noses practically touching. "Is that so?"

"Next date better not be in public, Jensen," she warned, challenging my resolve and my ridiculous need to keep the flirtatious game we were playing going.

"I don't have much say in the matter, it's your pick, remember?" I smiled at her and watched her hazel eyes get a little bigger, the mischief reflecting back at me like stars.

JENSEN

> **UNKNOWN:**
> Do you touch yourself when you dream of me?

> **UNKNOWN:**
> Do you suck dick on the first date?

> 11 Missed calls from Unknown

I had woken up to an onslaught of harassing texts and an empty bed. I wasn't sure what was worse but dropping Adeline off at home after our night out felt like a new form of torture. I had left her another set of dice in her mailbox on the walk back to the car. Small baby blue ones with ducks in them that I thought would put a smile on her face.

I dragged my ass to practice the next day and then to class, and then back for the game tonight. All the while she was radio silent on the phone and I was just hoping that she would show up to the game so I could see her face.

"You took her to Kojo's without us?" Cael whined, faltering in his stretch and bringing me back to reality. "You haven't taken any of us there in months!"

The stadium was hot today and half of us were already sweating just from warm-ups. Cael sank into the grass next to Van who was stretching his hamstrings across from me.

"You've been a little busy," I said, "and you're a terrible dancer."

"Wow," Cael feigned offence, clutching the space over his heart dramatically.

"You are," Van agreed, pulling his hat over his eyes to shield from the sun. "I'm kind of impressed you have her doing anything. Cosy says she's normally pretty one track with rugby and work."

"Jenny must be damn good in bed to have a girl changing her schedule for him," Cael teased.

"We haven't," I said, rolling over to stretch out my other hip.

"She's just like willingly hanging out with you?" Van laughed.

"Why is that funny?" I scowled, actually offended.

"I mean you're nice and all man, but… you have a track record with women and it doesn't involve multiple dates or a vow of celibacy," Van said, rolling up on his knees and stretching out his arms over his head.

"*You're a whore*," Cael blurted less eloquently, "he's politely calling you a man whore."

"Coming from you," I scoffed, rolling my eyes.

"I'm a changed man," he laughed, staring at me like I was the idiot.

"Yeah well if you can change, so can I," I said with a shrug.

"Whatever you're doing, I've never seen my sister come to so many games, so it can't be that bad," Van noted, waving up to the stands. Cosy was joined by Kaia, Zoey and Adeline. She was staring down at me, her hair blowing around in the wind and a big smile on her face.

It was distracting how good she looked in my jersey, she was wearing a black tank top and had tucked one panel of the jersey into a tiny pair of jean shorts that showed off her hips and her tattoo.

Cael started to laugh from beside me, crawling to his feet he walked toward me but I couldn't be bothered by him. My full attention was on her and the way the sunshine made her cheekbones shimmer.

My head was tugged backwards roughly by the hair and I swatted his hand away feebly, squinting in the sun with a snarl on my lips.

"You're in love," Cael whispered with a nasty smile on his face. "That's why you haven't slept with her," he teased, his fingers still gripping tightly to my hair and pulling at my scalp.

"Let me go, idiot," I said trying to fight him off but he just laughed.

"Admit it," he ordered and Van groaned from beside us.

"He's not going to let you go until you tell him what he wants to hear," he noted.

"No, no," Cael said, shaking his head. Tuff of blonde hair shooting out from beneath his cap and a wild look in his eyes. "Tell me the truth," he whispered. "Do you love her?"

"We've been on two dates asshole," I grunted, reaching up and digging my nails into his wrist making him release my hair a little. The problem was every time I saw her I asked myself the same idiotic question. "It's just fun, now let me go," I demanded.

"Fine, but I don't believe you. And I'm consulting Ella on the matter because I know I'm right and if she agrees then you're screwed," he said, going to step back but I grabbed his ankle and he tumbled into the grass.

I pushed out of the grass, grabbing my mitt and wandering to home plate to do some catches with Reyes who was talking to Arlo while Josh gave everyone dirty looks from the dugout. He'd been on the bench for the game to let his elbow flare up die down but it meant today's game would be hard won. And man did we need it.

Before setting up I turned to the fence, "what did I tell you about that jersey?" I yelled over to her and she shrugged.

"You haven't gotten me a replacement," she said back, popping a candy into her mouth.

"If you keep wearing it to games I'm going to take it back with force," I warned her with a smirk.

"Oh," she cocked her head to the side and all that messy brown hair spilled over her shoulder, "do you promise?"

"That was a threat," I huffed, running my tongue out over my bottom lip just trying to control myself in public.

"Even better," she smiled back at me, blowing a kiss before sinking back into her chair and leaving me more worked up than before. "Go do something cool," she smiled at me.

"Just because you asked so nicely," I said, giving her a wink. When I turned around Cael was standing in his space behind Reyes with a smug look on his face.

I flipped him off and went back to warming up.

When the Ump called for the game to start it was like a flip had been switched. We all set aside our personal lives and came together as a unit. We knew what the stakes were and we couldn't come off the field without the win.

If we lost, the season would be over.

And all the stories about us would be true. We couldn't win without Arlo.

Coach gave some speech about playing our best and Dean followed it up with an equally tired rant about believing in each other. Everyone was exhausted but determined. The thought of a bi-week tickled our heels and fueled us forward through the game.

"Focus on shutting them down," Arlo instructed Reyes and me. "End the game on the mound. Make sure you keep it clean and don't throw the same pitch back to back. We want them tripping over the unpredictability."

"Yes Coach," both of us gave him a quick nod. Taking the field was easy, leaving it without a field would be devastating.

The stadium thrummed with unintelligible enthusiasm only silencing as Reyes set up to throw the first pitch of the game. I sank low to the ground, steadying myself in the clay and getting my fingers dirty as the batter readied him for the pitch.

Reyes was bad for just throwing, his communication lacked the finesse that Arlo had spoiled me with. Josh could be brash at times, but he always gave me a warning before doing something insane.

The ball was released and before I could adjust it smacked into the back of my glove with a deafening echo. My eyes flickered up to Reyes who looked proud of himself but I scowled. We needed to be on the same page or this would go south, and fast.

The second pitch came off just as hot but the batter was already stumbling over the unexpected curveball that came at me and the Ump called the second strike. I could feel everyone's eyes on us, this first batter would set the tone for the rest of the game and if Reyes could manage to shut him down...

I threw it back, taking a slow and calculated breath before sinking back down and rolling out my neck as Reyes pulled back on the mound and released the last ball. The batter swung and I swore the stadium collectively held their breath as the ball whipped through the air and the sound of it slapping clean into the leather of my mitt rang out through the air.

"That's it boys," Arlo's voice boomed from the dugout next to Coach's loud clapping and suddenly the confidence was refreshed. The team shone a little brighter and I could feel the hope bleeding through the concrete walls of the stadium.

With the tingle of belief running through our bloodstream, the game came easy, it was like we were playing with newfound energy and the team had found our way back to what we had been before.

Everyone was completely focused and by the time the last inning rolled through the stadium was on fire and we were running fumes but up by six whole runs. We had managed to pull off the win.

"Six fucking runs!" Cael clapped his hands together.

"We haven't played this good all season, no offense Josh..." Todd groaned.

Josh grumbled something under his breath, anger rolling off him and for a second we all braced for another fight between the two of them but Arlo was quick to come to his defense.

"Todd, shut the fuck up." Arlo snapped, and it wasn't his usual playful tone that he used with us either. It was authoritative and loud. "It wasn't Josh holding you back," he said, "you were all so caught up in your own heads trying to recreate a season that you forgot that we *always* go forward and what was last season, *isn't* this season."

"Why are you ragging on us, we won," Cael argued and for a second I thought that Arlo might put him through the wall. But he just shook his head in disbelief. Coach Cody stood back, leaning against the wall with his arms crossed, letting Arlo take the lead on the speech.

"You won one hard game, we have three more series to go through if you want to win it all. This was the easiest game you'll play in weeks." Arlo said and the dugout fell quiet. "Blaming hardship on each other isn't how we do shit and you *know* it."

"It was just a joke, Arlo," Todd tried to say but Coach cleared his throat to silence him.

"All fucking season every single one of you has been trying to prove a point to everyone... the news, the experts, the fans, your families. Not once have you gone out there to prove to yourself that you can do this," Arlo sighed, pulling off his hat and running his fingers through the dark strands of his hair. "You won today because you remembered who you were, what this team stands for but if you let it slip your minds again, this will be the last happy memory you have of the season."

All of us stayed quiet, our chests still rising and falling irregularly from the last inning, sweat pouring down our skin, our muscles sore and aching.

"Two steps at a time," Dean was the first to find his voice, his fingers coming up to his chest and the team fell in quickly and without hesitation. It was going to be an exhausting month but if it felt anything like today, every single battle was going to be worth it.

SARAH

"You sure you'll be okay?" Cosy asked in the parking lot, her hand on the frame of her open door.

"Yeah, location is on and if I stop moving for more than ten minutes Kaia will call so..." I laughed and Cosy took that as insurance enough that she could leave me to wait for Jensen.

I was standing on the concrete pad outside the stadium listening to a group of girls squawking over the team. It was only when they started ranking them that I started listening closer.

"Everyone knows that Cael is in the top five," the redhead said but her friend clearly disagreed.

"If Van Mitchell didn't have a girlfriend he'd be number one," she said.

"Cael Cody has a girlfriend..." one of the others added and the redhead scoffed. "You're all sleeping on the catcher," she said.

"Jensen?" The brunette grumbled. "He's a playboy and way too cocky for a catcher," she said and I had it in my right mind to turn around and let them know exactly how I felt about their assessment of my favorite Hornet.

Instead I shoved aside my jealousy and pulled out my phone. Their rankings didn't matter much anyways, not when I had direct contact with my number one.

> We really need to work on your public image. You're being left behind in the Hottest Hornets rankings.

I giggled and shoved the phone in my pocket, ignoring the next two buzzes as the door opened and players started to flood out into the parking lot. The group of girls immediately turned on their best smiles and turned to where some of the players piled into a line to wave.

I heard Jensen before I saw him, his laughter loud above the rest as he walked backward play-fighting with Van Mitchell. There was a cheesy grin on his face and his hair was damp from showering. It was stupid, but he had the ability to take my breath away.

I stuck to fingers between my lips and whistled loudly, catcalling his pathetically adorable ass like a sexually frustrated fiend. His eyes moved around the crowd, landing on me eventually and I scrunch my nose up at him as he pushed through the line of players toward me. His smile grew with each step and it set fireworks off across my chest.

"How's this for public image," he practically purred, dropping his bag to the ground, his arms wrapping me up and lifting me off the ground. His lips found my neck and jaw as he bombarded my skin with kisses and I giggled to get free of his grip.

"Put me down." I tugged on his damp hair and he lowered me to the ground.

Once my toes were touching the concrete I pushed his face toward mine and stole a kiss before he could protest otherwise. I had been extremely patient waiting for one all week and I wasn't going to be denied just because we were in public. A camera flashed and I could feel his smile against my mouth as I relaxed my grip and lowered completely to my flat feet.

"You're going to get us put in the school paper," Jensen whispered, his teeth grazing my bottom lip.

"Well we might as well give them front page news," I chuckled as his fingertips dug into my hip and he stole one more heated, languid kiss that left my knees weak. But he wasn't finished because he ran his mouth over my jaw to my ear.

"I'm taking that jersey back tonight, with or without your help," he whispered, my toes curling in my shoes at the thought of it.

I swallowed tightly peering up at him through my lashes as he pulled away, his hand cupping my jaw and his criminally soft brown eyes watching me with the most lustful intentions. His chest rose slowly as he wet his bottom lip and finally broke our eye contact. He looked around at the guys, signing calendars and photos, while my eyes fell on the group of girls who had been talking about him earlier.

The brunette's mouth was open in shock and I couldn't help myself but give her a petty wink as Jensen finally let go of my waist. He was looking for someone, his back angled away from me but his hand still hovering close to my thigh as he looked.

"Hey," he called out to Van when he finally found him, "you got room in your truck for Adeline?"

Van looked at me over and smiled, "I always got room for Addy, she'll have to play lap monkey if she's coming to Delta though," he said, breaking focus to take a picture with a young boy.

"Think you can keep your hands to yourself for five minutes?" He turned back to me and I shook my head. Jensen huffed a quiet, "*brat*" under his breath but scooped up his bag from the ground and linked his hand in mine.

Once the crowd had thinned out and most of the guys had started to filter out to the parking lot Jensen led me over to Van's truck that was already packed with bodies.

"Fuck off Todd, get in the bed," Jensen grumbled, grabbing one of the guys who aimed to steal the last spot in the cab.

"Why don't you and..." Todd paused to give me a dirty look and Jensen slapped a hand to his face.

"Don't finish that sentence if you're about to insult her," he warned. I'd never been one to need a guy to stand up for me but I'd be lying if I said I wasn't immediately turned on by the sight of Jensen doing so for the most minimal of insults. The guy hadn't even said anything yet.

"I was going to do the opposite," he laughed as Jensen's hand tensed around his jaw. "I was gonna tell her she could trade up and sit in my lap if she wanted a ride to Delta."

I waited for Jensen to lose it but the explosion never came. He looked over his shoulder at me, his hand still tightly wrapped in mine and smiled.

"Hey Van," Jensen said, turning his attention away from me and Van turned around in the driver's seat, "You think Todd needs some exercise? He was looking sloppy out there today"

"Sloppy is being nice... he could go for a run," Van called back with a shrug and turned back around starting the engine of the massive truck.

"You heard Van, have a good run." Jensen looked Todd over before shoving him out of the way and climbing into the truck with his hand out to me. I gave him a sympathy smile before using the step to haul myself up into Jensen's lap. "Keep your eyes off my fucking girl, Todd." Jensen slammed the door in his face and Van pulled out of the parking lot.

My girl. The temperature rose in the cab and I could feel the tingling sensation that swirled around in the base of my stomach as his hand gripped the tattoo on my thigh, his fingers sinking between. I pushed my fingers into the back of his hair, just needing to ground myself to keep from spreading my legs for him like I was in heat. Waiting for him to make the first move was going to kill me, I just knew it.

"Was that necessary?" I asked him, swallowing down the sticky sensation in my throat as everyone started up in conversation.

"Nope," he said, staring at me with an intensity that made me feel shy.

"Your girl hey?" I said next, my tone low and serious. He nodded slowly like it was the most obvious thing in the world. "Were you planning on talking to me about this?" I asked him quietly and he shook his head no, just as slow.

The air around us was suffocating and hot.

"You don't seem too mad about it," he said after a moment.

The problem was I loved it.

It made me feel giddy and watched.

Van pulled the truck into a vacant spot on the street and killed the engine, "everyone get the fuck out, I have a date."

I pushed the door open and climbed from the truck with Jensen on my heels, his hands found my hips and he pulled me against his chest nuzzling his nose against my neck.

"I've never been to a frat party," I confessed and Jensen snorted. "What?"

"Adeline Sarah, rugby prodigy, has never been to a frat party?" He mumbled as his lips found the space behind my ear, he inhaled my shampoo without shame and spun me around in his arms, continuing to walk us across the lawn toward the loud house.

"I have something to tell you," I said, biting down on my lips and dragging his gaze to them. "I'm a massive nerd."

"*You*?" He laughed, his hands splayed out on my back as we came to a stand still. I didn't give two seconds to the commotion around us when he was staring at me like that. It was like the world faded away when he locked in on me, my heart raced, my breath shortened, thoughts dissipated. He made me stupid in love without even being aware of his effect on me and I hated him for it.

"What kind of nerd?" He lowered his voice and leaned closer, tugging our hips together.

"The worst kind," I whispered, stealing a kiss that made him smile and turned me even further into a puddle. "A smart nerd, I didn't care about parties."

"That must have killed Keegan," Jensen laughed quietly, his tone low and husky. It was just for me and him.

"It did," I said back, "she tried every night to get me out of the house but I'd rather be there in bed, with the ugliest fuzzy socks and reruns of Jeopardy."

"I should have seen this coming," he said.

"Oh yeah?" I scoffed.

"You play Dungeons and Dragons once a week with your friends, it was pretty obvious you were a dork, I was thinking like Milhouse dorky...not Lisa Simpson," Jensen teased.

"Wow," I gasped and shoved him away playfully, but he caught my wrist and pulled me back, his mouth colliding with mine as his hands wrapped around my waist, holding me in place. I tilted my chin up to him as he deepened his grip on my lips and his tongue slid into my mouth, allowing the world to fade away around us. I wanted to live in that bubble forever, his hands on me, our bodies pressed so tightly together you couldn't tell where one began and the other ended.

I sighed against his lips as he retreated, not wanting him to leave.

"If I don't take you inside, you'll never experience your first frat party," he groaned.

"Why's that?" I asked with a tiny breath.

Jensen wrapped his hands around my face, pressing my hair into my cheeks and bringing his face close to mine. "Because I'm so fucking hard right now I'm half tempted to take you to the closest quiet corner just to get a moment of peace," he said.

"Romantic," I giggled and he huffed loudly in frustration but stole another kiss before I could grumble against his lips. "Take me inside."

SARAH

All of my suspicions were correct. I hated parties.

Even with Jensen close the noise levels were insane and every drunk person that bumped into me activated my fight response. Every time I whirled on someone, Jensen laughed and straightened me out.

Jensen was determined to get me dancing and it wasn't so bad. I liked the way his body felt against mine and everyone was so busy with themselves that no one noticed the loverboy glances he threw my way. The music was still too loud and the people too drunk but it was easier to distract myself with Jensen's hands engulfing me possessively. Eventually Todd turned up, pissed off and looking for a drink but Jensen just laughed at him when he tried to start shit.

We celebrated wins at the Hollow. Free drinks, live music, and crowd control crowds. Frat parties were like that, but one hundred percent worse.

"I'm thirsty," I said to him after a while and he nodded, turning me around in his arms and pointing me toward the kitchen. Once we got there, it wasn't so horrible. There weren't as many bodies, and I knew most of the players hanging around and a few of them introduced me to their partners. I was talking to Dean Tucker when Jensen's hands started to roam again.

I gripped his fingers in mine as they spread out over my stomach, stopping him before he made the fabric of my shirt ride up too much. "We've had a few pre-season games but our season opener is next week," I said to Dean when he asked me if we were playing. "Stop it," I whispered to Jensen who feigned innocence with his lips on my shoulder.

"No," he responded quickly and continued his assault on my already warm skin.

"Lucky us," Cael Cody smiled from his perch on the counter.

"I can get you tickets, I'll send them..." my sentence turned into a yelp as Jensen's fingers found my hip again. "I'll send them over to Dansby House."

Dean laughed, clearly very accustomed to dealing with Jensen's antics and went back to talking to the people around him. I turned my head and my nose brushed against Jensen who was resting on my shoulder watching his friends pour shots.

"You're a nuisance, I'm trying to get to know your friends," I said to him and his eyes flickered to meet mine. "What's gotten into you?" I asked him.

"Just happy," he said, surging forward to steal a kiss. "I need to run up to grab something from the Nest, come with me?" He asked, and how could I say no to that face.

It took us forever to get out of the house, every person that saw him stopped us to congratulate him on the game and with each conversation I could see his patience wearing thin. The next guy that approached him got a scowl and a quick "yup" before I was gently tugged out the front door into the fresh air.

"I didn't think it was possible to get that many people in a house?" I laughed as we started across the grass to a path.

"That's not even a big party," Jensen said, relaxing a bit the further we got from the noise.

"How far is Dansby House from here?" I asked him, looking at the path. It was dark and I wasn't exactly a fan of it.

"Ten minutes tops," he said.

"Let's make it five," I challenged, stepping back from him. "And it goes all the way up to the house?"

His lips curled into a smile, nodding slowly as his hungry eyes raked over my body.

"I'll race you," I said. "If you beat me up the hill you can have the jersey back."

"Oh, I'm going to have that jersey by the end of the night regardless of a silly bet from a beautiful girl." Jensen stepped forward and I stepped back away from his grasp.

"It's okay to be scared to lose to a girl," I said, teasing him a little as I stretched out my calves, "fragile male egos."

Jensen scoffed, "you aren't going to insult me into racing you up the hill in the dark."

"Just say you're a coward then," I said, pushing him a little further and I could see him cracking.

"I'm not a coward, and I can beat you in a foot race but it's pitch black outside and I don't want you getting hurt," he argued gently but I wasn't having it.

"Says the baseball player to the rugby player," I laughed, "if anyone is made of glass here, it's you, baby."

"Don't," he swallowed tightly. His entire body pulled under the moonlight, his muscles hardened beneath the thin fabric of his t-shirt.

"Don't what?" I giggled realizing what it was that got him all tense, "call you *baby*?"

"That's—" he stepped forward again, his neck red. It was clear to see that it was affecting him. I loved the shade of pink his cheeks turned being called it and I started backward. "Adeline." His voice was low and warning.

It wasn't going to stop me though, I took off running before he could stop me. *Sprinting*. I knew I had a decent head start when it took another two minutes before I heard his footsteps pushing up through the path behind me. Twigs snapped behind me and it only fueled the urge to move faster.

Sure baseball players were fast, but I had spent my entire career running to avoid getting caught by someone bigger than me, stronger than me. I sprinted over a hundred yards every single practice, this hill… in the dark was child's play.

I controlled my breathing and it wasn't until I popped out the other side of the path into the backyard that he caught me. His arms wrapped around my middle and hauled me over his shoulder like I weighed nothing.

"I win," I giggled when his hand flexed tightly around my thigh. "You should do more cardio," I teased, giving up fighting against his restraints and letting him carry me up the back steps into the house.

"I'm about to," he grumbled, kicking the door closed.

"It's pretty in here," I noted, pushing up to look around at the kitchen as he stomped through it and down the hallway. Everything was dark but it was obvious that the house was gorgeous and old. I was completely unbothered by the fact that Jensen was clearly on a mission as he took the stairs. "Where are we going?" I asked after a moment.

He wandered into a dark room, closing the door behind him and locking it.

"You have a roommate? That's so cute," I laughed as he set me down in the center of the room. Jensen grumbled something and kicked off his shoes. "Are you going to talk to me or just stalk me like an animal?" I asked him.

"Take off the jersey, Adeline."

"Oh we're doing that? Now?" I smiled at him, heat building in my chest as I retreated out of his reach toward his bed. He had warned me that he was going to get it back one way or another and now that he had come to collect on that threat, I was giddy about it.

"Do you know how many texts and calls I've gotten?" He said, his eyes dark. "All because you refuse to take it off?" He was complaining but from all I'd learned about Jensen he was the type of guy who fucking loved the public display. The fact that I had been parading around wearing his number in more ways than one, riled him up.

"But I love this jersey," I purred and Jensen's jaw ticked.

"I'm not asking, I want it off," he took a step closer, his eyes never leaving mine. The tension in the room was palpable, the temperature rising. "Last chance to remove it willingly," his voice dropped lower.

"Come get it then," I whispered, raking my eyes over his impressive form. *Fuck*, I had waited too long for this and I could feel the sexual frustration vibrating through my muscles like an electrical charge. "Aren't you supposed to be competitive or something? Make your move." I challenged him.

Jensen smirked, unbuckling his belt slowly. "Damn it, Adeline," he groaned. Without it the pants hung low around his hips giving me a clear view of the hardened lines of muscles leading down beneath. He took a step closer, his voice low and dangerous as he dropped it to the floor with a soft thud. His eyes never leaving mine, he surged forward closing the distance between us. He wrapped his strong arms around me, lifting me off the ground and tossed me back to the bed.

"You asked for it," he said, the sound more of a groan from deep in his throat as he climbed over me and gripped the hem of the jersey.

"I've been waiting for it," I whispered.

Jensen's pupils dilated, his breath hitching slightly at the admission. His fingers flexed against the jersey, slowly inching it up my stomach. "For me to take back what's mine?"

"The jersey. Among other things..." I groaned, my hips pressing into the bed as his knuckles brushed against my stomach.

His eyes snapped back to mine, filling with lustful intensity. "Other things?" Jensen repeated, his voice barely audible. His hands stilled in their exploration, the jersey pulled up to my ribcage. "Like what Belle?" He demanded, his face inches from me. "What else is mine to take?"

Belle âme. The name tingled at my fingertips when he said it like that.

"You said I was your girl," I said, "prove it." The demand was simple and it caused his body to lower against mine.

"Adeline, you've belonged to me since the day I met you," he said with conviction.

And it should have scared me. The idea that he was claiming stake was far beyond a simple fling but... it left me breathless and without words to combat the intense feelings that stirred up deep inside my chest.

"But if it's *proof* you want," his face hovered over mine as he pulled the jersey up further, his voice rough with desire and possessiveness.

I nodded gently, words escaping my thoughts and being replaced by incoherent fantasies of what he might do if I just pushed a little further. "Show me," I demand, curling my leg around him to bring him closer.

Jensen wasn't lacking encouragement or confidence. With a throaty groan he pulled the jersey open, not bothering with the buttons. The force of his tug sent them flying across the mattress and dragged a funny yelp from my lips. He laughed at me, kissed my jaw before he pushed it over my shoulder and down my arms.

His body pressed against mine and I could feel his heartbeat racing in sync with mine.

"Is that what you wanted?" He asked.

I giggled, feeling exposed and too warm under his gaze, "a little underwhelming," I smirked.

Jensen's eyes flashed with amusement and something darker. "Underwhelming?" He repeated back to me, taking the jersey in his hands he sat back on his knees still keeping me pinned to the bed. He bundled the jersey around his fist, yanking hard on the fabric until it tore down the center with a loud rip.

"Oh,' I said, pressing my hands beneath the hem of his shorts to touch his thighs. I needed the contact, the warmth. My heart was pounding and the heat in my stomach was unbearable. I giggled, dragging my bottom lip between my teeth at the impressive show, unaware of his intention until he was wrapping the two scraps of jersey around each wrist and tying them to the headboard with surprising gentleness.

"Still underwhelmed?" He asked, pulling back on the knot to make sure it was secure, his chest brushed against mine and he kissed me like he was trying to steal the air from my lungs, I followed him as he pulled away, a smile forming on his lips.

"Who knew there were so many uses for a baseball jersey," I said, wiggling my hands but there was no chance of getting free. I rolled my hips beneath him, unsure about how I felt being restrained but the look in his eyes gave me the confidence I needed. Jensen would make sure I enjoyed it.

"Mm, apparently they're good for tying up smart-mouthed girls too," he murmured against my neck, tracing kisses against my collarbone. "Should I continue proving how useful they are?" His hands trailed down my side making me squirm.

"*Please*," I replied, the word coming out more of a moan than a word.

Jensen chuckled at the sound, loving every second of it.

"Good girl," he praised and that was the final blow to my attitude. I clenched beneath him as my toes dug into the sheets. He pulled back, standing off the bed and shucking out of his shorts before helping me out of mine. His fingers were like ice on my hot skin as he trailed them down my thighs and back up my calves.

He leaned down, his lips kissing a hot line across the tattoo on my thigh.

"These are in my way," he said, brushing his fingers down my stomach, stopping at the bottom to push my tank top up. His smile grew shaky as he took a long breath before hooking them into the top of underwear.

"Do something about it," I said, barely able to get it out between the short breaths I was taking.

"Bossy," he muttered, slowly dragging them down and tossing them aside to leave me completely exposed to him. He tapped the inside of my calf lightly, his eyes fixated, "spread your legs for me," his voice was commanding now, his self-control clearly hanging by a thread, made obvious by the shake in his hands.

"Don't stop until you prove your point," I said, encouraging that control to snap as I tugged on the restraints around my wrists.

"God, that mouth…" He traced a circle around my stomach, making my back arch into his touch. "The whole Nest is about to know who you belong to." He promised darkly and settled between my thighs. He pressed soft, open-mouthed kisses along my inner thighs, deliberately avoiding the pool of heat between them. His large hands gripped my thighs firmly, pushing them wider as he continued to tease kisses up my leg. Then without warning or a comment he closed that cocky mouth over my center making my entire body arch off the bed with a loud gasp.

"That's my girl," he purred against me, the heat off his lips tangling with my own.

"Good to know that mouth is good for something other than being smug," I teased between another sharp moan. I hated that I couldn't touch him, I wanted to pull on the strands of his dark hair and rake my fingers across his scalp.

Jensen chuckled, the vibration sending shivers through me. "Keep talking like that and I might have to find other uses for that jersey," he teased, sucking gently on my clit, making my body tremble beneath his touch.

"You wouldn't dare," I gasped as his teeth grazed my core.

"You know I would," he paused, looking up at me, his eyes burning with desire and possessiveness before sucking gently on my most sensitive spot. I was too busy fighting off the tingling sensation of euphoria to answer him. He used his tongue to lick a slow, long stripe up my center and it racked through my body in a tortuous wave of pleasure.

Like he knew my ability for coherent thoughts was gone, his tongue circled my clit slowly and unraveled me without a second of hesitation. His hand slipped beneath me to give my ass a rough squeeze before wrapping around to my hip to hold me against the bed.

I moaned, pressing back against the mattress, desperate to touch him and fighting against the orgasm building in the pit of my stomach. I hadn't been with many guys but there hadn't been a single time when I was in danger of finishing with a guy between my legs.

"Jensen," I gasped as he curled his fingers against me, applying pressure as he continued his maddening circles with his tongue. I was shaking, just trying to wriggle free and catch my breath before I completely came undone but Jensen wasn't having it. His arm wrapped around my thigh, his hand gripping the tattoo like it belonged to him and held me in place as he continued to drive me over the edge.

"Yes, Adeline?" He purred against my clit.

"Don't stop," I begged him and felt him smile against my skin.

"Finish for me," he urged, his voice muffled against my core. He pulled me into his mouth and sucked, his fingers pressing against the perfect spot inside of me that painted stars across my vision. "Now."

Without words, my body answered his demand. I was a shaking mess as he held me through the orgasm, his tongue and fingers working me until nothing but a string of breathless moans was seeping from me and my thighs were quivering around his head. When he lifted his head, his face glistening in the dim light of the room, he cleaned off his lips and popped his fingers into his mouth. His eyes never left mine.

SARAH

There were literally no words to describe how feral the sight of Jensen, hard beneath his boxers, lust-blown pupils and messy hair, made me. He crawled up my body, his teeth finding the hem of my tank top with a smirk.

"Don't," I warned him but he didn't listen.

"It's in the way," he grumbled, ripping the fabric with his teeth at first and then tearing it away from my body. His eyes widened when he realized that I hadn't worn a bra that day.

"I liked that tank top," I moaned as his lips pressed kisses to my bare stomach.

"I'll buy you a hundred more, just be quiet Adeline," he begged, his mouth trailing up between my breasts.

"That's never happened before," I said, watching him pause to look at me.

Jensen smiled softly, his eyes crinkling at the corners as he pressed up to kiss me on the lips, "what an orgasm so good it made you speechless? Cause I deserve a medal for that," he said, his smile turning smug.

"Cocky," I scoffed, tugging on my hands a little against the scraps of fabric, "can you let me free now?"

He laughed, smoothing a messy strand of hair away from my face. "No," he said, kissing my nose, deliberately tormenting me. "You told me not to stop until I proved my point," he dragged a finger lazily down my torso.

"You can prove your point *while* I touch you," I pouted, "You're just being cruel now." I had never whined so much in front of a man in my entire fucking life.

Jensen smiled at me, clearly enjoying my frustration. "And you're being a brat," he leaned down to nip at my earlobe, "but I have to admit seeing you all tied up and wanting is a sight I could get used to."

"That's a lot of destroyed jerseys, baby," I whispered, feeling his body tremble against mine. The way that word affected him was the only thing holding me together in the moment.

A mischievous scoff fell from him, "We'll just have to keep buying more than, won't we?" His fingers trailed back up my body, stopping to circle my sensitive nipple with his thumb. "They'll be a reminder of how pretty you look when you're begging to touch me."

I scrunched up my nose at him, trying to stifle the moan building in my throat as my hips rolled to meet his. He leaned down, capturing one of my peaks in his mouth, sucking and teasing with his teeth and tongue until I was nothing but a writhing mess beneath him.

Fuck. "I think you like that idea, being tied up at my mercy…" he said, his voice muffled against my skin.

"I hate it," I argued, but in reality it was reigniting the heat between my legs.

"Liar," he smirked. "You love it, needy and waiting for me to touch you."

"Then touch me, Jensen," I snapped, "quit running that mouth."

His smile gave away just how much he loved my attitude. He enjoyed pushing buttons and it showed. "Maybe I should just ignore you," he said, his fingers tickling my overly sensitive inner thigh. I'd kill him if he did and he knew it. It was all over his face.

"Can you?" I teased, even indisposed and bound, I could remind him just how we got in this position. My eyes flickered downward between his legs, I could feel how hard he was beneath his boxers.

Jensen let out a low hum, his fingers tickling the skin close to my core. He wasn't ready to give up control just yet. He spread my legs with his knees, giving himself better access. "Can I, what? Leave you all wet and wanting" He purposefully avoided touching me, his fingers ghosting over my skin.

"You're only tormenting yourself," I bit out, trying to constrain the slight tremble. "You could leave me here, sure…" I teased, "but eventually your roommate will come back." My eyes cast over to the closet, where another Hornets jersey hung.

Todd.

Even the idea of it caused him to tense. Jensen paused momentarily, following my gaze. A flash of panic crossed his handsome features before he caught himself. He leaned down, and growled softly from the base of his throat, "Low blow, Belle. Very low."

He shifted back off the bed and shoved his boxers away. I had it in my right mind to let the whiny whistle of adoration leave my lips at the sight of him. His heavily tattooed body built of hard ridges and thick muscle, all bathed in the moonlight shining through the window.

I couldn't find the words to tease him because in that moment the only thoughts stringing together in my mind were, *large, thick and is that going to fit...*

And then, *Kaia is going to have a field day with this story.*

"You're drooling," he chuckled.

"Shut up and fuck me already," I snapped but the command was laced with soft laughter.

He stood there for a moment, his chest heaving. Clearly torn between continuing to tease me and his need to assert dominance in the situation. A feral grin spread across his face at my blunt demand. He quickly grabbed a condom from the nightstand and rolled it on, his eyes never leaving mine.

"Say please," he teased, coaxing himself with his hand.

"*Please baby,*" I said, giving him all I could as I arched my back against the ties and spread my legs wider. He wasted no more time, positioning himself between my spread thighs, gripping my hips tightly as he thrust inside me in one smooth motion.

"Fuck, that 'baby' shit will get me every time," he pushed in deeper, filling me fuller than I'd ever been in my entire life. My body trembled at the intrusion, adjusting to his size as he pumped out slowly once.

"Breathe," he whispered and he meant well, but fuck, the tone of his voice and the look in his eyes made me come undone around his cock. His strong hands squeezed my thighs in reassurance as he slowly pushed in again, hitting every sensitive wall and leaving nothing untouched. I was struggling to breathe through the small ache of how much my body needed to stretch to accommodate him. "You can take it," he praised, pulling out again.

When he rolled back, his shaft brushed the raw inside of my g-spot and dragged a vicious moan from me that blanketed the dull sting and left room for the pleasure to flood in. Jensen let out a satisfied groan as I clenched around him.

"There it is," he moaned with me, his hips moving in a deliberate rhythm. He was hitting the right spots and making it his mission to continue to do so.

"If this is you.. proving a point," I gasped as he rolled against me again. "It's only going to make me more of a brat." I curled against the restraints, my ass lifting off the mattress into his hips as he surged forward.

His thrusts picked up pace as he watched my body writhe against the restraints. A low dark groan of pleasure escaped him as he slammed into me, the force of his thrusts making the headboard slam against the wall.

"Then, I guess I'll just have to keep you tied up and fucked stupid more often," he said, all the restraint he had snapped in that moment. "Might improve that smart mouth of yours."

"You think?" I gasped as my vision started to get fuzzy and my head started to feel light.

"I know," he groaned, his fingers digging into my thighs painfully as he continued to smack his hips against my ass. Everything was tangled together creating the most toxic mix of pain and pleasure that was going to push me over the edge for the second time that night.

My walls fluttered around his cock and his smug smile told me that he could feel how close I was to the edge. His pace became brutal and the room was filled with the sounds of slick skin and the creaking bed. My breathing was ragged and my heart was pounding faster than I'd ever felt it on the pitch.

"Baby," I gasped for air, my ass flush with his hips as he touched every inch of me. I could fucking feel him in my stomach. "I'm going to..." my words died out as the pleasure ripped through me.

Jensen's eyes flashed with dominance as he pushed me to the edge, reaching down between our bodies his thumb pressed against my clit applying just enough pressure to throw me over.

"You wanted to be a brat, now show me exactly how much you can take," he groaned, battling with his own building release. "Come for me." His demands were insane and made my skin so hot his touch burned.

Whatever words I managed to form died on my lips as the second orgasm wracked through my body even more violently than the first. It came in hot flashes that felt like electricity coursing through my veins. I yanked desperately against the jersey on my wrists, all I wanted to do was touch him.

I came completely undone beneath him and like a rubber band snapping he was quick to follow. He buried himself as deep as possible, and unleashed himself. His hips shook erratically as he spilled out, the sensation of the heat against my walls almost overwhelming as I fought to hold it together.

Jensen's abs contracted as he watched me fall apart, my cries echoing through the room. "Fuck," he groaned, pulling back slowly, both our bodies trembling.

"You untie me right fucking now, Jensen," I demanded, needy to touch him after all of that. A lazy smirk formed on his face, breathless and spent he sat up on the bed and started to unknot the jersey from around my wrists, his fingers massaging the red marks from where I had pulled too hard.

Once I was free I crawled into his lap as he leaned back against the wall and wrapped his arms around my back. Settling down against him, it felt like bliss to have his skin beneath my fingers. I pushed them up into the thick hair sweaty around his neck and kissed his jaw until I couldn't breathe. He didn't mind though, his hands roamed up my back and he caught my mouth as I pulled away, offering me a slow, deep kiss that did nothing to help the fuzziness of my head. I cupped his chin, turned his face away from me and kissed the delicate lover tattoo behind his ear, reciprocating the moment, making sure he knew it was mine.

"That was the best sex I've ever had in my entire life," I whispered, pulling back and Jensen's hands found the sides of my face. He was searching my eyes for signs of insincerity or teasing but he wouldn't find anything because I was staring at him with genuine adoration and complete satisfaction.

"I didn't know it was possible to feel this relaxed," I leaned back in his arms, letting my head fall back and closed my eyes as the last of the sensations rolled through me. I was so fucking content in his arms. He nuzzled his face against my collarbone, pressing his ear to my chest and listening to my heartbeat slow back down to its normal pace against his cheek.

Jensen shifted, pressing a kiss to my chest as his eyes looked up at the shredded jersey hanging limp from the headboard. "Coach is going to fucking kill me," he mumbled and I started to laugh, wrapping his head up in my arms, tangling his hair between my fingers and pulling him tightly against my chest in a pile of laughter.

SARAH

Kaia stood at the end of the bench with her arms crossed over her chest and her eyes burning holes into me while I did my rows. I'd been trying to ignore her for most of the workout, but she saw right through me.

"You're in too good of a mood, it happened didn't it." Kaia's hair was pulled up on either side of her head in frizzy space buns that showed off her tight, elongated jaw.

"What happened?" I said, struggling through the last set. My focus wandered when my eyes caught sight of shirtless Jensen, working on his back. My brain was a mess of stupid girlish thoughts. Wanting to be under him almost every hour of the day was fucking with my life. I knew exactly *what* Kaia was referring too but it was more fun to string her along, pretending I didn't. I liked when her face got serious and her eyes went dark.

"You *know* what," she snapped at me.

"Say it out loud, Kaia," I giggled and set down the weights.

"You got laid!" She said, far too loud. Both Rhea and Sunday turned to look at us in the middle of their sets. "She got laid," Kaia yelled, pointing at me.

"Why don't you tell everyone in the gym?" I said to her, a week ago I might have been nervous about it, even hiding the fact that it had happened from her long enough to come to terms with it. But I was on cloud nine, I leaned back on my palms and stared at her with a smile on my face.

"My beautiful, brave little slut! You're glowing!" Kaia moved forward and slipped onto the bench, straddling it with her legs. "It must have been good, you're like a fucking fat cat right. Are you purring?" She teased.

"Shut up," I scoffed. "It was really fucking good," I whispered. "Jensen is very much above average," I laughed, holding out my hands and her eyes widened.

"Yeah, just know that this conversation is not over, and I want every single detail later," Kaia demanded, like she didn't have her own love life and was vicariously living through me.

"Finish your circuit," I said to her.

"I really don't want to," Kaia groaned, "Physio was brutal this morning…can't we keep talking about Magic Mike's massive dick?" She whined but she would do it anyways, she had never quit anything in her entire life. Even if she didn't want to do it. Kaia would pull herself off the ground and do it anyway.

I climbed off the bench, putting distance between me and Kaia. "Finish and I'll take you for breakfast," I said to her even though it was two in the afternoon. Kaia's favorite food was bacon, it could motivate her back from the dead if need be.

"Fine," she groaned, falling back against the bench and rolling off it lazily to return to her abandoned weights.

I racked my weights and moved across the gym, desperate for a moment to think. I eyed the pullup bar and despite my hatred for it, the machine was secluded near the back of the gym away from all the noise.

Next week our season officially started and so did the sprint to the finish line. Scouts were going to flood Harbor and they were all coming to watch us. The hope was that more than one of us got noticed and one day, even though we'd be separated by miles, we would meet each other on the field again.

I looked around at the girls, Rhea laughing as she spotted Sunday and Kaia yelling out insults at them for some sort of fucked up motivation. My heart hurt. Moving to California hurt but it was inevitable. I would end up there, I had too. I had worked too hard my entire life not too. If I let it, that sadness would eat me alive. I pulled myself up the bar, focusing on what I could control.

I hadn't even noticed him come up from my left as his hands wrapped around the bar and he lifted through the next pull up, matching my speed.

"Why are you sad?" He asked and it caught me off guard.

"I'm not," I grunted through the next one but paused as his face crossed the bar and captured my lips in a quick kiss.

"Right," he said with a smile, I did one more pull-up alongside of him before wrapping my legs around him and hanging there while he kissed me again.

"You know I'm trying to work out?" I said, breathless as he pulled away.

"Three more," he said, lifting with me and kissing me over the bar.

"You're annoying," I groaned, but obliged him on the next one.

"There's nothing wrong with assisted pull-ups, Adeline," he teased, lifting both our weight through the motion again. "Doesn't make you weak," he said. I knew he wasn't talking about my strength, he was trying to pry out the answer to his first question. It wasn't going to work, my impending sadness and inevitable distance wasn't for him or this relationship. Instead of answering I stole a kiss while he did the work and it helped to push away all the other thoughts.

"One more?" he whispered, taking my bottom lip between his.

"One more." I agreed, shaking my head at his show of strength as he lowered himself back to the ground. His hands wrapped around my ribcage as I let go of the bar and he set me back on the ground.

I could tell that he wanted to push the topic of me being sad, but thunder clapped loudly outside and broke his attention away from me. It was pouring. The next explosion of lightning caused the lights in the gym to flicker. Jensen chuckled, one hand still on my hip, he looked down at the watch on his wrist.

"What?" I asked. With the power flickering the girls had paused their sets and were standing around watching the rain beat against the glass.

"We need to get to the Nest," Jensen said, giving my hip a squeeze. Kaia perked up like someone had offered her a million dollars.

"Is it happening?" She asked and luckily Sunday was as confused as I was. A bright smile formed on Rhea's face.

"Can someone fill me in, please?" I asked, wandering closer to them.

"Kaia made friends over the Christmas break," Rhea said, leaning on Sunday's shoulder. Their size difference was ridiculous when they were side by side.

"What exactly does that mean?" I said, wiping the sweat away from my neck and coming to stand next to them.

"It means the boys at the Nest like to get messy, and it's finally wet enough to see just how much," Kaia practically vibrated the words from her body.

I had never seen her so excited.

"Slip and slide," Jensen said.

"Can we go?" Kaia turned to Jensen. "Please?"

With zero clue of what was going on it was weird to see a silent conversation between my best friend and my— I stopped myself before the thought was even able to form. It was just another reason to be sad about California when I should have been happy. I could have sex with Jensen without it being more, that was the point. It was supposed to be light, relaxing and fun. I was capable of that.

"We haven't finished our workout and if we miss practice later, Coach will have our heads," I said, reminding them that we had responsibilities.

"Coach won't make us practice with lightning and you know it," Rhea grinned.

"Conspirator," I said to Rhea.

"Minty please," Kaia begged, *Kaia never begged.*

"Minty?" Jensen looked over at me.

"It was one..." I stopped telling the story and chuckled, "Foul play," I said to her with a pointed finger. "Fine, let's do it."

Kaia jumped at me, picking me up off the ground and throwing me over her shoulder with a spin. Everyone collected their stuff and piled into Jensen's old man car, Rhea sliding in behind me as I moved my seat forward for her and Jensen's hand wrapped around my thigh.

He winked at me as he pulled from the parking lot and took the five of us back up to the Nest. "Cosy is gonna hate that she missed this," Kaia was jabbering from the backseat.

"No she won't, she hates fun," Rhea laughed and threw her arm around Sunday. "When was the last time she came out with us for karaoke? Or drinks, or dancing..." Rhea's list was endless.

"I wish *I* knew what was fun was supposed to be going on," I grumbled and turned my head to look out the window. The rain was coming down hard and pelted against the windows as he parked the car outside the Nest. I still wasn't entirely sure how they could reduce such a regal home like Dansby House to something called the Nest, but every time I referred to it by its actual name, Jensen scowled or ignored me all together. I had been silently bullied into calling it by the dumb nickname in record time.

"Addy 'I hate surprises' Sarah," Kaia said, leaning forward on the seats and tugging at my hair. "You're going to *love* this."

She was the first out of the car and like clockwork, Dean Tucker was coming out the front door. He held his hand out to her and I watched as they bumped their fists together, top, bottom, side, side, wiggled their fingers before bumping their opposite elbows together.

"Is this the Twilight Zone? That's what this is, isn't it?" I said, watching with horror as she just disappeared into the house with him. "How does she know him?" I asked.

"I told you," Rhea said, getting out of the car with me, "she made friends."

"They have a secret handshake!" I said to her and Rhea shrugged. She didn't say anything but she was right, Kaia made those kinds of friends wherever she went. It was impossible not to love her, she was loyal, loud and when it came down to it she always had your back.

Rhea led Sunday up the stairs and into the house leaving me standing in the downpour with Jensen. The rain soaked his dark hair, and when he ran his hand through, it left the strands sticking up in droopy curls leaning in every direction.

"Scared of a little rain?" He asked me, his eyes watching my expression carefully. How did we go from him wanting to jump my bones to being acutely aware of my every thought? It sent a tingle of nerves through my muscles.

"I'm going to need the tanned, strictly sunshine baseball player to stop making assumptions. I *love* the rain," I said to him. "I do not like being out of the loop."

"Is that all it is?" He asked, taking my hand and leading me toward the house. The implications of his question were clear. *Why were you sad?*

"That's all." I gave his hand a squeeze, trying to convince him and myself that it wasn't the time or the place to have the 'I might not be here in six months' conversation with him.

"I can fix that problem," he said.

The worst part was, he could probably fix it but I was too much of a chicken to talk to him about it. I surrendered to his gentle tugs and curled myself against his side as we wandered through the house. We walked by all the empty rooms to the wide open back door and ventured into the rain after a brief thirty-second pause from the downpour.

"What the hell is that?" I asked him.

"A slip and slide," he said, his lips crooked and showing off a portion of his brilliant, sharp smile. "Come," he hopped down off the step and held his hands up to me, grabbing my waist and pulling me down before I had time to register what the hell was happening.

Several members of the Hornets baseball team were spread out across the lawn in dirty clothes, and half naked, covered in grass and mud. I watched in amazed horror as Van Mitchell the outfielder tossed his massive, muscled and very naked, very muddy torso down the hill with reckless abandon.

"What?" I laughed and inched forward to watch, from the angle we were at I couldn't see over the hill but I knew it was steep. We climbed it just the other night. As I got closer it was obvious that they had been doing this for years. Down the backside of the hill, carved into what was a beautiful patch of grass was a dirty path that had turned into a mud pit from the rain.

It was a thick, slippery slope that they were sliding down.

"Oh my god," I said as Kaia tore off her pump cover, her muscles were still tense from our workout, her back flexing as she spoke to the first baseman with a smile on her face. He was telling her how to do it without getting hurt, but I still flinched as she took the thin plastic sled from him and launched herself down the hill. Her screams of laughter filled the air as everyone cheered for her.

Jensen tugged off his shirt with one hand, and between the rain and the gym pump I nearly moaned. Every muscle on his body was tight and overworked, the tattoos stretching over his tanned skin. Combined, it made me clench my thighs together. *He was turning me into an animal.* He looked over at me and lifted my chin with the crook of his finger, "eyes up here, Belle."

"I'm having withdrawals," I grumbled and grabbed his wrist before he could pull away.

That made him laugh, his chest rumbling as he brought me closer, "*later*," rolled off his lips as he leaned down and his lips met mine gently, the rain making the kiss slick.

"Tease," I said as he pulled away, his fingers finding my wrist and backed toward the edge of the hill.

"I'll just watch for now," I said to him, between the rain, the mud and the sharp slope... Everything about the slip and slide they all loved so much looked like a surefire way to get hurt before my season even started.

"No." Jensen shook his head.

"No?" I said as he tugged me toward his chest, his hand snaking up under my t-shirt to fan over my stomach. *Cheater.*

"You talk such a big game about how much tougher you are than me, you're going down that hill," he said as his hand roamed, his fingers brushing the edge of my gym shorts.

"That death trap doesn't prove how tough I am," I said to him with a grin on my face, hiding the fact that my stomach was churning over, needy like an idiot for his hand to trail lower.

"Fine," he said, and pulled his hand away. "You don't wanna have fun, I can take you home," he said, and he was dead serious.

"Good, we can have more fun in private anyways," I said, pulling on his arm.

"Oh no, Adeline." He looked me over, mischievous and two steps ahead of me. "I'll drop *you* off at home. I won't be staying... no fun means no fun."

"That's not fair," I said, trying to control the whine in my voice. It would give him way too much power in the situation. "You can't leverage sex to get me to do something dangerous," I grunted, narrowing my eyes on him as the rain dripped down my face.

"I can't?" Jensen's lips curled to the side and he closed one eye, his face scrunching up to keep the water out of his eyes. "Isn't that exactly what I'm doing?"

"I'm not going down that hill, Jensen!" I yelled out to him as he got further away from me.

He shrugged his broad, toned shoulders at me, the ink rippling across his chest, "have it your way but I'm cutting you off, having only one thing on your mind is making you cranky."

Kaia appeared from the bottom of the hill, out of breath and soaked in mud from head to toe. "You gonna let him talk to you like that?" She hollered over the sound of thunder.

"Don't be a chicken, Minty," Rhea called out to me.

It cracked through the air and I knew that I didn't have a choice.

"What are you going to do, Adeline?" Jensen said as I walked toward him on mission, I didn't bother removing my shirt before I lowered my center of gravity, wrapping my arms around his core and shoving him backwards. "Hey!" He called out, unprepared for the tackle as we both hit the ground at the edge of the hill.

"I'm not a coward and I'm not cranky," I huffed, breathless from the excretion. I was strong but Jensen was pure muscle from head to toe, he barely grunted hitting the ground. He laughed wildly, as everyone stood around cheering us on as he rolled me through mud. The wrestling match was short-lived between the rain and slippery terrain, we lost our grip on the edge and went tumbling down the hill.

His arms wrapped around me as we picked up speed, my laughter a combination of screams and tiny yelps that turned quiet as we slid to a lazy stop in the mud.

"Are you okay?" Jensen huffed, running a hand through his mud-drenched hair. His soft eyes traced over me quickly, "I didn't hurt you?" He sounded panicked for a moment as I adjusted in the mud, my hand slipping out from under me and splashing around us as I started to laugh. "Adeline!" Jensen's voice was tense when I didn't answer.

"Can we do it again?" I asked.

Jensen's concern dissipated as his lips curled outward and showed me the brightest smile I'd ever seen from him. "You're crazy," he grumbled, pulling me up from the puddle and wrapping his dirty hands around my jaw. His lips tasted like dirt and grass but I leaned into the kiss he provided and let the world go fuzzy.

JENSEN

> **ADELINE:**
> I can't. I feel like crap. I'm just going to sleep it off.

Her response to my text about going out for dinner had me walking through the front door of her apartment with a paper bag full of vegetables and other random crap that I thought might help her feel better.

Adeline was sick because of me.

The storm had lasted almost four hours and we had spent the majority of it covered in dirt and grass until the girls had to dart away for rugby practice... which they also held in the rain. She had been cold and wet the majority of the day and while I was smart enough to know that most likely wasn't the result of why she was sick, I still felt terrible.

I knocked quietly on her apartment door and waited just hoping that I caught her in a moment where she wasn't sleeping it off. After five minutes my plan of taking care of her had started to turn into taking the groceries to my mothers, making soup and bringing it back... but as I was working out the math the lock clicked and the door creaked open to her flushed adorable face.

"What are you doing?" She asked, her bottom lip jutting out in confusion.

Her dark hair was messy from her nap and rogue curls were sticking every which way around her reddened cheeks and nose. Her eyes looked hazy as she took me in, squinting from the hallway lights.

"Taking care of you," I whispered quietly, it was pretty clear that her head was bugging her by the way she kept switching which eye she was using. "It was on my list, remember? Take you on dates, feed you, keep you happy..."

"Take care of me," she finished the silence with a small smile but then shook her head. "No, you can't, I don't want you getting sick."

"I don't get sick," I said to her and pushed on the door with my shoe.

"Everyone gets sick," she grumbled, her voice raw and she turned away to cough it clear.

"Not me," I said.

And I wasn't lying, I couldn't remember the last time I was properly sick. Even my stomach was made of steel. Tested true by the amount of times that Todd had actively given the entire Nest food poisoning and I was the only player left standing to clean up the puke bowls.

I wasn't taking no for an answer.

Let me take care of you.

I knew that she was trying to hold me at arm's length for a reason, what this was... whatever we were. Neither of us had expected it to happen and unlike me who's goals started and stopped with the Hornet's baseball season. Adeline had plans and I hadn't been a part of them until a few weeks ago.

I wasn't stupid. She was scared of getting attached and I didn't blame her. We were at the age when chasing our dreams and making the hard decision to let some die was on the forefront of everything we did. And Adeline had massive dreams.

I'd made peace with the idea that rugby came first, and I knew that somewhere along the line it probably meant that the sport and her future in it would play a trump card over our situation-ship.

I was a big boy. I could handle it.

She wiggled her toes on the tiled floor and I watched a shiver rattle through her. She looked so tiny when she was sick and all I wanted to do was scoop her up and curl around her in bed until she was back to normal.

"Let me in, Adeline," I coerced.

Those sick and exhausted hazel eyes turned vicious at the demand but she relented and the door swung open gently. She padded backward in her tiny shorts and sports bra, her body littered in bruises that I had to constantly remind myself were part of the job.

Moving through her dark apartment I set the bag down on the counter, leaving it behind for a brief moment. She locked the door again and as soon as she was in reach I had her face in my hands, she grumbled at the contact but I felt her body relax into my touch.

"You're really warm." My tone dropped, and one of her eyebrows perked up in response. "Back to bed," I said, pressing my lips to her hot temple. Another string of groaned unintelligible words followed before a dim, warm light flickered on and lit up the countertops along the kitchen wall. She eyed me for a second, her brows furrowed as she took me in.

"Bed," I demanded when she remained still, her whole body trembling from the cool air of her apartment.

I watched her wander across, taking in the wide space. Everything was open except a door that no doubt led to the bathroom off the main entrance. The living room was drenched in dark colors and vintage artwork, with a T.V. and record player against the far wall. Nestled against a large row of windows was her bed opposite of the massive sectional that took up the open space perfectly.

I unpacked the groceries as she crawled back into her covers and pulled them up around her face, closing her eyes completely unbothered that I was moving around her kitchen. It took me a second to orient myself in her kitchen but eventually I found everything I needed to make her dinner. After a little while the smell of simmering vegetables pulled her from her exhausted, sick state and she was glaring daggers at me from her pillows.

"You're grumpy when you're sick," I laughed, filling a mug with soup and grabbing a spoon for her.

She didn't respond but she pushed up in the bed and curled back against the headboard with a pillow under her arm and the blankets pooling around her waist. I watched as she pushed the sweaty waves away from her neck and tucked them into a bundle out of her way.

Her hands shook as she took the mug and for a moment I considered holding it for her and just feeding her myself but the look on her face told me that I shouldn't even try. She brought the hot soup to her nose and inhaled slowly, her chest rising in a shuddered breath as her eyes started to water.

"This smells amazing," she mumbled and brought the mug to her lips without bothering the spoon. "What is this?"

"It's avgolemono," I said, resting against the side of the bed on my knees and bracing myself with my elbows on the mattress. "Lemon chicken soup."

"What is that Italian?" She huffed, taking another sip. I could get used to grumpy, sick Adeline in all the best ways. Her brows were crumpled together in a cranky line and her jaw was tight in frustration, hating being on the outside of something. I loved how bothered she got when she wasn't the one with the answers, always having to be the smartest person in the room.

"Greek," I corrected her.

"Oh, so the Greek god crap isn't a rumor... wait, Jensen isn't a Greek name," she added before drinking more broth.

"It's not, it's Scandinavian," I said, "My mom's side of the family is very big, very loud and very much Greek..."

"Is this her recipe?" Adeline asked me, finally reaching for the spoon in my hand to fish out some of the vegetables.

"No, that's Ya-Ya's, no matter how often my mom likes to claim it's not," I laughed and her eyes flickered over to me, silencing the sound, "What?"

"Nothing," she whispered, "It's just nice hearing about your family."

"Everyone that's lived in Harbor long enough knows about my family, I'm not used to having to fill in the gaps," I said to her, snaking my hand behind the covers on her bed to find her thigh. I brushed my thumb across her hot skin as we both went quiet and she finished her cup.

"I grew up all over the place," she said when she finished, setting the mug on her side table. "My parents divorced and we sort of bounced around for a while before Mom settled in Harbor and got remarried."

"You didn't grow up here? You and Kaia make it seem like you've been friends since you were kids," I said to her, and it was true. If she hadn't told me I would have just assumed she was a Harbor native.

"Kaia beat the shit out of a high schooler on my first day of school after he almost hit me with his car in the parking lot. He was twice her size and up until that day I'd never seen a man cry that hard," Adeline smiled at the memory. "We've been attached at the hip since."

175

"So you have a step-dad?" I asked her, desperate to get into the bed with her but waiting for the invitation.

"I've had *four*, she's on... boyfriend number six?" She said, shrugging her shoulders. "I don't even remember their names half the time. I think this one is Ronald? Or Roger?"

"Ronald is a horrible name," I teased and it brought a tired smile to her face.

"It is, but at least he has a first name. Unlike you," she chuckled.

"I have a first name, you just haven't figured it out yet," I shrugged.

"I know it starts with an M," Adeline said, sniffling.

I reached out and handed her the box of tissues on the table.

"Is it Matthew?" she asked, blowing her nose, "or Marcus?"

"Nope," I said. "Way off base."

"Are you going to give me any hints?" She asked.

"Nope," I smiled at her.

"Fine... I'll figure it out eventually... Martha," she added, making me smile but I shook my head no. "Can I have more?" She asked after a minute, and the question was simple, but the admission to being looked after was clear. I nodded, pushing off the floor, grumpy about having to remove my hand from her skin but happy to look after her. "It's the first thing I've eaten in two days and I think it's actively fighting this cold single-handedly," she said to me as I wandered across the apartment.

Looking over my shoulder at her I watched as she flipped through her phone, the screen lighting up all my favorite features on her face. She tossed it aside, seemingly frustrated as she slumped against the headboard.

"What's wrong?" I asked her knowing the chances of her lying to me.

"I've missed two practices, and the season opener is right around the corner. The scouts are coming down this week. I need to be back on the field but my entire body feels like it's made of brittle bones and open wounds." She took the mug from me and closed her eyes as she inhaled the smell again. "It's my last chance to impress them."

"Finish that," I said to her and wandered away from the bed before she could start asking questions. The bottom half of the grocery bag I had brought was full of random craps that had landed in my cart while on call with my mom.

"Get her Epsom salts, and nothing that stinks... do scentless and then go over to the flowers and get her eucalyptus, but you have to roll it out to get it to work with the steam," she bossed me around through the phone. "And stop by the house before you go over and get the herbal honey in the cupboard above the counter, by the tea."

"Mom," I groaned and she tutted in my ear, silencing my protests before talking to someone on the other end of the phone.

"Get her new socks too..." she mumbled between instructions to her assistant. "Are you listening to me Kai?"

"Yeah Mom," I stifled the laugh that bubbled up in my chest. "New socks, honey above the counter, eucalyptus and Epsom salts. Now is there dill in Ya-Ya's soup?" I asked the question that had started the phone call in the first place.

"My soup, and no." She said, "I have to go," she mumbled, "fresh eucalyptus Malachi, nothing synthetic," she scolded like she knew I was standing in the bath aisle looking at the selection of scented bubble baths. "I love you," she said quickly, waiting for me to respond before she hung up.

"What are you doing?" Adeline asked as I collected the rest of the supplies and walked toward her bathroom.

"Finish your soup," I ordered her, ignoring the question and clumsily flicking on the light in the bathroom. I started to follow all Mom's instructions and it wasn't long before I could feel Adeline's eyes on my back. I rolled up my sleeves and checked to make sure the water was hot, the steam in the bathroom tangling with the eucalyptus and making it smell incredible.

Adeline looked like she was going to cry when I came face to face with her.

"Arms up," I said to her, ignoring the way her thankful, sick expression made my heart clench in my chest. Her grip on it was growing tighter and I was afraid of what would happen if she ever let go. She listened without protest, letting me pull her sports bra off. Careful to respect her space and how achy her body felt I helped her out of her shorts only pausing to kiss her hip bone with tenderness that made her body shiver.

"I'm not taking a bath with you watching," she scowled.

"I'll help you in and leave," I said, just trying to behave as she stood naked in front of me.

"I'm sick, not dying and that tub is massive," she nodded with a familiar playful smirk that had me stripping from my shirt so fast she giggled at my movements.

I groaned at the hot temperature as my skin hit it but I hid my discomfort, holding my hand out to her. "Come here," I said, holding her hand as she sank into the water.

"Wait until Kaia finds out that you can cook and run bubble baths," she moaned as her body lowered beneath the surface in front of mine. "And it's hot," she relaxed against my chest, with my legs straddling her and closed her eyes. "Thank you, baby," she purred, practically falling asleep as I raked my fingers through her scalp, just grateful for her invitation. I'd been missing the way her body fit so perfectly into the shape of mine.

"It's the least I can do for getting you sick," I whispered to her and kissed the top of her head.

SARAH

My body was still recovering from being sick but for the first time in a week, my lungs weren't burning from taking a walk. I pushed through the locker room doors to find most of the girls getting ready for the game. Doechii blasted over the speakers in the corner as everyone pulled into their gear slowly.

At least it was nice out today, the rain had cleared up and the sun returned to dry up all the fields, restoring them to grass instead of the giant mud pits they previously were. I tossed my duffle into my locker and stripped from my tights as Sunday plopped herself down between Rhea's legs to get her hair done.

The scouts would be here today, they'd be here all week. But I was desperate to make a good impression. Rugby wasn't just a sport, it was an outlet, a dream, a way of life for me.

I remember the day I saw the forms for the high school team sitting on the teachers desk in the gym office. I had come off the field from track and a little feral voice told me to pick that form up. I brought the form home, maybe hoping it would warrant a reaction, I didn't really care what kind. Maybe mom would flip out and tell me no or Dad would give me the talk about how dangerous it was.

But instead they floated around me and forgot to sign the forms the night before try outs so I forged their signatures and brought it in.

Coach Gunthry immediately created space for me, he was quick and attentive with every player on the field. He worked hard to help foster our skills and there was never an instance where I felt left behind or forgotten. My brothers made it to two games that year, and even less the following. But even after graduation, the girls from my high school team attended every college game I played. They never missed one.

My parents never attended one.

Rugby wasn't just a fun way to keep active. It was the family I never had, it was mine and no one else's and it made me feel unstoppable. Kaia clicked her teeth beside me, "How are you feeling?"

"Better, I can't believe no one else got sick." I groaned, shoving my feet into my cleats.

"You just have a sweet baby immune system," Kaia said, reaching out and pinching my cheek. I swatted her hand away and growled a warning. "Touchy," she hissed. "I know it's not your stupid brothers, the only thing that might rattle you is your parents. Are they here?"

"Hah," I huffed. "Never. Mom would sooner be caught dead than sitting in the stands."

It was true, even as I got better and started to get noticed for my talent, none of them cared. It was always fake enthusiasm and lack of interest, they were just too busy to pay attention and their lack of attentiveness only made me work harder.

"Okay, well." She grumbled and grabbed my chin, forcing me to look at her. "If that scout is already under your skin, we're going to lose today."

"The scout is not under my skin," I said to her, my eyes never leaving hers, "and we aren't losing today."

Kaia scanned my expression and when she determined I was confident in my response she nodded and loosened her grip on my face to tap my cheeks with her fingers. "You hear that, girls?" She raised her voice, her eyes still on mine as a smile formed on her face, "We aren't losing today!" She surged from the bench and started jumping around the locker room to the music.

The scout was most definitely under my skin.

Today mattered more than any other day.

I rolled out my shoulders, following them out onto the field for warmups and scanned the crowd. It was one of the rare occasions that a Hornet's game overlapped a Hillcats and my heart sank unexpectedly not seeing him in the stands but I couldn't let it get to me. We had to win.

Our strengths lied in the fact that the Hurricanes would underestimate our abilities to keep them pinned down but Cosy and Rhea had been running new drills and we were more than ready to shut them down out there. The logical preparations did ease the rampant anxiety that flowed through my chest as the stands rumbled loudly and the team talked amongst themselves.

"Do you see them?" Kaia asked, sinking to the grass beside me. I shook my head. "Okay, you looked once, that's enough. Keep your eyes on the field now, play like they aren't here."

"What if I don't impress them, Kaia?" I asked her, stretching my arm over my chest.

"Why is that even an option in your mind?" She countered, following my motion.

"Because it's an option rooted in reality. There's a chance that no matter how hard I play today, they just don't care. Maybe my style isn't what they're looking for..." I could go on but my words died on my tongue. I flipped over, pushing my hips into the ground to get them loose and Kaia mirrored my movement coming face to face with me.

"You're the fastest girl on the field, Minty." She said and I narrowed my eyes on her because Kaia Keegan would rather die than admit I was faster. She was being too nice. "I mean it, today I mean it. No teasing, or joking. It's you, if anyone is going to get to the big leagues, *it's you*."

"You're sugarcoating it to make me feel better," I sighed.

"I'm being serious," she responded with a sigh. "You are exactly what they want. You're trying to lower your standards so you aren't disappointed and I get that, Addy, I do. But you've worked so hard to get to this game and it would be a waste of all that time spent proving everyone wrong to give up now." Kaia stared at me with her mean, dark brown eyes and waited for the confidence to click back in place. "This is the one place you aren't invisible, you made sure of that. You wanted this attention, now own it."

I inhaled and held my breath before letting it out again with a sharp nod.

"That's my girl."

It was a long game of back and forth. The second the whistle was blown to start, the Hurricane's were all over us. We were and always would be a team of speed but it didn't mean we weren't prepared to defend ourselves when the time came.

Kaia and Rhea had taken back to back turns in the sin bin after Amber had found a spare second to take a cheap shot on Sunday. Shortly after Amber was subbed out for another girl and the game went back to fair play but their blood was already boiling and both teams were more concerned on protecting then they were running.

We needed to refocus if we wanted to win this game.

"Watch for Kiely," Cosy was out of breath as we pushed back to allow Sunday to kick the ball. We needed one more good drive and we'd win with a comfortable point gap but the Hurricanes were playing like the intense cardio wasn't affecting them and all of the Hillcats were running on steam.

Sunday looked to me as we clicked into place in unison and she kicked a high, hanging kick that floated through the air and gave me time to rush the field. Rhea stayed on my tail and protected my body as I surged through the air to get the ball in my hands and regain possession before Kiely, the Hurricanes best back, charged to do the same. When my toes hit the turf, she was there but Rhea was faster, blocking the lunge and taking the tackle to open the lane on my right.

I could hear two more Hurricane players narrowing in on either side of me from behind, barely a yard out and the sound of their cleats ripping into the earth fueled me faster. I could see Kaia out of the corner of my eye, and passed the ball hard. It hit her with a slap and she was able to avoid the tackle with precision before swinging back around and passing it backward into me. The crowd was electric for the two of us, but we still had a little to go without getting caught up for the confusing play to be worth the trouble.

"Left," Kaia yelled and I pushed off that foot chucking the ball to her. She moved in a smooth one eighty just like we had run a hundred times and popped out on my right with a determined grin on her face. She didn't have to say a word, she hurled the ball toward me from the right and I extended my arms as it slammed into my stomach and I wrapped it up. I didn't stumble a single step as I took off, mere yards from the line and perfectly centered beneath the uprights.

I slid out of reach of the attacker and rolled until the ball was between me and the grass and the try was called fair. A loud barrage of whistling and screaming came from behind me in the stands and I turned to see half the Hornet's team, sweaty and red faced screaming in celebration. My heart was racing, they must have come straight from their game to catch the tail end of ours.

Jensen was bear hugging an excited Van, his hair damp from a quick shower but his gaze snapped to mine and he gave me a wink as I backed away slamming into the chest of Rhea and Kaia who were ready to do celebrating of their own.

"You caught it!" Kaia screamed as Rhea hauled me up onto her shoulders. "You caught it from the right side, you beautiful bitch!" She slammed into Rhea who took the hit with grace and managed to keep me balanced as we traipsed to center field to shake hands.

She set me back on the ground for Cosy and Sunday to wrap me up. "Stunning," Cosy hissed with a smile, "feels good to win this one."

"Damn right it does, now let's party." I hollered and wrapped my arm around her shoulder as we filed into line. We shook hands and as we made our way back to the tunnel a set of arms wrapped around my middle tightly. Jensen's lips nuzzled against my sweaty neck as he lifted me off the ground against his chest.

"Hi Belle," he purred, turning me around and lifting me off the ground until I was wrapped around his waist with my hands resting on his shoulders.

"Hi Lover," I said with a whisper, before I grabbed his chin, angled his head to the side and kissed the *lover* tattoo behind his ear. "You must have won, look at the smile on you," I said, stealing a kiss from his lips, one hand wrapping around my middle his other finding its way up my back to my neck as he deepened it. He smiled against my lips as he broke away with a tiny chuckle.

"By three runs," he hummed. "You looked incredible out there."

I scrunched my nose up, "Let's hope it's enough to impress the scouts." I blurted without thinking and watched as something flickered across his face that he hid well but not fast enough. I hadn't really thought about what I was losing if everything worked out the way I wanted, but I pushed aside the feeling and kissed Jensen again, distracting us both from the unknown.

JENSEN

> **UNKNOWN:**
> Is your backdoor open?

> **UNKNOWN:**
> How much for a handjob?

I shoved my phone back in my pocket and climbed from the car. I was one more invasive, disgusting text away from changing my numbers. The only texts I wanted were ones from Adeline and the one I had gotten before practice had me rushing through drills just to get to her.

I was in so deep, I could feel her in my sleep.

Of course, Adeline looked like a fucking dream.

Her hair was loose around her shoulders and all the color had returned to her skin since being sick. She was wearing jeans that hung wide on her legs and a tiny cropped mesh shirt that showed off her toned stomach and begged for me to touch. Kaia was leaning against her in a minidress and a rough-looking jean jacket with a concerning smile across her usually stern face.

"You're late, fuckboy," Kaia snipped.

I ignored her jab completely, wrapping my arms around my girl and peppering her skin with kisses until she begged me to stop in a fit of breathless giggles.

"I had practice and I'm two minutes late," I said to Kaia, setting Adeline back on the ground. "How are you feeling?" I asked her.

"Better," she said, keeping her hand knotted into the back of my shirt.

"Alright what's this big surprise?" I asked as another car whipped into the parking lot.

Adeline's body went rigid and I followed her gaze to the slamming door as Kaia pushed off the car to meet the guy stomping across the asphalt toward us.

"That's Christian," she sighed, pressing her face into my shoulder, meeting my gaze. "Kaia's boyfriend."

I wanted to ask her why we didn't like the guy because it was written all over her face that we didn't but he was in ear shot and I wasn't going to tempt starting an argument with a guy I'd never met before over my girlfriends silent disdain.

"Jensen," I introduced myself, holding out my hand to him. He was tall, with a wiry frame and dark hair, his lip pulled to the left in annoyance as his beady brown eyes flickered down to my hand.

"Chris," he grunted in return but didn't shake my hand, leaving me hanging awkwardly. "Is this the latest conquest Kaia won't stop talking about?" He asked Adeline, and talked about me like I wasn't standing in front of him.

"Stop," Kaia scoffed, "I wasn't talking about him last night while my mouth—"

"Don't finish that sentence," Christian said, cutting her off as his hand wrapped around her throat and roughly kissed her to keep her quiet.

I could feel how uncomfortable Adeline was by the way her body pressed tightly into mine and she completely avoided the weird display of affection between the two of them.

"We're going to a pop-up at the Hollow," Kaia said, "Adeline's oldest brother has a band and they're playing their first live gig tonight."

"You have a brother?" I looked down at her and she sighed.

"She has *two* brothers," Kaia laughed maniacally. "There's your *surprise*."

"Consider me shocked," I said quietly and dug my fingers playfully into her side to draw a smile out of her. "You were just going to throw me into the deep end tonight with your brothers?"

"Oh, baby," Adeline scrunched her nose up at me, "they're not the deep end."

"Zane and Taylor are easy..." Kaia interjected, "it's the Hollow that should scare you."

"The pub downtown?" I looked at her confused.

Kaia didn't answer, a smile spreading across her face. Suddenly my relaxed state was on high alert. Even though I was sure that I had passed the best friend test long ago, Kaia being the main instigator between our relationship it was clear that tonight had been created to test me.

She wanted to see how far she could push me before I broke.

But the joke was on her, there was nothing in the world that could trip me up. I wasn't going to mess up what I had. Not for anything. It was also very obvious that Kaia's boyfriend was another test, I just couldn't quite figure out what one. Was I supposed to get along with him, or did I follow Adeline's hushed body language and keep my guard up?

We all piled into Kaia's car, Adeline forcing me to sit in the back with Christian. The second she hit the gas I knew we were in trouble. Kaia backed out of the parking lot with one hand on the wheel and the other on Adeline's seat.

She was going at least twenty over the speed limit as she pulled the car into a quick one-handed drift around the corner on a red light, her right hand never leaving its relaxed position behind Adeline's head. She slid in and out of traffic causing Christian to grumble something from beside me. Adeline was flipping through music completely unconcerned with the friend's lack of safety as she ripped through the streets of Harbor.

"Let me guess, the *Fast and Furious* obsession extends to you?" I said between the hiccupped radio channels.

"You afraid of a little speed, fuckboy?" Kaia laughed, and I swear the car moved faster.

"I didn't say that," I said, leaning forward to snake my hand around the seat and find Adeline's skin. I needed contact, craved it like a lovesick idiot.

"You can say it... it's okay if you are. I'll show your girl a good time if you're too much of a coward," Kaia teased with a honey-like giggle.

"God Kaia," Christian groaned, his eyes on his phone.

"I surrender. Sorry Belle, you don't need me, you already have the perfect boyfriend." I rose both hands to Kaia, our eyes meeting in the rearview mirror.

"Dude," Christian's voice was like sandpaper on everyone's good mood. "Stop flirting with my girlfriend in front of yours."

"He's not flirting, and neither is Kaia..." Adeline scowled.

"Sounds like flirting," Christian stared her down and it took everything in me to stay quiet while Adeline dealt with his attitude.

"How would you know what flirting is?" Adeline said.

Christian glared at her, his eyes narrowing as she challenged him.

"Just because you flirt like limp cardboard..." Her words died out as she turned into Kaia's arm, leaning over the console as Kaia kept her foot on the gas pedal. Her lips caught her jaw in a languid open-mouthed kiss that made Kaia turn her gaze off the road to focus on her best friend. I shifted on my seat, cursing them both for needing to prove a point to such an asshole because my dick stiffened in my jeans as Kaia's mouth captured Adeline's in a quick, playful kiss that left smirks on both their faces. "Doesn't mean everyone else does."

We were all going to die in a fiery crash and I'd be happy for it.

Her eyes met mine quickly as she pulled away from Kaia, a cute smile on her mouth that made me warm and feral. I needed out of this car with these two before I exploded.

"Don't fucking kiss my girlfriend, Addy," he snapped and my hand tightened on the seat. There was something in the tone of his voice that made me want to put his smug face through the backseat window.

"We've had this conversation, Christian. Kaia is *my* boyfriend, before she's your girlfriend. I get first dibs and you shut your mouth," Adeline teased and my heart grew two sizes in my chest. *What the fuck was this girl doing to me?*

"Can Kaia be my boyfriend too?" I said teasingly and Adeline giggled, sitting back in her seat and giving Christian the middle finger without looking back at him.

Unfortunately for everyone, that was the end of Christian's good behavior, if you could even call it that. The moment we arrived on Main Street and Kaia was parked, *backward without even flinching into a spot far too small for her car*, the back door was slammed unreasonably hard and she was chasing after Christian.

"Is he always like that?" I asked Adeline after opening her door for her.

"Worse," she said, fixing her hair in the window before turning to me with a bright smile. "Thank you for not losing your cool."

"Oh my boxers are damp and sticky," I joked and Adeline tipped her head back in laughter. "I don't know why you're laughing, it's not funny. I have to meet your brothers with cum shorts," I laughed, chasing after her as she backed up to the crowded sidewalk and out of my reach.

By the time I caught her, she was flushed and giggly, begging to be fucked senseless and I was starting to think that maybe I'd rather just keep her locked up to myself forever. I kissed her neck as my arms wrapped around her waist, not stopping until my teeth found her ear and her ass was pressed tightly against my semi.

A husky voice cleared their throat to our left and Adeline stiffened in my arms, her smile turning into an embarrassed line as her eyes drifted up.

"Hi Taylor," she said, straightening herself out.

"Addy," Taylor said. It was like looking at two of them, side by side it was very clear that they were siblings. Her brother was taller but not by much with a wider jaw and darker green eyes but they shared the same complexion and wavy, brown hair.

"This is Jensen .." She said, wiggling out from my grasp and nudging me.

"It's nice to meet you," I offered my hand to him and he took it.

"Taylor, and you're the Catcher."

"Is that a bad thing?" I laughed.

"No, I just remember a very embarrassing conversation between my sister and my brother a few weeks ago-"

"Shut up, Taylor!" Adeline snapped with a smile on her face.

"Testy," her brother smiled back at her. "Have you seen Zane yet or were you too busy necking the dreamboat?"

"Thanks man," I said, appreciating the compliment even if he hadn't meant it to be one.

Taylor stared at me like I was insane but Adeline laughed and it made me wanna kiss the sound out of her but I controlled myself, slipping my hand into the back pocket of her jeans.

"No, but Kaia is here somewhere..." she said.

"Yeah, I saw her arguing with Christian in the alley," he said, "She's still with that asshole?"

"She's not a quitter," Adeline mocked Kaia's tone.

"Right..." Taylor rolled his eyes, backing away from us, "I'm going to go get a drink and see if I can find Zane before his set. It was nice to meet you, Jensen."

"That went horribly," I said to her and she just turned her face into my chest, laughing.

"At least your tongue wasn't down my throat," she shrugged and all the color drained from my face at the thought. "It's okay, we aren't like that..."

"Like what?" I asked, confused by her statement.

"We aren't really close, Zane is seven years older than me and Taylor another four," she said, "We're cordial, but we're more passing friends than we are siblings. Their opinion of you doesn't matter to me," she clarified, "That's all."

"Good because there's no way I'm keeping my tongue out of your mouth all night," I whispered, calming down her racing heart and kissing her gently until the tension in her shoulders disappeared. "Should we save Kaia or..."

"If anyone needs saving, it'll be Christian. She'll be okay," Adeline said, tugging on my arm and pulling me inside the busy pub.

The Hollow was a fascinating place. From what I knew about the bar, it was a space for first responders created by two brothers who both had served the public for a number years before opening the bar as some sort of haven. The location had been in the papers more than once for awards. Live music filled the enormous space from wall to wall. A long bar ran down the middle of the large rectangular dimly lit pub. The walls were floor to ceiling black tile with a vault roof of exceptional dark red architecture. None of it should have worked but it felt moody and gothic while still so alive, packed with people at all the tall standing tables and shoved into the leather booths.

There were more than six employees behind the bar all dressed in the same black t-shirt with 'The Hollow' sprawled across their chests in red printing. It was busy tonight and the back corner was alive with a band and the dance floor was flooded with bodies.

"It's incredible in here," I yelled to Adeline over the music as she pulled us toward the bar. I recognized Sunday behind the bar almost instantly, her small frame darting in and out of the sea of other employees with a smile on her face and a bottle of vodka in her hands.

"Hi!" She screamed, climbing up on the bar.

I watched as she stepped over an empty glass with precision, kicking it backward with the heel of her boot right into the hands of another employee.

"Is that?" I leaned into Adeline in shock, watching as the guy moved around behind the bar. I recognized him from T.V. and like a little kid I couldn't contain my excitement about the sight of that tufted blonde hair and angry look. "Judd Loveday, like *the* Judd Loveday..."

I was completely ignored as Sunday wrapped her hands around Adeline's face, vodka bottle and all. She kissed her quickly before tapping her chin and without skipping a beat Adeline tipped her head back and opened her mouth.

"Sunday!" A voice boomed from the other end of the bar.

"Drink faster," she urged Adeline, who had downed at least three shots since Sunday started pouring. "Quick he's closing in," she laughed and Adeline almost choked but kept drinking.

Two hands reached out to grab Sunday but she was faster, "Catch!" she yelled to me and hurled herself off the bar top.

I barely had time to react before throwing my hands up to grab her by the waist and pull her down into me in a bundle of blonde panic and spilled vodka.

"I fucking warned you," the guy said from across the bar.

"Oh calm down big baby Brighton," she mocked him but did it just out of his reach. "It's one bottle!"

Brighton Black. Sunday's brother.

He was tall, taller than I expected him to be against how little Sunday was. It was like he had stolen all her height. He had to be at least six-four in shoes, if not taller. With sharp blue eyes that narrowed on his younger sister and a tight jaw that was clenched so tight all the muscles in his neck and shoulders popped. He was an animal.

"Bright!" Someone called and his attention was diverted off his sister for a moment. Sunday took her chance and darted away from the bar, weaving through the crowd until she was climbing over a booth in the back and falling over Rhea in laughter.

"Does the back of her t-shirt say 'You have to fight my brothers for my phone number?'" I asked Adeline and she nodded, opening her mouth to say something but was silenced.

"Where'd she go, Addy?" Bright turned back, his grip on the bar violent.

"Dunno Brighty," she mocked, licking the drops of vodka off her lips with a smile.

"Don't call me that," he warned, "and if you find Sunday, bring my bottle back or I'm making you pay your tab!"

"Quivering," Adeline teased and he rolled his eyes, throwing the towel over his shoulder down on the bar and disappearing. The back of his shirt had more writing on it in red, and said 'Thing One' which made me laugh. "Welcome to the Hollow." Adeline beamed with pride.

"What the hell was that about?" I turned expecting to find Bright, the voice matched but the face did not.

"Jensen, this is Boone," Adeline said, her mood shifting from menace to friendly in a matter of seconds. "Thing two, Boonie-baby to Kaia," she laughed and the guy rolled his eyes. "Or as Sunday affectionately calls him *Bobo*. What's up Bright's ass tonight, the bar is packed he should be happy."

"He's pissed, I told him I'd wear the thing two shirt today but I couldn't find it so now he's walking around on a mission to make everyone's night horrible," Boone laughed, the lines around his blue eyes crinkling as he leaned on the bar beside us. He was covered in as many tattoos as I was but gave off a giant teddy bear kind of vibe in comparison to his rabid grizzly bear brother.

"They're twins," Adeline explained.

Boone stood up to his full height and for the first time in a long time I felt small. He was somehow bigger and wider than his brother, his wingspan alone, must have been seven feet. The Hollow shirt he was wearing was too short on his torso that it might as well have been cropped but he didn't seem to care as he stretched out and grabbed two beers from behind the bar. He handed me one, cracking the other and holding it out to Adeline.

"Slow." He warned and she just shook her head at him. "Fraternal, and yes, I'm taller if you were wondering." Boone smiled and showed me a perfect set of teeth. "If you see Sunny, make sure she finishes the bottle before she shows her face. It's better if there's no evidence." He patted her on the head and started off through the crowd. The back of his shirt said the same thing as Sunday's and I couldn't help but laugh.

"Hey Boonie," Adeline's mood shifted quickly as she followed his path and waited until he faced her again. "Kaia is outside with Christian," she said. I watched his face fall as he looked over at the front door, he didn't say anything but I could tell from his body language he felt the same way as Adeline.

"Go have fun, say hi to Zane for me," Boone said, running a heavily decorated hand through his dark hair. "It was nice to meet you," he nodded to me and disappeared.

"I'm scared to ask why he had the look of murder in his eyes, that's a big dude to piss off," I asked her and lifted the beer to my lips.

"History," Adeline said, her smile returning to her face. "He's usually the only one that can keep them from fighting too badly, she listens when he talks."

"So why don't we like Christian and why isn't Kaia dating Smokey the bear?" I asked her and she giggled, leaning forward to capture my lips in a small, very welcomed kiss.

"Christian is a jerk, but he's Kaia's jerk and we respect that," she said, tucking into between my legs as I leaned against a stool and wrapped my arm around her waist.

"Did Boone get that memo?" I pointed to the broad glass windows, each huge pane framed in black and just beyond was a clear view of Boone towering over Christian as he walked backward on the sidewalk, Kaia nowhere in sight.

"Fuck," Adeline said, quick to move and I was quick to follow.

"I fucking warned you," Boone's voice boomed. "What did I say?"

"Go to hell Boone!" Christian said but he had nothing to stand on and he was running out of sidewalk. His back slammed into the black fenced in patio that ran along the left side of the bar.

"Go get Brighton!" I heard Adeline call out to Judd behind the bar as she looked around for Kaia. "Do you see her?" she asked me and I shook my head. "Boone!" She called out but he was too focused on his target.

"The last time I saw you, she was crying and I told you if you ever made her cry again I'd give *you* something to cry about!" Boone was back in his face and

Christian had nowhere to go. "You either get the fuck in a cab and fuck off or I'll follow through on that threat right here and now," he said, somehow looking even larger than before.

"Whatever, I didn't want to be here tonight anyway," Christian said, starting to move around Boone toward the street. "You're pathetic you know that," he added as he called for a taxi mindlessly, "always playing second fiddle, she'll never see you like that and you're an embarrassment."

The laugh that came from Boone's chest was deep and baffled at the insult.

"You're a very small-minded individual," he said, stepping forward he lunged and Christian missed the curb stumbling out between the two parked cars. "I could blow on you and you'd walk yourself into traffic," Boone snapped, "but she would kill me so I'll be the bigger man."

"Ha, ha," Christian snarled. "Just keep your fucking massive head out of our relationship, it's not my fault she chose my dick over yours."

Boone's face went cold.

"Hey," I stepped in between their bodies just praying that Boone had sense enough not to swing on me but ready to take the blow if he did. "Listen man, tonight isn't your night and instead of running your mouth how about you go home with a full set of teeth so that you can live to shit talk another day?" I said to Christian who seemed less than impressed by my antics.

Boone, on the other hand, laughed from behind me.

"Fuck you too," Christian flipped me off, moving toward the taxi and climbing inside without another word.

"You're not going to hit me are you?" I turned back to see Boone watching the cab pull away from the curb. I flinched when he stepped forward and threw his arm around my shoulder.

"I'm going to get you a drink for being a brave little soldier like that, most people wouldn't dare step between me and him," he declared. "Baddy Addy, I fucking love this one."

Bright was standing in the doorway with a scowl on his face as we reentered, stopping his brother with his hand. "Thank you for taking it outside," he said to him and looked over at me.

"He was already outside, I can't take too much credit," Boone smiled and pushed through the doorway, taking me with him. Adeline was standing just inside with a red-faced Kaia who was putting on a brave face. Boone loosened his grip around my shoulders as Adeline swooped in to show me love, tugging me away just as Boone paused.

He lifted Kaia's face to him with a single finger, the motion oddly intimate but no one around them seemed to even take notice as he whispered "What do I always tell you?"

Kaia's mood shifted from the words, whatever it was that Boone preached when they were alone fell silently between them and she nodded while taking a deep breath and giving his cheek a playful slap. "Let's get fucking drunk!" She yelled, shaking off the tense mood as she beelined for the bar.

SARAH

"C oach laid the package out on the desk, "They want you in California at the end of season."

"Are you serious?" I took the folder and started to flip through the contract.

"Absolutely," Coach smiled at me, "You've been impressing the hell out of everyone Addy, they were bound to take notice eventually, and you earned this shot."

"End of season?" I said again, rubbing the page about temporary housing between my fingers.

"They want you leading the Premier League next year, this is big," Coach reminded me like I wasn't aware of the pressure it placed on my shoulders.

"Do I have time to think about it?" I asked her and she nodded.

"Get back to me by the end of the week so we can start the paperwork officially," she added as I stood up from my chair.

"Thanks Coach... for everything," I said, waving the papers in the air with a smile on my face, leaving the office I whipped out my phone. My fingers took me to texting Jensen but I stared at the phone with a heavy heart...

"He's genuinely perfect, Minty, not a damn thing wrong with him." Kaia cooed from the living room floor as she nursed her hangover the night after the Hollow. She refused to talk about what happened with Christian but I knew that the fight had been bad if Boone was willing to step in.

Usually he would buffer, make jokes and shuffle them inside for a drink. Despite what was so clearly obvious to everyone else around him, Boone did an alright job lying to himself but we all knew how he really felt about Kaia. They had gone home together last night and despite Kaia denying that anything happened, it was never with certainty that it didn't.

"Maybe he has crooked toes or doesn't eat bananas," I shrugged, hanging upside down on the couch with a popsicle between my lips. It had been unbearably hot the last few days in Harbor and my apartment's air conditioning was broken, leaving both Kaia and I to sweat out the booze from our system.

"He doesn't, and he does," she said, rolling onto her stomach with a grunt. "Just admit it, Jensen is perfect and you're fucked."

"If you weren't here, I could be," I groaned and Kaia lost it laughing.

I hated how right she was though, staring at my phone I realized just how fucked I was.

> **So wait, the dude died and they CGI'd his face onto the brothers to finish the movie? That's messed up.**

> **Do you eat bananas?**

> **What?**

> **Bananas, do you eat them?**

> **Yeah...**

> **And your toes are straight?**

> **Are you being kidnapped because if this is some secret code, I'm confused and you'll never be rescued at this rate.**

I closed our messages and opened one from Taylor, asking him to meet me at the Hollow. It was quiet inside during lunch, only Brighton was around while Boone dealt with the lunch rush in the back. He nodded to me, bringing me a drink and silently went back to what he was doing.

"Addy," Taylor said, coming around the table and taking his normal spot beside me. "What's with the emergency texts?"

"This," I pointed to the folder and heard Bright greet Zane behind my back.

"Holy shit," Zane slipped into his chair, "is that?"

"A Cali contract."

"Damn, Addy," he flipped through it, shoving his glasses over his nose and putting on his best lawyer face. "This is fucking intense, they're offering you so much money."

"It feels...unreal?" I said.

"It's definitely real," Zane said, "Why do you sound scared?"

"Because she has a life here and she's not Dad..." Taylor snapped.

"Yeah, because Mom is a saint, Taylor." He rolled his eyes and suddenly the conversation was all about them again.

"At least she didn't move across the fucking map just to get away from us," Taylor grumbled. It was a tired argument they had often, Taylor always took Mom's side, Zane always took Dad's and I was always forgotten.

"Okay well, I don't have kids or a husband so if..."

"Dad moved so he could pay for the house Mom refused to sell," Zane reminded Taylor who only scoffed. I got up from the table, knowing I wouldn't be missed and wandered over to the bar.

"What do you think of California?" I asked Brighton as he appeared from the kitchen.

"It's hot and dry," he shrugged, pouring me a glass of water. "Why?"

"I got the contract," I confessed.

"Shit," Bright said with an understanding nod. "When do you leave?"

Not asking *if* I was going or *if* I had made a decision yet. No, Bright had jumped straight to *when do you leave?* I swallowed tightly.

"End of season," I said.

"I'll have to get Rugby One so we can watch the games," he said without skipping a beat, showing me the confidence I had expected to receive from my brothers and didn't get.

"Thanks, Brighty," I said with a smile.

"Don't call me that, Addy," he said, tapping the bar and disappearing again.

> **What are you doing tonight?**

> **You if I'm lucky**

> **You might as well be a four leaf clover with those odds.**

I giggled, making my way back over to my brothers who were still fighting over our parents and hoped that Jensen was about to give me an out. I might have asked them here but it was very obvious how wrong I was in doing so. They weren't going to be any help, Bright was kind and oblivious. Who I really needed was Kaia.

> **We have the night off and we're going to Hilly's for trivia, I can pick you up?**

> **Please**

An hour later Jensen was in the parking lot of my apartment wearing a half buttoned black silk t-shirt and a pair of beige pants. His tattoos were the perfect accessory to his dark messy hair and bright smile.

"Belle," he purred as I walked out in my lightest sundress and a pair of sneakers, giving him a twirl that made the dress fly up around my thighs and ass. "You better be prepared to fight cause I can't mess up these hands and if anyone hits on you tonight…"

"You wouldn't fight for my honor?" I teased and fell into his arms with a soft groan as he wrapped his arms around me.

"I'm a lover," he mumbled into the crook of my neck, the words tingling over my throat. I pulled back to look him in the eyes, both hands pushing up into the back of his hair as he captured my lips in his. It numbed all the worry in my body and calmed all the fear that I was feeling over unmade decisions. Tonight wasn't for that though, it was for us. Rugby could wait six hours.

"Come on," he whispered against my lips, stealing another before opening the door for me and letting me tuck inside. He found the last parking spot in the lot of a very busy Hilly's with a string of curse words for Dean Tucker's parking job on the left side of him.

"He thinks just because he's the size of a bear he can double park," Jensen grumbled as he held the door open for me. My favorite thing about him is that no matter where we went, no matter who we were with his hand was always on me. Currently pressed gently into my lower back, but in the car it was wrapped in mine or tucked into my thigh. Like he couldn't help himself but be attached.

"Hey Addy!" Van nudged my side as we slid into the booth next to him and Zoey. She handed me a beer with a smile before turning back to pay attention to the host at the front of the restaurant talking loudly into a mic.

Hilly's was quiet compared to the Hollow, less packed with sweaty bodies and drunk assholes. The music was quieter as the host explained the rules of trivia night and everyone gave her most of their attention. It seemed I had been tossed into the deep end of Hornets culture without warning and I couldn't help but think it might be payback for our night at the Hollow.

"I'm Ella," a pretty blonde girl with a bright smile and big brown eyes held out her hand to me, "I work with the team."

"I work with the team," Van snorted, "she's Arlo's fiance."

"Like the Arlo King?" I said and Jensen stiffened beside me. "What? Everyone knows Arlo King..."

Zoey giggled, I had met her long before tonight. Any sort of family event that Cosy held, her siblings attended if they could. Van and Zoey were a matching set.

"I just didn't think you'd be a fangirl," Jensen said, his eyes practically rolling into the back of his head.

"Isn't everyone? It's Arlo King." I said, knowing it would rile him up and right on cue I felt his fingers move across my back and dig into my hip playfully.

"She has a point, I remember the day you met him. Pretty sure you fainted," Van teased Jensen and he flipped him off. "And then the week after all he talked about in the locker room was how fluffy Arlo's hair was and how cute he looked hollering at us during practice."

"Shut the fuck up Mitchell," Jensen said, a tiny amused laughed spilling from his lips. "If you're all finished, you've met Cael and Clementine." He pointed to the blonde shortstop and his adorable brunette girlfriend whose cheeks were rosy from her second beer. "Dean, Josh," he said, pointing to Dean Tucker and his boyfriend, the newest pitcher for the Hornets. "Todd…" He grumbled and the guy sighed, bringing his beer to his lips.

"Where is he anyways?" Jensen asked Ella, who was intently listening to the rules of trivia. She turned to look at him with a small shrug.

"Him and Silas are holding up in the garage," she said, rolling her eyes.

"That can't be good," Cael said and Ella agreed.

"Their loss, our teams would be uneven if Arlo was here anyways and Todd needed a partner," Ella said leaning forward to mess up his hair. He looked over at her in annoyance. "We can trade, you can have Cael if you want…"

"No," Todd answered quickly. It was pretty obvious that Ella was competitive, she was already more focused than all of the rest of them and as the questions started to come she was quick to answer them.

After a few beers, I started to get more comfortable, and I was starting to beat Ella to questions that she clearly knew the answers to. Jensen and I were in the lead for points as intermission came around.

"You know a lot about sports?" Ella asked with a smile but it was obvious how annoyed she was about losing.

"I grew up in a household where any sport was a good sport. It was the only channel ever played. " I explained as Jensen's fingers tickled across my thigh, I spread my legs letting him sink deeper and closed them over again, trapping his touch against mine without thought.

"You're quick," Ella said, "I hate losing but I like her. Todd get your shit together, if we lose this because you're eighty percent liquor I'm going to make your life hell in physio tomorrow."

Todd shuddered and set down his half consumed glass of rum and coke. "It's not my fault she's a living breathing sports fact machine," he grumbled.

"I'm embarrassed to admit that baseball is my weak spot," I said, "I know the least about it."

"It's a tough sport to follow," Todd said, his eyes barely lifting to meet mine. It was clear that he wasn't exactly as welcoming as the rest of the group. He seemed like he didn't even really want to be there and unfortunately for him, I enjoyed arguing with grown men.

"Not that tough," I said, "just not really that interesting."

Todd stiffened, and Jensen laughed, turning his head into my hair to cover the sound but the warning to leave it alone never came from him like I had expected it too.

"Are you serious?" Todd's glare deepened and he sat up a little more. It was almost surprising how much life he suddenly had in him.

"Well your games last two hours and a half hours? Sometimes longer and a lot of the time the defense is so strong that it's just two hours of pitching. In rugby it's a matter of seconds before something happens and it's never just a one off, we run that field for eighty minutes straight." I said.

"You're glorified soccer players," Todd argued. "And don't you play sevens. You play for fourteen minutes." I'd give him that win, but I wasn't backing down.

"Our pitch is bigger than a soccer field," I countered with a smile and everyone at the table waited with small laughter and smiles for Todd's rebuttal. "Just admit that rugby is the better sport," I said.

"Never," Todd was quick to respond to that, "because it's not. It's a sport where the main objective is to hurt the other guy, there's no tact to it. No skill."

I leaned forward on the table, and Jensen's grip on my thigh tightened gently.

"So you're saying anyone could play it?" I asked.

"A toddler could play rugby," Todd said, taking back the rest of his drink. Everyone watched as he slammed his empty glass down. "It's not that hard."

"What's the average age of a college baseball player?" I asked, but the question was directed at Ella who just laughed.

"Twenty two," she said, "in Todd's case, thirteen?"

"Traitor," he mumbled, "I could out play you in any sport, you're a girl. By nature, I'm bigger and stronger than you."

"Fair," I said, the smile creeping back to my face as I fought to ignore his egotistical insult. He had no idea just how strong I was, and given his addiction to booze and his lazy plays on the field. He wasn't an athlete, he was barely a man. "Prove it then," I said, taking it a step further.

"What?" Todd asked, his voice laced with confusion.

"If you think you're a better rugby player than me, *prove it*."

Jensen's chest rumbled with laughter.

"Hillcats VS Hornets," I said, turning to look at him.

"Hey now," Cael was the first to protest. "How did we get dragged into this? I didn't say shit, you're plenty strong and very smart, very—" Clementine dug her elbow into his side to shut him off. Her face was full of amusement at the challenge.

"Playing against just Todd would be an unfair advantage," I said, "If he's going to prove his point, he needs a team… Unless you're scared."

Van chuckled, "I'm in. Cosy's been trying to pull something like this together for years."

"Me too," Jensen kissed my shoulder, his lips lingering.

"Next Friday," I said, "we have practice but I'm sure Coach won't mind some hands-on time. You need fifteen guys," I told them.

"How do we convince ten more guys to play?" Dean asked, looking around the table.

"Just tell them that I called them pussies, that should do it," I smiled and the laughter that tumbled from the girls at the table was infectious.

"This night got infinitely better when you arrived," Ella said.

"Agreed," Zoey said, leaning into my side.

"This is fucking stupid, you guys are going to get hurt," Todd said to me.

"Have you ever seen a single game of rugby?" I laughed, my brows coming together tightly. "Or are you just bull-shiting because your manhood was threatened by a pretty girl?"

Jensen snorted, his face still pressed to the side of my head.

"This will be a piece of cake," Todd said with unbridled confidence.

"Friday, six o'clock." I said, I would need to shoot a text to the team but there's not a chance any of them would back down from tossing around the baseball team.

"Have you seen the size of Rhea Drake? She's like Van with boobs!" Cael interjected, trying to talk some sense into them. "She alone proves Todd wrong," he said.

"I can take Rhea," Todd slurred and the entire table erupted into laughter.

SARAH

It had rained most of the morning, the field was slick and covered in mud for the throw-down game between the baseball team and us. Coach had been on board instantly, but she lived for a good *'put men in their place'* moment, so I knew I wouldn't have trouble convincing her to be our referee.

"Should we like... make them sign waivers or something?" Sunday asked, doing up the laces on her cleats. "I feel like someone is going to get hurt."

"You can guarantee Todd and his fragile male ego are going to get hurt, Rhea's in a mood today," Kaia quipped, her eyes focused on Rhea stretching her Hillcats jersey over her massive shoulders. "We might want to ask if they set aside funeral expenses..."

I laughed as my fingers raked through her hair, tightly twisting them together into thick braids that met at the nape of her neck.

"Just be careful with Jensen's face, I'm kind of attached to it," I teased quickly and Kaia looked up at me with a soft expression I wasn't expecting. "Don't look at me like that."

"Have you told him yet?" She asked, leaning back against me in the locker.

"About California?" I asked. The answer was no, I hadn't. I had given my answer to Coach. I was going come season end. It was too big of an opportunity to pass up, but even the thought of talking to Jensen about it made me sick to my stomach.

"Not about that," Kaia said, poking my cheek. "About how you feel about him."

"There's nothing to talk about it's just a casual thing between us, he knows that and so do I." I pushed away from her gently, double checking my laces and the tensor wrap around my knee. I could feel her glare, the heat pooled between my shoulder blades and it was laced with judgement.

I thought about defending myself from her onslaught of silent arguments when Sunday opened her mouth again, "do you think they have mouth guards?" She asked.

"God I hope." I paused, before turning to the team. "Alright I know today is goofy, but we have a point to prove and I am not letting those boys leave this field without a decent amount of bruises, a win and Todd *has* to cry."

"Which one is Todd?" One of the girls asked.

"You'll know," Rhea, Kaia and I all said in unison.

We made our way out to the field to find the Hornets stretching on the other side dressed head to toe in Hog colors.

"Who the fuck gave them those?" Rhea was the first to ask, breaking out of the line up and stepping onto the field with a dirty look.

"That fucking asshole," Cosy grumbled, her middle finger extending out to a waving Judd Loveday, who was standing next to Boone and Brighton on the other side of the field.

"God, he sticks that beautiful thick head in everyone's business and if he didn't look like a Viking god, I'd probably share your sentiment..." Kaia hummed, her body leaning into mine as she swooned.

"Are you going to be able to concentrate?" I asked Kaia and she smiled at me.

"Are you?" She countered, her eyes sweeping the Hornet's team and landing on Jensen, bent over tying his cleats.

"Holy fucking shit," the words tumbled from me before I could stop them. It was like a slow-motion scene out of a romantic comedy, we all lined up in silence to watch him in the misty weather. Every inch of him damp and shiny from the rain. The rugby shorts hugged every muscle in his strong thighs and ass. Every single tattoo was on display and every single girl on the team gave him their full attention as he straightened out.

"Fuck," Sunday mumbled as he smiled at me and started across the field. His hair was damp and hung on his forehead in funny, messy curls that begged to be touched. "At this rate, *I* won't even be able to concentrate."

"Nice gear," I said as he got closer and he looked down at himself.

"It's a little snug," Jensen groaned, pulling at the hem of his shorts around his thighs.

"No, they fit perfectly, baby..." I looked down at his thick thighs and wet my bottom lip. I couldn't figure out if I wanted them on him forever, or permanently off him...

"I guess someone told Boone about the game today, him and Judd came down to the stadium with a box of crap for us to use," Jensen explained, his hand reaching out to wrap around my waist but Kaia interjected, slamming a rugby ball into his stomach with a glare on her sharp face.

"No fraternizing with the enemy, get back to your side of the field fuckboy," she said with a smirk, but it didn't stop Jensen from leaning around her with his hand on the ball to kiss my jaw gently. His direct defiance of Kaia's orders only riled her up further but he wasn't paying her any mind.

Jensen dared to tease as he pulled back. "What we're we supposed to play in, our baseball pants?"

"No," both Sunday and I chimed in and Jensen laughed at the ridiculous show of love for the rugby shorts.

"You involved the Hogs, that's foul play and we haven't even started," Kaia argued.

"We had to make sure that the game was played fairly, you didn't think we were going to let your coach solo referee us?" A smug look formed on Jensen's face and I could feel the heat rising in Kaia beside me.

"Boone Black is the biggest cheat on this field, he doesn't put a toe on it. You want fair, you can have Brighton. He's a stickler for the rules and won't make bad calls just so you win," Kaia argued and Sunday giggled as Rhea paced around behind us like she was going to war.

"You're taking this way too seriously." Jensen looked over his shoulder at the Hornets, all waiting for instruction.

"Maybe you aren't taking it seriously enough," she said, watching him like a hawk. "*Maybe* there needs to be higher stakes," she snapped.

"No more bets." I shook my head, trying to stop what was coming but Jensen and Kaia were paying me no attention and there was no stopping what came out of his mouth next.

"We win, you all show up to the next baseball game, painted head to toe with pom poms. The Hornets need some new cheerleaders," he said to her and I sighed as she started to laugh.

"Alright." Kaia nodded, her laugh dying out as she looked up at him, "but if you lose, the bet stands only you all show up to our game... painted head to toe with pom poms."

"In nothing but rugby shorts." Sunday added so quickly her words strung together.

"In nothing but rugby shorts for Sunny, because she asked so nicely," Jensen said, not looking away from Kaia as he extended his hand to her.

He started to back away when I stepped forward, "also if we win by more than three tries, Bright, Boone *and* Judd all have to come," I warned loud enough for them to hear me. I watched as their expressions changed from confident to worried.

"And how do you expect me to convince them of that?" Jensen asked me, purposefully stretching his arms over his head and showing off the hardened ridges of his stomach as his jersey rode up.

"You're the charming one, figure it out." I scrunched my nose up at him before turning back to the team. "We *cannot* lose." My tone dropped and I narrowed my eyes on all of them.

"Your lack of faith in us is rattling, Minty." Rhea grinned, showing all her sharp teeth as her hungry eyes scanned the line of men on the other side of the field.

"Not a lack of faith, questioning our focus. We can't just rough them up, we need to *win*." I warned as the girls started to huddle around. We ran over a few plays, hyping ourselves up as Coach talked to Brighton at center field.

"We're playing sevens because the Hornets couldn't find enough players," Coach said.

"Pussies," Kaia coughed out.

"Do you know how hard it is to talk anyone to go up against godzilla?" Van said from the other side of the line. "Rhea has better personal records than half the guys on our team."

Rhea beamed at Van like he had just called her every sweet thing in the book and gave him a little wink before her face dropped back into focus and narrowed in on Todd who was rearranging what little cock he had smuggled into his rugby shorts.

"Statement stands." Kaia shrugged.

They had collected the usual suspects, and I recognized a good handful of the lined up baseball players. Jensen, Dean…Cael and Van… Todd. But their ringer was Arlo King himself standing at the end of the line with a grumpy expression on his chiseled face. The three other guys all looked equally terrified as Coach ran through the rules for them.

"I want Kaia's wraps checked," Boone said over the noise of conversation. His white shirt was damp and stuck to the rolling form of muscles, giving show to all the patchwork tattoos that littered his massive toned body beneath. The growl that left Kaia was feral and she glared at him like her eyes could burn holes in his skin. "Don't give me that look, Killer. You're just as much of a cheat as I am," he purred with a bright, knowing smile.

Kaia, unwrapped her left hand, wiggling it at him before flipping him off with a bare set of knuckles, "The brass is reserved for dickheads," she sneered.

"Mmhmm," Boone eyed her with that same smile before backing off to join Judd on the sidelines.

"Let's get this game started before the rain gets heavy," Coach barked, her whistle slipping between her lips. "Play safe, play fair… if I see anyone out there getting too rough this game is being called. I am not bringing the ambulance down here today or risking a bunch of D1 athletes over a bet, do you understand me?" She looked over both teams and we all nodded in agreement.

As soon as Sunday's foot touched the ball it was apparent that the Hornets had been given a crash course on rules from the guys. They were nowhere near ready for the onslaught of contact and within seconds Sunday had slipped between Dean and Van like she was invisible, both of them grabbing at her but too slow to turn on their heels and she was gone, jogging into the scoring zone and tapping the ball on the ground between the posts.

"Easy like a Sunday morning." Kaia dog whistled at her.

Even Boone was clapping from the sideline.

"Whose team are you on?" Jensen asked him, kicking at the grass with a bright smile as he whipped around to look at me.

You're screwed, I mouthed at him and he nodded, running a muddy hand through his hair. I patted Rhea on the ass to get her to move into position, forcing her to abandon her current round of taunting.

"Rough start, Todd," Rhea said, her eyes on him trying to push himself off the ground, stomping her foot in a puddle and kicking up the mud into his face. He clambered from the puddle and found his footing just in time for the next play to start.

Three more easy tries were scored before the Hornets started to find their groove, Arlo slipped back into a leader position easily, his voice loud and commanding as he organized them back into their line and Sunday tapped the ball.

Rhea was quick to protect, her body wrapping around Van, who was the only Hornet with any tackling experience and with all her strength lifted him out of Sunday's route. The two of them hit the dirt hard, Van laughing loudly as they rolled around in the mud to get loose from each other. *Good hit*, was chimed out as I skipped past them to fill the gap. Cosy was quick to cover the pass, intercepting Jensen with a hard hit that sounded painful as they went down but it left Sunday to hurdle them with a semi-clear path to the other end of the field.

"Moose," I called to Sunday, who was running straight into the arms of Dean. Her eyes darting over her shoulder, the blonde strands sticking to her face as she flicked the ball back into the gut of Kaia.

Kaia took the ball and goose-stepped around Dean only to run straight into the broad chest of Arlo. *Shit*, he was quick and as she scooped her knees higher to dart around him he reached out and wrapped one arm around her waist and pushed her to the ground, careful not to use his full weight.

Before she could get control, the ball skipped from her fingers, popping out with force and bouncing out of bounds.

"Fair," Bright called, stretching his impressively long arms out at his side. He had stripped down to his training pants and a light t-shirt that was billowing in the wind much like the dark waves of his hair. He stared at me with dark blue eyes and smiled, because we had fucked up. "Ball out."

"They're going to get hurt, they don't know how to do this properly," I warned him, skirting around him as he turned his nose up at the mud covering my jersey.

"Worry about your own line up, Addy," he clipped in my ear.

"Whatever, you're the one that has to drive them to the hospital when they break a bone, Brighty." I flashed him a grin over my shoulder and snuck into line behind Rhea, ready for the ball.

Sunday positioned herself between her and Cosy, her face set into a hard glare as the Hornets clumsily tried to follow suit. I bothered my lip seeing the state of Jensen's face. The hit he had taken from Cosy resulted in a small but sharp gash that cut through his eyebrow and was bleeding into his eye. He wiped the blood away with the back of his hand, seemingly unbothered as he watched his team with caution as Dean and Van tried to convince Todd that it would be fine, they could hang on to him.

"All you have to do is grab the ball from her in the air when Kaia throws it in to play, then pass it out to Jensen," Boone explained from a distance.

"Shut up," Kaia snapped at him, "if they couldn't be bothered to learn the rules…"

"Are you okay?" I whispered to him, pointing to my own eyebrow as Kaia continued to argue with Boone about his backseat rugby playing.

"What, this?" He patted a finger to the cut with a small hiss and nodded, "Doesn't even hurt," he blinked away some more blood as the rain started to fall again. My heart was pounding in my chest at the sight of him, covered in dirt, muscles straining against his jersey, blood dripping down his face. It sounded insane but there was nothing like a damp, dirty and damaged man flushed with adrenaline and madly in love to set me over the edge.

Kaia was still arguing with Boone on the sidelines as Jensen closed the gap and took my chin between his fingers, "really I'm fine," he whispered, taking my lips against his. I truly wasn't worried, he was mistaking my absolute infatuation for concern but if I meant that he wanted to try to kiss the worry back from the forefront of my mind, I'd let him.

"Free bird!" Kaia's voice broke through the adoration and tingling happiness. I knew that play, my brain switching back to rugby just as quickly as it had turned off. I shoved both hands against Jensen and pushed him back far enough that as I launched toward the ball, tickling from Sunday's hands, he couldn't get steady enough to catch me.

I darted down the field, open and free for an easy score. I could hear Jensen behind me, struggling to keep up but he was right on my heels as I slid over the line and tapped the ball down out of breath.

He crumbled over, laying on his back just trying to catch his breath as the rain beat down over the field. "Fuck, you're fast," he gasped, closing his eyes as I stood from the ground and hovered over him.

"You tried to distract me." I tapped my cleat against his muddy ribcage, "cheater."

"Almost... worked..." he huffed and grabbed my ankle, tugging roughly and causing me to lose my balance. He dumped me into the mud puddle beside him with a smirk on his face.

"I have it in my right mind to jump your bones right here and this is how you treat me?" I teased, rolling over until I was straddling him in the dirt. It didn't matter who was paying attention, I didn't care. I just needed contact before I drove myself insane with needy, touch-starved thoughts.

He opened his mouth to say something more when yelling broke out in the air through the rain, Rhea was furious about something and where Rhea was big in bark, Kaia was bigger in bite.

"Fuck," I swore, slipping in the mud as I tried to get up.

"What did you say?" Kaia snapped, charging across the field in front of me. Rhea was face to face with Todd, drenched in mud and clearly talking shit when he had no right too.

"I asked the terminator if she was packing a cock in those tight little shorts," Todd made the mistake of repeating himself. Rhea tried to stop Kaia but it was too late, he had signed his death warrant as far as she was concerned.

"More dick then you! You fucking—" Rhea stepped forward but Brighton saved his life and put himself between them completely forgetting about Kaia.

"Wrong Hillcat," I sighed loudly, stopping in my tracks, knowing exactly what was coming.

"Fucking waste of space," she declared before her hand snapped out and caught Todd across the cheek without remorse.

"Hey!" Bright and Arlo yelled at the same time, everyone staring in shock.

"I mean..." Jensen sighed, his chest coming to my back as I froze.

Boone moved on instinct, throwing Kaia over his shoulder before she could do more damage. She kneed him in the chest but kept his grip on her as she screamed murder and he carried her off the field.

"Get up," Arlo growled at Todd who had dropped to the dirt so hard his body left an imprint in the softened grass. "Learn some manners," He shoved Todd by the jersey off the field as Coach called the game.

"Sorry, Hornets..." She shrugged. "I guess we'll see you all at the next game," she added with a wink, collecting the balls and getting some of the girls to help. Cosy stood with her brother, talking to Bright with a dirty look on her face as Judd approached.

"That was a wash, I'm going to have to sell my soul to get them to the game." Jensen chuckled, his head coming to rest on my shoulder.

"Nah, they show up every game..." I confessed and he sighed.

"I think I learned something about myself today," he whispered, his lips finding my neck. Heat pooled in my stomach as his hands pressed up under my shirt against my stomach.

"What?" I asked, my eyes drifting to Boone absolutely ripping into Kaia as he checked her hand. Hopefully, it wasn't broken, we couldn't afford that six-week loss if she needed to heal.

"I like it rough," he smiled against my skin and dug his fingers into the cold, dirty skin beneath my jersey dragging a throaty moan from my lips.

SARAH

The apartment door slammed wide open as Jensen fumbled with the hem of my wet jersey, tugging it up and over my shoulders. He tossed it away, kicking the door closed behind us as the fabric hit the tile floor of my kitchen with a loud plop.

"We should..." he tried to get out between frantic kisses and tiny gasped moans as my fingers raked through his wet hair. "Shower... so muddy," he moaned as I tugged gently.

"That's what washing machines are for," I snapped, and his worry over making a mess snapped as his hands scooped down and lifted me against him effortlessly. His strong arms wrapped around my thighs as he carried me toward the bed, ignoring the trail of mud we were leaving behind.

He chuckled against my lips, a husky sound laced with amusement and desire.

"Brat," he teased, nipping lightly at the sensitive skin of my throat. I leaned back in his arms with a lusty smile on my lips and exposed my throat to him. Taking advantage of the new position, he trailed open-mouthed kisses down my neck. His teeth grazed my collarbone before he bit down lightly, soothing the sting with his tongue.

The way his eyes fluttered shut as he savored the taste of my skin drove me insane. The dirty, grassy smell of his skin, the trickles of water that dripped from his hair and the stain of blood that dripped down the side of face was making me feral.

I needed him right that second or I was going to lose my fucking mind.

"Jensen?"

He opened his pretty brown eyes at the sound of his name and focused on me with blown pupils.

"Show me what you learned today," I whispered as my lips curled up mischievously.

He understood the task, today had been about flexing our strength, full of aggressive tackling and heated moments. I wanted that dominance and intensity and I knew he was willing to provide it because a devilish smirk curled to those pouty, kiss-bitten lips.

"And the shorts stay on," I said as he dropped me to the bed, crawling over me between my spread legs. My hands roamed over his muscle tense back and pushed beneath the band of the tight shorts until my hands were roughly positioned under his ass giving me room to dig my nails into his skin.

Jensen's breath caught in his throat, a deep sound rumbling from his chest at the sharp contact of my nails. His hands found my wrists, holding them firmly in place with just enough force to show ownership. He pressed into my touch, grinding slowly against me. The rough fabric of his shorts created the most delicious friction and my hips lifted to meet his as I pulled him close enough to pepper his jaw with warm kisses. I trailed them down and over his throat until his entire body was tense and vibrating.

He let out a shuddering breath as my lips found his collar bone, his hands sliding under my back to hold me flush against him. Jensen started moving his hips in a slow, deliberate rhythm that was only furthering the tingling sensation that was growing at a rapid pace between my legs.

"God this is stupidly hot," I confessed, "I shouldn't be this turned on," I said with a badly timed giggle that turned into a tight, gasping moan as he rolled forward again.

Jensen watched as I threw my head back doing my best to suppress my laughter. "You're the sexiest thing I've ever seen," he snapped his hips forward again, harder that time. Almost as if he was testing my reaction, but I was a puddle in his dirty, sweaty hands as his rough shorts brushed against my thighs.

"Okay okay, I surrender," I gasped, "shorts off, shorts so off...I can't..." I was on the verge of begging.

He chuckled darkly, hooking his thumbs into the waistband of the shorts and pushed them down himself in one shift movement. Completely freeing his hard length and earning a delicious moan from my lips as my eyes trailed over his dirty gloriously toned and tattooed body.

"Fucking perfect," I whispered, pushing up on my elbows in nothing but my bra and rugby shorts to take him in completely with heavy chested sigh of appreciation.

Jensen drank me in, sprawled beneath him, the tiny sports bra barely restraining my breasts. A smirk tugged at his lips as he leaned down, bracing himself on one strong forearm beside my head. "Perfect, huh?" He hummed, rolling his hips again.

Every delicious inch of him brushed against my thigh and my eyes fluttered closed, "I know I didn't stutter, baby." A tiny strangled gasp left my lips as his teeth found skin, his lips curling into a proud smirk. He sucked the spot above my breast lightly, sure to leave a mark.

His smile only grew as he felt me shiver beneath him, his teeth grazing sharply against my collarbone before soothing the burn with a languid lick. I closed my eyes and felt him pause, hearing the wrapping tear and I was moments from begging him just to give it to me when he shifted his hips, letting the head of his cock tease my entrance through the rough fabric of my shorts. He wasn't even inside of me and I couldn't stop the noise that tumbled from my lips as his hips rolled again, slower that time, letting his length slide against my inner thigh over and over.

"How much longer can you hold out, Adeline?" He asked, his voice low and teasing.

"Who's being a brat now," I growled, digging my nails into his bicep and bring him close for a frantic, messy kiss.

Jensen laughed against my lips, deep and rumbling from his bare chest. He bit into my bottom lip, hard enough to make me gasp as his hips snapped forward against without warning making my back arch sharply into his touch. "Touch rough, kiss hard, talk shit," he mumbled, "Unbelievable," his voice was husky with lust.

Jensen watched me, knowing that I could hold out longer than him if it truly came down to it. He slowed his hips, making his movements shallow and teasing, actively trying to keep his touch soft, his kisses sweet against my fevered skin.

"I was never going to win this game was I?" He asked.

I shook my head slowly with a lazy smile, my thoughts dizzy with need and waited for him to break as I slipped my hands free and pushed my damp shorts off. Jensen's eyes darkened as he watched my movement, swallowing hard trying to hold on to what little control he had left. But when my hand slipped between my legs and I started to touch myself, he lost it. The resolve in him snapped, "Fuck Adeline, you little—"

I gasped as he surged forward without warning, burying himself completely between my legs with a groan that sounded strangled. His fingers dug into my hips as he held tight, stunned into momentary silence as I stretched perfectly around his shaft.

"Quiet now, aren't you?" He teased, roughly watching me fall apart beneath his touch as he pushed even deeper.

It was practically impossible how good he felt rubbing against every searing, frayed nerve inside of my body. I could feel him in my fucking stomach as his hips snapped and the bed buckled under his force. My face contorted in pleasure as I rolled up to meet his thrust, his hands gripped my hips tightly, fingers digging into the soft skin. He was hitting spots that were making my vision blur.

"And you were going to make me fuck you slow," he panted.

"I was delusional, never listen to me again.. I talk nonsense—"

My teasing words were replaced with a string of stuttered gasps as the orgasm built violently in the pit of my stomach and coursed around unchecked through all my muscles. A tiny snarl left his lips as I fluttered around him in pleasure. Jensen's hand wrapped around a thigh, hauling it up over his hip and gripping it tightly as he opened me wider and started in a new angle with an unrelenting pace.

I gripped the sheets as my head fell back, unable to control the noises flooding from my overstimulated body. Jensen groaned loudly, our moans filling the air in a symphony of pleasure that only spurred him on further. He shifted again, hitting that spot inside of my already needlessly soaked core and sent stars bursting behind my eyelids.

"That's my beautiful girl," he purred, his breaths short as my body arched and my mouth fell open in a wide silent scream. He snapped his hips forward relentlessly, fucking me through the orgasm and drawing every delicious second out of it like it was his favorite form of torture.

"Take it." He demanded, "Swallow me whole," he encouraged as I clamped down around his cock. "Fuck, just like that Adeline," he groaned loudly as I squeezed around him. His hips jerked erratically as he chased his own release, leaning down and pressing his forehead to mine as his fingers dug painfully into my thigh.

Jensen's body convulsed around mine, a string of breathless words falling from his reddened lips, he grunted, his body tensing as he finally let go. He stayed buried deep inside, his hips jerking with the aftershocks of his orgasm. His breath was so hot and ragged against my skin.

"So perfect, baby," I whispered, kissing his sweaty, dirty face over and over again until his body relaxed.

He nuzzled into my touch, his arms wrapping around me tightly, still half hard inside of me, his hips making slow lazy thrust as he worked through the last of the aftershocks. He let out a shaky breathing, his body slowly coming down from the intense high. He pressed soft kisses to my lips, cheeks and forehead mirroring the affection.

Jensen looked up at me with such a softness that it was there in that moment that the words almost slipped out. They hadn't even been on my mind but it was such a small, delicate moment of weakness I couldn't help myself but smile. His big brown eyes, drunk on sex, our bodies disgusting from rolling around in the mud all morning.

Who was ever going to love me the way Jensen did?

"You're incredible," I said instead, burying the thoughts away and brushing my fingers through his hair. "You smell like a wet dog though," I teased.

He let out a small laugh, the sound rumbling across his chest. He pulled back slightly, looking down at us with a smirk. "And you smell like sweat, dirt and..."

he rubbed his dirty, bloody face across my chest, leaving me giggling and begging him to stop. "Blood."

"That's nothing new for me," I cooed, leaning into this touch, always needing more. My body was addicted to his and was continuously finding ways to be in constant contact with him.

He shook his head, rolling his eyes playfully. "No, no it's not," he agreed, leaning down and pressing a kiss to my nose as his finger squeezed my sides gently. "You're fucking gross," he teased, his voice soft and full of fondness.

"Well, if someone had let us shower before. ." I teased.

His hand gently raked down my side, giving my ass a soft pat as his smirk widened. "Who's fault was that again?" He asked innocently.

"Shut up and kiss me," I pouted to get out of trouble.

Jensen chuckled against my lips as he closed the distance. The kiss was slow, and deep, his tongue teasing mine lazily. He pulled back just enough to murmur, "brat," against my mouth before capturing my lips again.

JENSEN

I set the oversized bowl of lettuce on the counter and turned to where Van was cutting vegetables with a knife two sizes too small for the size of his hands.

"I'm so ready to be back on the diamond tomorrow," I grumbled, rolling out my shoulders. "I'm starting to feel antsy."

"Yeah I agree, it's going to be a long series. Lorette is going to fight hard," he said.

"I still can't believe they made it this far, with Yuri on the mound they're playing sloppy defense and barely keeping it together on offence."

"Weirder shit has happened, at least we don't have to play Portland yet, that's going to be vicious." Van turned to the fridge and started unloading bottles of salad dressing onto the island.

"Lorette will take care of them, and we can handle Lorette, we know that offence in our sleep." I countered and Van shrugged in agreement. "It's Portland that's going to give us trouble."

"Why are you dressed up? It's Mario Kart night," Van eyed my clean maroon shirt and jeans. "Addy." He came to the conclusion before I even opened my mouth. "All you playboys are growing up and getting hitched, it's adorable," he said with a smile.

"I'm not getting hitched, we're just going out," I said, my brows pinching together at his accusation. Adeline bristled at the word boyfriend, there was no way she wanted anything more than fun. *Right?*

"Sure," Van said. Giving me a dirty, all knowing look.

"What?" I asked.

"Nothing, you just seem to really like her but anytime someone brings her up in a manner that's more serious than I don't know a booty call or a fling you clam up like someone asked when the wedding was… that's all." Van explained.

"Is that all?" I scowled at him. I didn't clam up. I panicked. There was a clear distinction. "We're having fun, no strings attached, easy and simple."

"Oh, come on Jenny, you and I both know Cael was on to something that day. It's alright if you see her as more than casual. Even fuckboys are allowed to catch feelings every once in a while," Van said. "And you definitely don't have to lie to me about it, I'm your best friend."

"I'm not lying."

"So you know about the California offer and you're not bothered by it?" Van asked, unknowingly sharing something with me that I definitely wasn't supposed to know about. "You're alright with her leaving?"

I swallowed the need to ask him what the hell he was asking about and put the pieces together as quickly as I could on my own. Adeline had been offered the trade to California. She had mentioned it in passing once or twice, but never anything serious. How long had she known about it?

"There are plenty of girls in Harbor," Van said, knowing that I was tripped over by the news but not willing to give me the satisfaction of backing out of the corner he had walked me into. I agreed with him. The problem was by the way my brain stuttered around the statement, it was obvious that my heart and mind didn't agree

There's only one Adeline Sarah.

"Like I said, *casual*." I repeated and Van watched me with his stupid, intelligent eyes seeing through the lie I was throwing at him.

Van just laughed as the timer on the oven went off. Whatever it was that Josh had started smelled delicious and when I pulled the massive sheet pan from inside the waft of Chicken Parmesan hit my nose like a tidal wave.

"He should always cook, it should be a law…" I mumbled, inhaling more of the smell as I set it down on the counter.

"His rotation is purely Italian food and hamburgers, we'll all be carb loaded and need to get our ball pants sized up," Van noted tossing the veggies into the bowl.

"Are you complaining?" Josh appeared from the living room archway with a scowl on his face and Van just smiled at him. It was still awkward at times, mostly because Josh didn't know how to be human. He was serious all the time except for around Dean and even then saying he was enjoying himself was a stretch.

And he was sneaky as hell, you never knew when he was around and he was always just… there. But he had started to warm up to the Nest, to the team. Just in time for us to graduate, sure, but he had gotten there.

My phone vibrated in my pocket and I took the momentary lull in conversation to check it.

> **Do you think you could come get me from practice?**

> **Me?**

> **Sorry I meant to text my other booty call, ignore this.**

I shook my head, I was wrapped around her little finger and she knew it.

"No complaints here," I said for the both of us as I scooped a hot chicken breast into a to-go container and shoveled some salad into a zip-lock bag. Van stared at me like I was insane but I just shrugged, "Salad in a bag…" I grumbled, squeezing in some dressing with a smile on my face. "I have to go, I'm meeting Adeline. Thanks for dinner, Josh."

"Jenny," Van called out to me and I stopped.

"What?" I gripped the door frame waiting for him to speak again.

"That's how I know," he said, "you're the only person that calls her Adeline."

"Everyone calls her that." I shook my head and tapped the wood.

"Not the way you do." Van stared at me and Josh looked over his shoulder with a smug smile.

"Fuck you both."

I was supposed to be picking up Adeline from practice but when I arrived their field was empty and the only sounds, I could hear were coming from the field over. I followed the noise past a row of seating and popped out the other side on the edge of another pitch. It was only when I heard Adeline's laughter that I knew I was in the right place.

The four of them were hanging over the bleachers, picking at food and talking as Rhea braided Kaia's hair. Not a single one of them noticed me approaching, their eyes on the field in front of them. Adeline's hair was loose around her face and frizzy from the heat, and her skin was still flushed, all pretty and pink from practice.

"One day we should tie all their cleats in knots," Cosy said without looking up from what she was reading.

"Then how will they run laps and get sweaty, Cos?" Rhea said like it had personally offended her.

"Listen I know you hate him but there's not a damn thing wrong with Loveday when he's damp and his mouth is shut," Kaia said. I turned my head to take in what they were watching to find the entire male rugby team running laps in the hot sun.

"Ladies," I said, leaning on the bleachers. "What are we doing?"

All four of them jumped out of their skin and started laughing uncontrollably.

"I call it hog patrol," Kaia said with the sickest smile.

"That's disgusting," Cosy said with a grumble.

"Hot dog cart? Quick lunch, piping hot?" Rhea added to the hilarity while Adeline slid across the bleacher toward me. "Two for one special?"

"How many hot dogs do you think I could shove in my mouth?" Kaia asked.

Rhea tilted her chin up and started to count on her fingers.

"Ignore them," Adeline whispered, her fingers hooking under my chin to bring my lips to hers. "Thanks for coming to get me, I need to go home and change quickly."

"Anything for you." It slipped out before I could stop it but it made her blush and suddenly I didn't regret a damn word. "Mind if I steal your girl?" I looked around Adeline to the others.

"Only if you feed her," Kaia said and by the smirk on her face there was an innuendo there somewhere that I couldn't find.

"I'll make sure she's satisfied," I said without hesitation.

"God, will you two stop?" Adeline groaned.

"Come on," I grabbed her by the waist, pulling her down off the bleachers into my arms and shuffled her back to my car. Two hours later, Adeline was fed in every sense of the word. Dressed in jeans and a barely there top that showed off her perfect stomach.

Once we got to the Hollow everything was a blur, it seemed to be where you could find any of them on any night. But tonight, the place was packed.

"You know the DJ isn't horrible." Adeline knocked back a gin and seven before smiling at my comment. My fingers pressed into the front pocket of her skin tight jeans and held her against my chest as I whispered in her ear. "I still prefer live music better."

"It's dance night," Her voice was muffled by the sounds of Boone ringing the obnoxiously loud bell above the bar when someone ordered a Hollow, some disgusting concoction made of jello and nine different liquors. "It's the only night of the week Brighton will let us play pop music," she whined. "Sunday worked hard to get us dance night, don't you dare complain!"

"I'm not," I raised my hands in the air and instantly hated the lack of contact. "Where is Sunday anyways?" I asked.

"She works nights this week at the hospital," Adeline explained, but was quickly distracted. "Oh my god, I love this song," she squeaked, darting in a zigzag line with my hand in hers straight toward where Rhea and Cosy occupied the dance floor.

That close to the speakers, the music was so loud it vibrated through my bloodstream and made everything feel fuzzy as Adeline ground herself up against me and the lights made everything unbearably warm. But with the music playing and my girl in my arms, it was easy to enjoy the small moment of bliss that the noise level provided.

"I'm going to get some water," I said to her, kissing the hollow of her neck before slipping back into the sea of dancing bodies to the bar. I slid in between two bodies and nodded to Boone who filled a glass for me.

"Jensen, this is Wren." Boone pointed to the guy next to me. He held out his hand to me with a bright, cheesy smile on his face. Framed by a set of deep dimples and paired with fluffy uncontrolled blonde hair that he'd stuffed under a black backward cap, he looked like he just stepped off the set of Point Break. "Best friend, liability, absolute joke of a human being."

"There's no shame in *being* a good time," Wren winked.

"He acts like he isn't the first to cause trouble," he said to me.

"What's with the flag?" I asked, pointing to what looked like a miniature red flag poking out of the buckle of his hat.

"Oh," he smiled even wider, "some girl has been handing out 'red flags' to men that try to hit on her... I personally don't think I deserved it. I'm head to toe with green flags." He motioned to his crisp white shirt and jeans.

I laughed, staring at him for a moment longer trying to figure out if I've seen him before. His big blue eyes darted between me and Boone. "I don't play for them, if that's what you're trying to place. Boone and I know each other from the academy. We were paramedics together before he ran off to France to be a cook..."

"I love how when you tell that story you always make it sound like you were abandoned for a spur-of-the-moment romance or some garbage, it was for school. I was chasing my dreams." Boone lifted the pop gun and sprayed it at Wren, who feebly blocked the explosion of water and sent it cascading around him, soaking everyone in the vicinity.

"I'm your dream, right here in Rhode Island," Wren whined, taking the bottom of his shirt up into his hand and wiping off his face. I kept a smile on my face as my mind wandered to the corners where I kept the news about Adeline and California. She would tell me when she was ready, it stung that she hadn't yet but I understood why. Every day I spent with her made it harder and harder to have a reasonable response to her moving across the country. I hadn't exactly lied to Van about what we were and weren't but now I was even more confused than before.

"Hey isn't that your girl?" Wren cleared the water from his eye and nodded to the dance floor.

I broke free of the thoughts and turned to find Adeline staring up at some drunk guy that had invaded their dancing circle. Leaning against the bar as the guy continued his attempts to get her to dance, she wasn't playing whatever game he was. She was two steps ahead of him and with a smile on her face she continued to reject his advances.

"Are you going to do something about that?" Wren asked, bringing a beer to his lips as Boone leaned over the bar between us.

"If she needs me," I said, watching carefully. "She'll tell me."

Adeline inched away just for the guy to reach out, making the mistake of touching her without an invitation. Adeline smacked his hand away but still she was handling it, her fingers pressed against his chest as she moved him backward and Rhea filled the gap that he kept sneaking into.

"Hey that was the girl that gave me a red flag," Wren said and Boone started to laugh between us. Rhea did in fact have a handful of toothpick sized red flags sticking out of the pocket of her leather shorts as she danced.

"He's a determined fucker," Boone noted as the guy circled back around them and grabbed Adeline's hip from behind. I tensed slightly watching her as she turned in his arms and stomped on his foot, *hard*. His drink went flying, his body language instantly turned aggressive and his other hand still had a firm grip on her. She looked over her shoulder briefly, our eyes barely connecting, but I pushed from the bar.

Sliding easily through the crowd, I slipped in between her and Kaia, wrapping my arm around her waist and pulling her back against my chest. The smile on her face was wicked.

"Buddy back off," the drunk stepped forward but I planted my feet as Adeline all but went back to dancing.

"Not a fight you want to pick," I said over the music pumping through the speakers.

"I ain't scared of some scrawny punk," he said, "I was here first."

"It's not me you should be worried about." I told him and his face twisted with confusion for a split second, replacing the drunk anger raging in his eyes. Adeline didn't need my help, that much was true as she drove her knee upward into the guy's groin and as he doubled over she poured what was left of her drink over his head. I gripped her tightly, spinning her back around to face Kaia and Rhea as the guy hit the ground fast.

Kissing her cheek I let go of her and turned back to the guy writhing on the floor. Kneeling down, I helped him off the ground, "I warned you," I said with half a smile, "let's get you a drink," I patted him on the back, as he nodded and tried to walk off his bruised ego.

Boone and Wren were both in stitches when I returned to them, setting the drunk idiot on a stool to lick his wounds. The girls had gone back to dancing completely unbothered by the intrusion that had happened.

"I keep telling Brighton the girls are the best security we have," Boone said, handing me a beer. "The drunks are more scared of them, than they are old Johnny," he nodded to the old guy half asleep by the front entrance.

"Is that guy even alive?" Wren asked with serious concern, "Oh no, he moved...we're good."

"No one would have blamed you for hitting that guy," Boone added, running a hand through his dark hair.

"And let him get out of this without a crippling blow to his confidence?" I said to them both. "You'll never see him in here again after that."

"Oh shit," Wren said, "I recognize her now! That's Adeline Sarah," he said, slapping Boone in the chest with the back of his hand. "She's like a big deal," he added.

"It's going to suck to watch the Hillcats lose her," Boone said, and the comment wasn't meant to be malicious, it was just conversation and one he didn't know was still festering.

It was going to suck.

I inhaled deeply, trying to control how I felt about it all, and forced a smile onto my face as I joined back into the conversation.

JENSEN

> Are you sure they're okay with me coming?

> Don't be a coward.

> It'll be 5v1, Adeline.

I shoved my messy hair under a hat and climbed from the car, grabbing the two bags from the back seat to haul inside Sunday's townhouse. She lived in the new development on the north side of Harbor, where every house looked the same and the street wound together in confusing circles. I had left the nest almost an hour early to stop for snacks, and treats hoping that if I managed to find her house on time that I could buy their favor with food.

I knocked on the front door, holding the bags in one hand, and the gift bag in the other. If I was going to crash their one night of the week that boys were strictly forbidden at, I was going to do it properly.

Sunday opened the door, her blonde hair framing her cute little face and she narrowed her eyes at me suspiciously until I held up a bag full of candy and junk food.

"I come with gifts?" I said, just hoping that she'd let me in.

"What's in that one?" She pointed to the gift bag in my other hand and looked back up at me.

"Why don't you find out." I handed it to her and watched her scurry back into her house leaving me to wander inside without her invitation. I laughed, looking around at the entrance, the wall covered in framed photos of her, the girls and her family. All of their shoes were piled around the front door so I kicked off my own and followed the sound of their voices through the house. Everything was exactly how I expected her house to be. It was covered in photos and art, bright-colored blankets and furniture that I'd never thought to put together but somehow it worked and made everything feel cozy. There was a small, well lit living room off the front entrance and a set of stairs on the other side of the hallway that led me back into a big kitchen and dining room area.

The dining table was covered in game pieces, notebooks and other knick-knacks, but the girls were hovering over the bag at the counter taking turns pulling out little packages each with their own bow and tag.

"Bribery is wild," Rhea said, perched on the counter with a wicked smile on her face and her little gift in her palm. "I like you Jensen," she said as she started to tear into the tissue paper.

Adeline gave me a little scrunch of approval before she gave Cosy the package marked for her. Cosy was not as sure about any of it as the rest of the girls, her signature scowl never faltering ever as she rolled the present out into her palm. A set of baby blue dice, inlaid with flowers and sparkles. They were the exact opposite of Rhea's dark grey dice with bright teal accents and tiny moons.

"Thanks Fuckboy." Kaia giggled, ripping into hers, muddy dice with pink flowers that resembled cherry blossoms. Sunday was next, her package filled with yellow dice that contained bright blue jellyfish and plenty of glitter.

"We aren't going to go easy on you just because you brought us presents," Cosy said, but there was a new lightness to her voice that wasn't there before.

"I wouldn't have it any other way," I said with a smile on my face. Adeline rolled her dark green set in her palm, a soft smile on her face that she extended to me as the other girls found their places at the tables with drinks in their hands.

"You didn't have to do that," she whispered, curling her hand around the set and looking over at me.

"It's just dice," I said quietly, completely lost in her delicate expression, "totally worth the stress of picking the perfect set for each of them to see that pretty smile."

"Suck up," she giggled and gravitated toward me. "Come on." She led me over to the table and I found a place in the empty chair between her and

Sunday. While the other girls chatted, Adeline tossed open her well loved leather notebook to a page near the back. "This is you," she said proudly. I looked down at the little sketch she drew, surprised at how good it was and back at her. "I know you asked for help but I couldn't sleep the other day and I got a little carried away..." she said.

"What's his name?" I asked her.

"I was going to let you pick," she smiled at me but I shook my head.

"I wouldn't even know where to start," I said.

"Okay good, cause I already picked one out," she beamed with pride, "Venali Elsk."

I could tell by the look on her face that there was a double meaning to that name, much like the tattoo that painted her thigh, that my fingers were constantly itchy to touch. She had ingrained something in the Dungeons and Dragons character that went beyond just casual. I'd Google it later and probably end up in knots when I remember that she's leaving.

"It's amazing," I cleared my throat, watching the gold in her hazel eyes light up. "Is he an elf?" I asked, brushing my finger over the sketched pointed ears.

"Well kinda, half-elf..." she explained. "Rogue, he's sneaky and disarming. But in a Robin Hood kind of way," she trailed off with a little laugh. "I even wrote down that he's got magpie tendencies and likes to bring gifts to his friends..."

I laughed, turning the page to see what else she wrote down, "you know too much about me Adeline Sarah, it's getting scary." I whispered under my breath as I continued to read and her hand snaked up the back of my shirt.

"It's an optimal min/max build so you can just have fun and not get lost today," she explained, her wavy hair falling over her shoulders as she tipped her head to catch my eye. "Is it okay?"

"Adeline, it's fucking incredible," I praised, "I didn't even know it could be this involved, it's cool." I watched as her cheeks turned a pretty shade of pink and if I wasn't sitting in a room full of her best friends I would have made sure that blush crept to every corner of her body with my lips.

"Here," Cosy interrupted, "it's a notebook, I wrote a few things in it on how you're going to stumble across the group."

I flipped it open and read what she wrote, "Really?" I laughed at her and all she did was nod. "Alright, I can do this. I took theatre in high school."

"Did you really?" Kaia questioned from the other side of the table, bringing what looked like a daiquiri to her lips.

"I was Puck in the senior play," I boasted.

"Like Shakespeare's, a Midsummer Night's Dream?" Rhea asked curiously.

"Yeah, and I was Soda-Pop Curtis in a production two years ago at Harbor U." I confessed, mostly because the look on their faces was hilarious.

"The jock is a theatre nerd," Cosy scoffed.

"I just like *doing* stuff." I corrected her, "If it's cool, I'm in."

"Alright dork," Kaia nodded, and I could see that the thought of going easy on me had gone out the window with my confession, "game on."

It took me a minute to grasp what was happening, between all the new names, powers and the confusion of starting in the middle of a story they had been running for only god knows how long. But after about four too many daiquiris and more than enough explanation, I was getting it.

Rhea was a half-orc named Evantha, who had doubled down on her class to make sure she could protect her squishy spell casting friends not only with her strength but with her intelligence as well. It was hilarious to watch her interact with Adeline, who was playing as a fairy she had named Sky Mapledash; a name that made me chuckle any time Cosy introduced her.

Adeline's notes were intense, it was like every time the group stumbled across a puzzle she was the first to have it figured out. Watching her put together the clues without hesitation was a testament to how smart my girl was and I beamed with pride.

"I'm pretty sure my first crush was Tinkerbell, you know," I brushed my lips against her ear, teasing her while she tried to roll. "That little skirt and bad attitude."

"Pay attention, fuckboy," Kaia's voice cut through my flirting. She moved her intricately painted figure across the board to a rooftop. She had explained to me exactly what she was but in reality whatever a Tabaxi was looked like a panther and it absolutely suited Kaia.

"You can't move that far!" Adeline pointed out, breaking off from my grip.

"Fastest in the west, precious Mapledash, I can move wherever the hell I want..."

"You aren't the fastest," Adeline's eyes narrowed.

"I am in this room" Kaia flashed a smile.

Sunday piped up, "Cosy got quiet she's going to jump us." She was at the end of the table chewing on the end of her pen as she waited for Adeline and Kaia to stop bickering. I think she said she was a Changeling with a ukulele? A bard maybe. I was losing track of my notes, my eyes running over what I had written down for Sunday. Mirage! That was her name.

"Be quiet," Rhea warned her. "You always give her ideas."

"If you're all finished?" Cosy looked over the panel at the map, her eyes bright with mischief and for a second I could see Van there. Her usual grumpy demeanor shed for enjoyment and at home in her element.

Cosy rolled a D20 across the mat and everyone held their breath as it tipped to twenty.

"Fuck," they all swore in unison.

"No, that's good, right?" I pointed to it. "She rolled twenty!"

"It's good for her, bad for us," Rhea explained.

And damn was she right, Cosy went on to almost kill every single one of us with a trap she had laid, triggered by our arguing the only way we would have survived it was if she had rolled lower than a twelve. *Maybe I wasn't getting it after all.*

Rhea had saved all our asses with a lucky roll and some hearty damage but she was in rough shape by the end of the game and Sunday was practically asleep in her lap.

"You're not bad at this," Cosy said as I helped her put away all the map pieces and Rhea carried Sunday to her bed. "Jensen," she said quietly as Adeline and Kaia giggled while washing dishes in the sink. "Adeline isn't the kind of girl you let go of," she said and I swallowed tightly, ignoring the way the liquor raised my temperature. "For the sake of you both, figure out if you're serious because she's never played better in her life. She's relaxed, she's happy... she's giggling," Cosy scoffed. "Just be gentle. She grew up being overlooked."

"She's on the news every Friday night," I said, trying not to sound like an asshole. "She's the darling of Harbor, the center of attention when she's winning games."

"She can't always win." Cosy's glare was quiet but deadly. "You have to be there to see her win or lose."

"I promise." The word came out of my mouth and I wasn't even sure what I was promising. Whether it be to take care of Adeline the way she deserved or some backwards threat tangled with approval from Cosy Mitchell, both options terrified me.

JENSEN

"Here," I held the door open for Adeline and let her slip into the dark stadium. The only lights in the concrete tunnel are the ones above the exit signs at the end of the hallway.

"You didn't bring me down here to fulfill some weird stalker fetish, did you?" She asked, her smile bright as she turned to walk backwards and talk to me at the same time. I locked the door and shoved the master keys into my pocket. I had to bribe Susanna for them with a week's worth of lunch, but it would be worth it.

"And what if I did?" I shrugged, mirroring her smile as I closed the gap between us and snaked my arm around her. She was wearing a tiny little shirt that was cut around the hem and showed off just a little bit of her stomach above the tight maroon gym shorts she had tugged on in a rush as I shooed her out the door.

She had been sulking.

Which wasn't something I was used to her doing. But the scouts had gotten in her head and it was affecting her game. She was missing passes, stepping clumsily, it was like her ability to play rugby like it was breathing had become clouded, and it was turning her sour.

"I could outrun you," she said so nonchalantly it made me laugh.

"You think you're faster than me?" I stepped forward and she stepped back.

"You're fast, but the majority of your skill set relies on you hitting the ball far enough to cover the bases without getting caught," Adeline all but purred, the smirk never leaving her lips. "I have to carry the ball. I *know* I'm faster than you."

"She's cocky, I like that in a woman," I said to no one but the concrete. "We'll see if you're faster though."

"I can beat you in a foot race, Jensen," she scoffed and I nodded.

"I believe that, how about we play some one on one?" I offered. The point of the night was to give Adeline a space to not worry about anything. Take her out of her environment and allow her to just have fun in a place that wasn't constantly reminding her about all the pressure she was under.

She didn't seem to care as long as I was involved.

"How do you play one on one baseball?" She asked, leaning back in my arms as my lips brushed against her neck.

"Without clothes," I grumbled and Adeline laughed, pushing me back.

"If you wanted to play with your bat and balls we could have stayed home," she teased, fluttering her lashes at me.

"Ha ha," I said, letting her go. "Come on."

I dipped down, hauling her over my shoulder with a tiny laugh dripping from her pretty lips before I carried her back through the arena to the field. I flicked on the stadium lights, and with a loud thrum they illuminated the perfectly cut turf and raked sand.

"I feel like a criminal touching it, it's so perfect..." she pushed her hands flat against my back, angling her head up to look at her surroundings. Setting her down she moved backward looking up at the stands. "It has to be intimidating... having that many people watching you?"

I shrugged, turning around to take in what she did. "I don't ever turn around..."

"You did," Adeline said, looking over her shoulder at me. "For me."

"Dire circumstances," I said, giving her a tiny wink.

"Mmm," she hummed, her eyes tracing a wide circle of the stadium. "Okay, explain the rules."

"All work and no play, Adeline Sarah." I clicked my teeth together and jogged over to the dugout. I paid Mikey, our newest equipment kid to leave out a crate and my bats after practice and nodded in gratitude to find them right where I needed. "Atta boy."

"I pitch, you hit, I chase the ball, you run the bases. Then we switch," I explained.

Adeline surveyed the field, no doubt running the numbers between the bases. I watched her brain tick gloriously fast as the smile crept to her lips.

"What is it, eighty-five feet between each base?" She asked, hands on her perfect hips as she turned to me with the question.

"Ninety, if you wanna be technical," I chuckled, shaking my head.

"Bring it on." She stepped forward so our chests met and smiled up at me, reaching down without breaking eye contact to wrap her hand around the bat. "It's bigger than I expected," she said, eyes casting downward in a snap as she lifted it, "and heavier."

I crossed my arms and cocked my head to the side, "you don't have to compliment my dick Adeline, it's already yours."

"I meant the bat, jackass." She rolled her eyes waiting for me to help her set up in the batter's box. I pushed my hand into the glove and waited as she pulled her hair into a ponytail, balancing the bat between her legs before she lifted it again and rolled out her shoulders. She stepped up to the base and angled toward me, with a sweet, soft smile. "Like that?"

"Yeah Belle, like that," I said, shaking my head and chucking the ball from my hand to the mitt. "You ready?" I asked her as she found her footing in the sand and she looked up, determined to prove me wrong.

I tried to keep a straight face but she looked so cute I had to inhale before pulling back and pitching her a soft ball that curved through the air in a lazy arch toward the box. She didn't even swing, her head cocking to the side.

"That's not how you throw during a game!" She snapped and I broke, laughing at her adorable annoyance.

"Fine," I said, "lift your bat and stop complaining," I snapped my fingers at her and she readjusted herself. The next pitch was straight, fast and whipped past her head only to slam into the backstop with a metal clang.

"Again," she said. Not letting the speed of the ball rattle her.

I threw another and it was perfect but Adeline swung and missed it.

"Breath before, not during," I said to her and she scowled.

"Don't man-splain how to swing a bat to me Jensen!" She argued. I waited for her to stop thinking so hard, and the second her back foot settled I threw another pitch.

"How do you do that?" She grunted in frustration as the next ball kicked off the backstop into the air. "It's like you know I'm ready to swing before I do and it's messing with my head."

"It's just basic body language," I said to her. "You fidget with your back foot as you count your own breathing, three and then your foot stops moving."

"Okay, okay…" One of the traits I admired about Adeline is that she always took something from a conversation, it was never just about the talking. She wanted to learn, to grow, to be better than she was seconds before. It was why she belonged in California. It was growth, it was her opportunity to be better, be stronger, faster.

"What's your tell?" She asked me, leaving the bat at her side.

"I don't have one," I said with a smile.

"That's bullshit, everyone has a tick… it's human nature." She shook her head in disbelief.

"I don't know what to tell you, Adeline." I shrugged. "I just don't."

"When you're about to kiss me the left side of your mouth lifts first," she turned her whole body to me that time. "When you're going to say something you think I won't like, you cross your arms… and when we're in the gym and you're starting to get tired but refuse to slow down because I'm not, you grind your teeth together."

"Is that all?" I laughed, enjoying the observations.

"You have to have one on the field, you wear your emotions on your face. I just don't believe you're somehow more evolved during games," Adeline said.

"You want to know the secret?" I asked her, and she nodded, making me laugh even more. "I've been watching everyone else for five years, the first season I learned the ticks of half the baseball players in the league and every time I step up to bat I use one of *theirs*. Never my own, never the same twice in a row."

Adeline stared at me, her eyes wide as she processed the information. She opened her mouth, not once but twice to speak and then closed it again to think about it some more.

"Say it," I encouraged as she sank her teeth into her lip.

"I'm just concerned that maybe you are a serial killer," she teased with a soft smile.

"I told you, I wouldn't have tattooed you if I was planning on cutting you up into tiny little pieces, Belle." I joked.

"You have to admit the whole 'I've been watching' thing is weird." There was no malice to her voice and her eyes were bright with playful curiosity.

"Coach thinks it's weird too, but it works. Makes me unreadable and it's the reason they bring me out when we're down." I said. "It also comes in handy when I need to impress the prettiest girl in Harbor."

"Wow so now I'm just part of your sick serial killer statistics?" Adeline threw her head back and groaned sarcastically.

"If it makes you feel better, you're the only girl I've risked a game for." I watched the recognition flicker across her face and I knew that I'd said something that triggered the sadness up in her chest again. *Shit.* "Ready up." I grabbed another ball from the crate at my feet and got ready to throw.

It whipped through the air and was by no means the perfect pitch but it flew true and straight. Adeline swung and she swung hard, the bat hit the ball with a loud crack that made me flinch delaying my reaction as she took off running down the baseline to first.

"Hey!" I called after her, trying to eye where the ball landed deep in the outfield. "That was cheating!" I started booking it to the small white dot as Adeline rounded second. It didn't matter how fast I was, she was faster. Her legs carried her quickly and before I even started running back to meet her at home plate she was pushing the line at third.

I started jogging as I got in and passed second base, keeling over on the pitcher's mound trying to fill my lungs with air as Adeline smiled at me from home base.

"Still think you could catch me?" She asked, and didn't even sound out of breath.

"You win, you win," I admitted defeat with a burning chest.

"Can we do that again?" She beamed at me, bathed in the bright stadium lights and for a second everything was alright. There were no pressures to make decisions, no one watching waiting for us to make the wrong move. It was just me, and Adeline.

"You're an animal," I choked out, straightening up. "Ready?" I asked her, palming the ball and she scooped the bat from the ground quickly with a funny little nod of excitement.

JENSEN

"There's no way you do this every day before practice," Cael whined.

"You've done one round of squats, Cody." Kaia glared at him, her hair braided down in thick cords that hung off her shoulders while she barked orders. "You asked to do this today, if I had known you were a pussy, I wouldn't have invited you."

"I like pussy, I'm not *a* pussy," Cael snapped his fingers at her. "Besides, Van hasn't done a single circuit and you aren't yelling at him."

"Yell at Van Mitchell? That angel?" Kaia smiled, showing all her teeth as she squatted down across from Cael. "It's okay if you can't do it, the girls will understand. This is a hard routine and maybe you're just too delicate?"

Cael set the weights down on either side of the bench he was perched on and leaned forward into her space with a matching smile and met her energy like a raw live wire sparking, just begging to be touched.

"You're baiting me, Kaia Keegan and I don't like it." Cael gripped the bench.

"Am not, just trying to get a work out in and there are baseball players lying around whining in my way," she was mocking him. Van scoffed as he lunged past them, his hair pushed back off his face with a bandana.

"I know all the tricks in the book so what do you want out of this? Us to cry, to tell you that you're stronger than us?" Cael wasn't phased by her and it was hilarious to watch their interaction as I spotted Adeline on the squat machine.

"I'm offended that you're more interested in that argument than you are my ass in these shorts," Adeline said, her voice strained from the weight.

"I can multitask," I whispered in her ear, stepping forward to help her find the hooks for the bar and wrapping my arm around her waist to pull her against me. My fingers dipped into the front band against her hipbone and drew circles on her skin. "And you can't tell me that isn't interesting. It's like watching a cat fight with itself in the mirror."

"I didn't say that, I said pay attention to me instead." She tilted her head back and I stole the opportunity to kiss a bead of sweat off her throat. She vibrated with delight and the feeling surged through me faster and hotter than any amount of pre-workout could.

"If I focus on your ass, I'll never get anything done," I groaned as she pouted up at me.

"Awe and here I thought I was your cardio," she said with a smile on her face.

"You are, but if you want me to keep those back muscles you like to dig your nails into then I also have to do weights." I kissed her nose. "Finish your circuit and maybe we can spend the afternoon setting a new cardio PR."

"Deal," she giggled, "One more?" She pressed to her toes and I obliged with a soft kiss. I smiled at her as she pulled away, memorizing every bright shade of her eyes. *She's leaving, stop pretending like she's not.*

Keep it easy, keep it uncomplicated.

"One more." I whispered.

Kaia and Cael were still at each other's throats, both poised to attack but both having too much fun to end the verbal sparring.

"I want your shirt," Kaia said after a few moments of heated deadlock.

Cael's eyes darted down to the grey sleeveless fuckboy crop he always wore.

"No," he laughed. I'd never seen true fear in Cael's expression until then.

"One full circuit, you have to fail out on your PR and you have to complete every workout I do," she said, "It shouldn't be hard."

"What's with the shirt?" Adeline asked, walking around to the lat machine and settling on the bench with her arms in the air. I stepped behind her, changing the weight and pulling the handles into her grasp without a second thought.

"That scrap of fabric is Cael's equivalent to a childhood teddy bear, or a ratty old blanket. It never leaves him, if it's not on him. It's in his backpack." I said, leaning against the machine while she did her reps.

"That's weird, but also not surprising."

"So you admit that you can't hold up next to a girl in a silly little workout routine?" Kaia pushed with a wicked grin on her face.

"Legs suck, Kaia!" Cael groaned.

"You aren't doing much to debunk the rumors that Harbor Hornets are pussies," she said, standing up to her full height. Cael pushed from the bench, towering over her with a tight expression on his face.

"Fine," he ground out, "one full circuit, if I can't keep up. You get the shirt."

"You sure? I don't want to make you do anything you aren't ready for…" Kaia teased and Cael took her outstretched hand in a rough handshake.

We continued our workout, moving around the gym as Kaia forced Cael through a grueling leg workout. Every machine was like a death trap to the guy who considered running bases his cardio for the week.

"I don't think I've ever seen Cael work out his legs," I said to Adeline as she racked a few weights that had been left on the floor by them.

"Good thing you don't have a game tomorrow, he's going to be bedridden," she noted, sitting down on the bench across from me.

I couldn't have cared less about the competition happening on the other side of the gym, Adeline's smile growing as everyone clapped for our friends after each rep. I was oddly at home and Cosy's words settled against my chest in the silence.

You have to be there to see her, win or lose.

"I see you Adeline Sarah," I whispered, wanting to make sure she knew.

She looked over at me like she always did, sweat running down her neck, cheeks flushed from working hard but today there was a softness in her eyes I hadn't expected and it knocked the wind out of me.

"What Belle?" I asked her when she didn't say anything, unsure if she heard the quiet omission, so much softer than the first time I had confessed to her.

"Nothing," she whispered back, her smile crooked and gentle. I could tell she was happier than usual and it made me want to wrap her up and find a closet where I could enjoy the sweat and heat in private.

"You have to finish!" Kaia hollered, interrupting our moment. She clapped her hands and cheered Cael on as he struggled with the squat machine. He grunted hard, pushing his strength into the last motion and managed to click the weight into place before rolling off the machine to the floor. "We've got one left, Cody! Don't you give up on me!"

"Fuck off, Keegan. I gotta reorganize my fucking guts after that," he crawled across the floor to the wall breathlessly, and Kaia followed him with a bottle of water. "Thank you."

She looked around the gym, her eyes scanning for something.

"What is she looking for?" I asked Adeline, who just smiled.

"Here we go," she said as Kaia clapped her hands together. The pair were completely in sync with one another without a single word shared. I watched as she leaned forward on the bench in her tiny sports bra.

"Fuck, Adeline. *Don't.*" A rumble left my chest at the side of her swollen breasts in the top. I shifted on the bench uncomfortably as my dick tensed in my workout shorts.

"What?" She smiled, looking down at her cleavage.

"Yeah," I grunted, just trying to get through the last of my bicep curls as she teased me.

"Want to go for a ride?" Kaia called out to her and without hesitation, Adeline popped up from the bench turning her back to the rest of the gym so she could smile at me.

Her eyes scanned quickly, looking for someone but fell back on mine with a smug satisfaction as her fingers came up under the hem of the bra and lifted it free of her glorious tits.

I dropped the dumbbell short of my foot at her brazen behavior, "you're a brat!" I called out just trying to control myself and my stupidly hard cock.

"Pay attention to my ass next time and I won't resort to war tactics," she laughed at me.

"You're going to pay for that!" I said, still tempted to chase after her as she situated her breasts safely inside, mouthed a tiny *I hope so* at me and jogged over to Kaia. I'd be stuck to this bench for at least another ten minutes.

I waited until Cael had collected himself to push myself off the bench and abandon my workout to see what Kaia and Adeline were up to. A crowd of Hornets and Hillcats had circled loosely around a bench in the university gym, watching the competition like it held higher stakes than a stinky old crop top.

"Add a ten," Kaia said to Rhea, testing the weight out. She was positioned to do hip thrusts on the bench, her long legs stretched out a cushioned bar flat across her hips. Rhea did as she asked, popping a five plate onto each side of the bar. "That's better," she tested it again.

"What are you doing?" Cael asked, sinking down beside her on the floor like he couldn't bear to stand any longer.

"Winning that shirt off your back by an unmistakable margin," Kaia teased. "Save a horse, ride a cowboy," she beamed up at Adeline, who had slipped off her shoes and was positioning herself over Kaia.

"What the fuck," Cael groaned, knowing he was screwed. Sweat soaked his blonde hair and the back of the shirt was drenched down the back and sides, turning everything the darkest shade of grey.

Kaia waited as Adeline perched perfectly, giving her space to get the bar comfy before she started to lower her hips, rising back up with barely any struggle. It was as if Adeline didn't weigh more than a feather.

"Four," Adeline counted out, staying perfectly still as her best friend thrust up and down without so much as a grunt of effort.

"This is cruel," Cael called out, "but I'm not a fucking quitter and you aren't getting my fucking shirt!" He snapped, but his voice was playful as he pushed off the ground. "Jenny, wanna sit on my dick?"

"No," I said in disbelief.

"Coward," Cael scoffed, looking around the gym. "You're the only one here that won't kill me! You can't actually expect me to thrust Van or Dean?"

"I'd add two hundred bucks to the pot just to see you try." I crossed my arms over my chest and he pouted at me.

"If I hurt myself before the next game you can deal with my dad," he threatened.

"Or you could just hand over the shirt and admit defeat," Kaia said with a smile on her face as the count reached twelve.

"She can do this all day," Sunday added, "we've seen her do it."

"Are you even a human being?" Cael leaned over with his hands on his thighs, bringing his face closer to Kaia.

"Fifteen," Adeline jabbed as Kaia continued to thrust. "Sixteen."

The count was pounding in Cael's ears, it was written all over his face.

"Seventeen," she sang out, pretending to yawn. The tiny movement shifted her balance and Kaia's face scrunched a little to hold her form.

Cael watched them both, no doubt trying to figure out a way to win but came up short, grabbing his shirt with one hand over his back and pulling it over his head in a shift motion before throwing it on the floor at Kaia.

"You win." He panted, completely spent by the activities.

Kaia didn't stop though, she just kept going to prove a point. Reaching twenty five she slowed and allowed Adeline to carefully stand up as Van consoled Cael.

"You gotta stop making bets you know you can't win," I patted him on the shoulder in passing.

JENSEN

"I thought we were going out for dinner?" Adeline asked me from the passenger seat. Days like today were my favorite. I had woken up with her face pressed against my chest, we had spent the morning at the gym, the afternoon destroying every surface in her apartment and when we were finished, she always demanded food.

"We are... at my mother's." I dropped the bomb, we were driving down through Harbor, the storefronts flashing by the car as Adeline's expression changed from excited to shocked. Which is why I waited until we were driving and she was locked inside to tell her.

"You want me to meet your mom?" Came out of her mouth, softer than I expected and it made my heart flutter in my chest.

"If I had it my way our first date would have been at the house but you had to go pick tattoos and chicken wings." I teased her but her face was so serious. "Marked me for life before you even met my mother..." I chuckled but noticed she wasn't laughing with me so I reached out to squeeze the tattoo on her thigh. "What?" When I tried to move back to the wheel her other thigh came down over my hand, trapping me against her entirely.

"You really want me to meet her?" She asked again, a little more nervous than the first time.

"It's just my mom, I mean dad will be there too... but he's nothing to be scared of," I said, pulling down the road to our house.

"It's a big step," she said finally, as I pulled into the driveway.

"It's just dinner, no expectations. No strings." I assured her and she sighed like she wanted to argue but she just looked up at the big house with fear in her eyes.

"What if they don't like me?" She asked as I killed the engine.

"Impossible," I said without hesitation.

"Improbable," she corrected, "there's a chance they don't."

"You're overthinking it. She invited me tonight, and I told her I was bringing you. She didn't make a big deal of it, and neither should you." I said, reaching over the console to her and grabbing her chin so she'd look at me. "If by some insane chance they don't like you, that's their problem. Not ours, because at this point I don't think I could stop liking you even if I tried."

"You mean that?" She asked me, and I nodded, only stopping because she cut me off with a gentle kiss. "Okay, I can do this, it can't be scarier than impressing rugby scouts?" She sounded more unsure then she had the day we got our tattoos. "The no answer is scarier than you trying to convince me it's not by the way." She steeled her nerves and grumbled at me as she got out of the car.

I rounded the car to put my hand in hers as I led her up the steps and inside, "shoes," I said to her quietly. She obliged before following me down the hall to the kitchen.

"Mom?" I called out and no one answered right away but there was muffled grunting coming from the cupboards where she was stretched up on a stool trying to reach the top shelf. "What the hell are you doing?" I dropped Adeline's hand, leaving her standing by the island to help my mom down.

"I know that tray is up there!" She swatted my hand away but got off the stool. "The one with the blue jays that your grandmother gave me."

"It's not up there." I shook my head, sliding the stool back against the counter.

"Why isn't it up there?" She eyed me.

"Dad broke it last summer while you were in Greece and claimed you'd never find out because you don't use it." I shrugged.

"Unfortunately for you and your father, I use it when we have company," Mom sighed and looked over at Adeline.

"Right..." I grimaced and turned to her. "Mom, this is Adeline," I said.

"You're prettier than he gives you credit for," she winked at Adeline, who laughed and gave me a death glare.

"At least he talked to you about me, I've been in the dark…" she said, still staring at me.

"Quit stirring the pot." I smirked at Mom with a shake of my head.

"Oh I raised you better," Mom scolded, but there was no malice in her voice. "Keep it up, and you and Dad can get crackers for dinner while Adeline and I enjoy the risotto and lamb."

"You made the lamb?" I stepped forward, and Mom stared me down.

"Not for rude little men without manners," she said.

"Who conspire with their fathers over broken plates," Adeline teased.

"It was a beautiful plate," Mom sighed.

"Can you two not team up on me? It's been two minutes," I asked, completely defeated but the color had returned to Adeline's face.

"You broke my plate," Mom smiled as her phone rang.

"I'll find you another one," I said softer.

"Watch that pot," she said, pointing behind her. "Excuse me, Adeline."

"See, not so scary," I whispered, grabbing the side of her head and pulling her temple to my lips. "Unless you break one of her favorite plates."

"Right," Adeline purred. "Is this where you grew up?"

"Kinda," I said, looking around the kitchen. "We travelled a lot growing up. Once Mom's business went international, she was needed all over the place to oversee construction and openings."

"She's a big deal," Adeline noted.

"She is, but not in this house. In here she's just mom." I said, it was a rule made a long time ago that when Mom was home, she was Mom. Nothing else. She had been putting me first my entire life, and it wasn't until lately that I realized how selfless she was. She had struggled and crawled her way out of the dirt, having a baby so young should have crippled her but she was smarter and more innovative than anyone gave her credit for.

It's why I was given every opportunity, why I always said yes. Because I had been raised by someone who never told me or anyone else for that matter, the word no.

"Canada, Greece, Japan, Spain and France," I listed them off for her and she gently shook her head in disbelief. I followed her as she started to explore the house. The walls were decorated with treasures from our travels and pictures of us against monuments and in museums.

"Were you ever in school?" Adeline asked in amazement.

"I was homeschooled for a while, but Mom wanted me to have some socialization other than rich businessmen and my dad," I said, pointing to a photo of her opening one of the hotels in France. "We spent the longest time in France. It was her first hotel from the ground up. Two years," I explained.

"Explains why you can speak it," Adeline grinned ear to ear as she took it all in. We stopped at a door on the end of the hallway with a do not enter sign on the first of it. Without a second thought, Adeline popped the doorknob.

"Wow, yeah just ignore the sign." I gasped as she wandered into my room.

"Holy crap," she said, ignoring my jab as she took in the shelves of trophies. "It's like a shrine in here, did you win all of these?" She stepped forward and pulled down one of the ones I got in sixth grade. "Dance?"

"I like to do stuff," I said like that was a reasonable explanation for the excess of hardware hanging from my walls and shelves.

"Jensen this is more than just liking to do stuff, this is competing and winning?" She laughed, admiring my childhood bedroom, "but you didn't stick with anything?"

"Until Harbor." I said, "I found a place there and suddenly I didn't want to keep trying other things. Baseball was enough for me."

"That's so sweet." She looked over at me as she set one of the trophies back. Her eyes scanned over more, the gymnastics, the water polo, the hockey... everything was there and nothing I had said was a lie. It had taken me a while to find myself in a sport, I like them all well enough but nothing ever felt like it needed me back. Until I started playing with the Hornets. Getting to play on the field with them every night was a dream, it was why I was taking burner classes just to hang onto that freedom for one more year before moving on to the next chapter.

I knew eventually I would join Mom with the hotels, I was more than qualified to do it and it had always been the plan but the second I told her I needed more time she put a smile on her face and responded with 'take your time Malachi.'

So I did, and luckily my turtle approach to life brought me Adeline.

Never part of the original design but with every passing day it was getting harder to see a future without my girl.

"It's annoying that all these trophies say M. Jensen," she grumbled.

"You didn't think it would be that easy, did you?" I said, knowing full well it was a matter of time before Mom pulled out my full name.

Adeline turned, "You know it's kind of cute that she has all of this still in your room. Look at your baby face!"

"I told you I was in the play senior year," I took the picture from her and smiled at it. "Do you think we would have dated in high school?"

"Absolutely not," she scoffed with a wicked smile.

"Ouch," I said, leaning over her to place the photo back on the shelf.

"Don't worry, I would have taken pity on you," she hummed, wrapping her arms around my neck.

"Oh yeah?" I returned the touch, tugging her closer by her waist and digging my fingers into her hips. "The popular girl and the homeschooled dork?"

"Even the homeschool dork deserves to get kissed under the bleachers," she teased, her fingers pushing into my hair with a smile on her face.

"Would the popular girl settle for a high school make out in his shrine of trophies?" I asked her, enjoying the lightness of the conversation.

"On his Power Rangers comforter," Adeline giggled, "so hot."

"Are you making fun of that relic?" I asked her and she raised an eyebrow.

"Absolutely I am," she said, looking over my shoulder at my bed again. "Do you even fit in that thing?"

Without warning, I scooped her up, tossing her to the mattress with a soft thud that made her bounce. I crawled over her as she sank into the pillow with a sweet smile across her face.

"You're right," I sighed. "I would have never survived having a girl this hot in my bed in high school." I kissed her jaw as it vibrated with amusement.

"I could have called you cum shorts," Adeline giggled.

"It was one time," I growled, hurrying my face into the crook of her neck while my fingers found the hem of her shirt.

"Would have been a regular occurrence. I can't imagine your willpower has come that far if you're still a five minute man," she teased.

"I'd threaten you, but it would just turn you on," I scoffed, tickling her harder and making her hips rise to meet mine.

"Awe you're learning." Adeline wriggled beneath me.

I nearly lost control when her lips connected with mine and her tongue slipped into my mouth dragging me down on top of her completely. It was easy to lose my focus when she was around, like the rest of the world didn't exist and for a second it didn't have a reason to. It was just me and her. Her hands in my hair, mine on her skin, our bodies pressed so tightly together there was no beginning or end.

"Malachi!"

My mother's voice echoed through the house.

"Malachi..." The triumph in her voice was vicious as Adeline pulled back from me. "Malachi Jensen!"

"Yeah yeah, shh now," I kissed her again to keep her quiet.

"Malachi means angel doesn't it," she pulled away a second time, leaving me to chase her lips.

"Yeah," I confirmed with a barrage of kisses around her face. "Do you want to keep asking questions or—"

My door flying open had me in the upright position in a second flat, Mom stood with her hand on her hip acting like I was sixteen again and got caught with a girl in my room. Which, to her credit, had happened because despite Adeline's assumption, I was never a dork.

"You were supposed to be watching dinner," she scolded, pointing at me, "He keeps the baby pictures in his bottom drawer," she said to Adeline before bringing the phone back to her ear and disappearing down the hallway. "Move it, Kai!" she called once more.

"How is it possible that she's still a cockblock when I'm an adult?" I rested my head against Adeline's and huffed gently. "Don't answer that," I cut her off when she opened her mouth to argue.

"She calls you Kai for short!" Adeline rolled from bed as I stood up just to smooth out my hair from her fingers.

"Yeah, since I was a kid," I said, still frazzled from the interruptions. "No one outside this house knows my name, Adeline."

"Why? Are you spies?" She giggled.

"No it's just—I go by Jensen outside these walls. Always have, Malachi is for my mom."

"That's so sweet," her bottom lip jutted out. "You're her angel."

"Are you done?" I smiled at her and her weird love of random facts, such as knowing the meaning behind names.

"For now," she cooed, hooking her finger into the collar of my shirt.

JENSEN

We made our way back to the kitchen, where Mom had her laptop out at the island, grumbling hopelessly over something. Adeline leaned against the counter at the opposite end as I made my way back to the stove. The pot I had been told to watch was fine, and I was sure that Mom was just being obnoxiously involved on purpose.

"Where's Dad anyway, isn't he your assistant chef?" I asked, giving the risotto some more liquid just like she had taught me.

"He's in a meeting," she said, "keeping stirring."

"Alright," I did as I was told as she tapped away on her laptop, clearly frustrated. "What's going on?" I finally asked. It wasn't like her to be doing work, especially not with company over.

"We're launching the new web service for the hotels and with it the mobile app but everything that could go wrong, is." She explained. "This app is cursed." She swore under her breath.

"Can I see?" Adeline piped up, straightening out as she pushed off the island to move around to help my Mom. "It's kind of my specialty," she said, her eyes scanned over the screen. "Oh, I know this program." She looked at the laptop, and my mom moved out of the way so Adeline could get to the keyboard. "If we rewrite this section of code." She pointed to the computer and showed her, "then this will streamline bookings and stop the issue of users being timed out waiting in line."

"You're IT?" my mom asked.

"Developer," she said, chewing on her lip while she typed something out. "We take clients and create their apps from scratch. Any of the assistance after is

IT." Mom looked over at me with a smile on her face, but her eyes were telling. *Oh she's out of your league.* The teasing was loud and joking aside, I absolutely agreed. Adeline Sarah was well out of my league. But there was something else there, a softer expression of *I like her*. And not that I needed the approval, but it made the corners of my mouth curl into a proud smile.

It was interesting to hear Adeline talk about work, she did it so rarely that I forgot she was a person outside of rugby. I can't help but keep my eyes on them. Adeline had been so scared to come over here, and now she was typing away on my mom's computer like it was nothing.

My mom looked up at Adeline and smiled softly, her expression full of gratitude and pride. "That's impressive, we've been trying to fix that for hours."

"Companies have been using artificial intelligence to run code and it's been a pain in my ass— I mean butt." Adeline grimaced when she swore.

"I've heard worse, Honey." Mom's attention was on the laptop screen when Adeline looked up at me with a smile. I gave her a small thumbs up, and she scrunched her nose at me sending sparks dancing across my chest. I couldn't help but stare, it was like she glowed the warmest shade of amber. I always wanted to be around it and the way my heart was trying to beat out of my chest. The words were on the tip of my tongue, I could feel them there wanting to slip out as a conscious thought. But that's not what we were, it was casual, simple. Fun.

I couldn't be in love with Adeline.

She spoke again and pulled me from my thoughts to check the risotto in a panic, only to see it nearly done. She was typing again, and my mom was watching intently to every move she made trying to figure out what she was fixing.

"That's what happened here, it just wasn't prepared for the test load that you sent through but I'd say if you expect that many visitors to the app on launch I wouldn't throttle the website." She explained it slowly and clearly as my mom took notes and nodded in understanding.

"You're incredibly intelligent, Adeline," she praised, and Adeline smiled.

"Thank you, Mrs. Jensen."

"Call me Lena." She winked.

"I didn't realize how many locations you had." Adeline crossed her arms over her chest.

"We've got a hotel in every major city across America now. Our newest locations are in Montana, California and Seattle." Mom explained, "Hopefully in the new year we can close a deal for a location in Mexico."

That was right, they had just opened a brand new location in San Francisco. Thoughts stirred around Adeline leaving and just like that insanity slipped in, leaving me wondering if she had just laid down a new path for me to follow. Without even knowing it.

Dinner went amazing, Adeline charmed her way into their hearts with nothing more than her smile and intelligence and I couldn't have been more attracted to her at that moment. The way she carried herself through every conversation with such an ease no matter what questions my parents threw at her.

> How am I doing? Do you think she likes me?

> How couldn't she? You're a dream.

I looked up to see Adeline smile at her phone before tucking it away as Mom returned with dessert. A few times Mom made eye contact and I knew from the soft expression that I had made the right decision bringing her here. It had been bugging me since I found out about California, and I couldn't figure out if it was because I was upset that she hadn't told me herself, or that I was stuck on not having a solution.

It was silly, but I wanted to keep Adeline. I wasn't ready to let her go.

I was starting to like the feeling of the strings she was tying me up in.

"I've never had lamb before, that was incredible." Adeline helped me carry the plates back to the kitchen after dinner was finished and handed them to me as I rinsed them off for the dishwasher.

"Thank you for enduring every single dad joke that was made," I said, kissing her temple before bending over to load the dishes.

"Worth it, I think I fixed the app for the hotel. I gave your mom—Lena... my work number so if she needs me when they launch I'm just a call away," she said to me, not understanding how much she was breaking my heart with her kindness.

"And you were scared," I teased her as her hand reached out to rake across my back absentmindedly.

"I wasn't scared." She rolled her eyes as she leaned against the counter waiting for me to finish so I could take her home, but I had one more surprise.

"Oh well if you weren't brave then I guess you don't need the treat I was going to give you," I said, looking at her out of the corner of eye. She perked up, tilting her head sideways to get my attention. "What?" I shrugged, "It was only there as bribery and I didn't have to use it."

"I like being bribed," Adeline pouted, "Bribe me!" She demanded and I laughed, closing the dishwasher to move in front of her.

"Ask me nicely," I lowered my voice. There were some things I didn't need to share with my parents. Like the feral need to drive Adeline nuts at every turn simply because I liked when she acted like a brat.

"No," she clipped.

"Oh well," I said, turning away from her but she caught my shirt in her fingers. "Use your words, Adeline." I grinned at her and enjoyed it as her cheeks turned red.

"What if I don't want to use my words?" She countered and I laughed.

"Your loss, it's a really sick surprise." I flicked a finger beneath her chin.

A grumble formed at the base of her throat as she narrowed her eyes on me, "please."

"Please what?" I pushed back.

"Please show me the surprise?" Her voice was sweeter than before as she turned on her charm and got her way with a pretty little smile on her face.

"Since you asked so nicely." I kissed her lips gently, taking my time until she impatiently leaned into the feeling and her arms wrapped around my neck. "Quick, before we get suckered into movie night." I gave her hip a squeeze and turned her in the direction of the hallway, leading her down the opposite side from my room and past my parents bickering gently in the living room over what movie they wanted to watch.

I popped the door on the garage behind my back as I blocked her way inside, "Close your eyes."

"No," she scowled and I waited until she decided she wanted to listen to instructions.

"You like that word today, hey?" I stared at her, kissing the corner of her mouth and taking her hand. I stepped down into the garage, grabbing her by the waist and lifting her down against my chest until she was inside with me. She was being unbelievably patient, and it was unlike her to be even entertaining my games. It wasn't until I clicked the button on the fob and the loud click of the doors unlocking echoed through the garage that she opened her eyes.

"Holy shit," She looked at the sleek black car and back to me. "Is that 2024 GR?"

She moved around me toward the Supra with childlike excitement on her face as her hand reached out to run over the smooth angled roof. "Is it yours?" She asked me, her eyes locked on the sports car. When I didn't answer, she continued to circle the vehicle, "Why do you drive that old man car? How dare you leave her sitting here!" She narrowed her beautiful, vicious hazel eyes at me over the roof.

"I'm not driving the Supra around Harbor, it's unethical." I shrugged, but I was enjoying her genuine shock that I had one.

"You just leave a sixty thousand dollar sports car sitting in your garage? Please, Jensen. Why?" She almost sounded upset over the fact that it was sitting here unused.

"I drive it up to the cabin, highways only. You can't even open the thing up in Harbor without hitting a stop sign. There's no point," I argued.

"*Her.* This car is a goddess and you're making silly excuses. Harbor deserves to hear her purr. You're a monster," she gasped.

"Catch." I said, knowing it would be enough for her to raise her hand, her reflexes were sharp enough and the keys landed safely in her palm.

"Are you serious?" She looked at the keys in her hand mischievously.

"As long as you can drive stick, Adeline. Dead."

She didn't need anymore confirmation before she was crawling into the front seat of the Supra with a wicked giggle. It took her another ten minutes of admiring the seats, dashboard and interior specs before she even started it and when it roared to life she looked like she had just won the lottery. Her cheeks were flushed, her smile was wide and bright. I was practically jealous of the glow it gave her as she pulled it from the garage.

"This is better than—"

"Don't you dare," I clapped my hand over her mouth as she revved the engine and the car roared beneath us. She licked the palm of my hand and shifted the car with a satisfied expression as it vibrated to life and she ripped away from the house.

For a girl so hell-bent on speed, she was good. Really good. It made me wonder where she learned to drive like that because there wasn't a moment of worry. She pulled the Supra out onto the highway without asking, and I was glad she did because the moment of pure joy in her body was like euphoria.

"Open it up," I said to her, reaching across to snake my hand around her thigh.

SARAH

I couldn't tell if I was pissed off or in love.

The car drove like it was flying, and the faster I pushed it the better it felt beneath my ass. I wanted to drive it forever. Jensen sat unbothered in the passenger seat, his smile unwavering even when I took a corner too fast. His trust was rattling.

It had been a long time since I drove manual and he didn't even flinch at giving me the keys, he just put his faith and his very expensive car in my hands.

And fuck was it hot.

We had to be almost an hour outside of Harbor when the road became truly quiet and I could push the engine to its capacity for a few miles. Jensen's smug attitude only made the rush of emotions ten times as strong. Meeting his parents was terrifying, and I'd never done anything like that before but I was pretty sure that I'd left a good impression. At least, I was confident I'd done so with his mother.

"There's a turn off up here," Jensen said, his arm stretching out to give me plenty of time to slow the car. There was a smaller road covered in trees that wound up around one of the many hills, it broke eventually to the coast line and gave the prettiest view to the ocean. Stars painted the sky like glitter as Jensen directed me down past another bend to a massive piece of unoccupied grass.

I turned off the car and ran my hands over the wheel, staring down at the console with pure excitement. "I stand by my statement, you're a monster for never driving her."

"Yeah, yeah." Jensen undid his belt and climbed from the car, shutting the door behind him and leaving me to follow. The air was chillier than before and I quickly tucked into his side as he leaned against the hood of the car. He watched the ocean tide crash up against the rocky shore but my eyes were on the stars and how bright they were this far out of the city.

"It's gorgeous out here," I said, my fingers brushing beneath his shirt around his stomach to steal the warmth radiating from him.

"Mmm," His abs tightened slightly as my fingers grazed over them. His arm tightened around me, "You cold?" He asked softly, his thumb rubbing my hip bone absentmindedly.

"A little," I said, scrunching my nose at him. "I didn't realize how cold it had gotten outside."

Jensen chuckled softly, his arm pulling me even closer until I'm sitting in his lap against the car hood. He spread his legs slightly so I could tuck between them trying to block the ocean breeze with his own body. "Here, use me as a heater." He whispered, his chin resting on my shoulder as he pressed his cheek to mine and wrapped me up against his chest as tightly as he could.

"Tonight was really nice, you know," I said, almost tempted to tell him about California at that moment. Warning him meant having a conversation I wasn't ready to have.

"It was fucking perfect," He hummed, voice low and rough sending shivers down my spine. He pressed a simple kiss to my jaw, his arms squeezing me tightly.

"You spoil a girl," I sighed, "How are you supposed to top letting me drive your ridiculously expensive car and a nightcap under the stars?"

"I'm sure I can think of a few things," he said and pressed a kiss to my neck.

"Oh yeah? Like what?" I pushed a little, my adrenaline was still pumping from the ride, and it was making me a little reckless. But I liked the way his hands felt around me and his mouth on my skin making every inch a little warmer than before.

"You really want me to list them all right here?" His voice dropped even lower, more intimate as his lips trailed over my shoulder, pushing the strap of my tank top out of his way. "Because I can think of some things that might involve this night having a few choice moments that aren't so wholesome."

I tilted my head back to look at him, catching his gaze and smirking, "who's around to tell us no?" I baited, wrapping my arms around him.

Jensen let out a low, husky laugh and his hands moved to grip my hips more firmly. He pulled me even closer, so there's no mistaking the heat pouring between us. "Exactly my point," he murmured against my skin, his lips finding that sensitive spot just below my ear.

"Who's the scaredy cat now?" I challenged, giggling from the feeling of his mouth on my neck.

He shook his head, his hands rough as he spun me around and gave my ass a squeeze as I slotted between his legs. "Oh, I'm not scared, Adeline. I was just trying to be a gentleman out here under the stars." His voice turned teasing and his fingers dug deliberately into my skin.

"The stars make a good audience." I pushed up onto my toes, wrapping my arms around his neck, brushing my fingers into his hair.

His dark eyes flashed with amusement and desire, his hands automatically moving to grip my thighs and pulling me up against him. "Is that so?" he challenged, his face inches from mine as he knowingly teased me. "What exactly do you want an audience of stars for, Adeline?"

"That list you're withholding. The not so wholesome one." I kissed his jaw and then his throat, working my way across whatever skin I could get my mouth on. He let out a low groan, his grip on my thighs tightening as he pressed me against him. My lips trailed down his neck and his chest rumbled with approval.

"You know what you're doing, don't you?" He managed to say, his voice tight with distraction.

"Is it working?" The words are muffled as I kiss the space where his neck meets his shoulder.

"Of course it's fucking working," he groaned, his head falling back as he gave me better access. One hand moved to tangle in my hair, holding me against him while the other found a handful of ass to pull me even tighter against his hips. I pulled at the back of his shirt, leaning away only enough for him to pull it over his head in a rough tug.

"Thank you," I whispered, returning to my job of running my tongue and teeth against every line of ink that marked his skin. Jensen let out a shaky breath, his fingers tightening as I explored his chest and abs with my mouth. His whole body is hardened, tense from the touch barely keeping himself together when I hit a sensitive spot on his rib cage.

"Fuck, are you sure?" He managed to say. I don't respond with words, my fingers finding the button of his jeans and popping it free without trouble as I focused on trailing lower with my mouth.

His breath caught sharply as my finger worked it open, his abs tensing under a long swipe of my tongue. His head is tossed backwards and I could tell he was fighting against his own urge to take control of the situation. "You're really going to do this out here?" He asked, nervousness laced in his voice.

Nearly on my knees, I hummed against his skin. Kissing just above the thin trail of hair leading into his boxers as my fingers rake down over his stomach. His hips jerked slightly at the feeling of my purr against his skin and my fingers trailing behind over his abs. His hand gripping the edge of the car so hard his knuckles were white in the dim light.

"You're killing me Adeline," he managed to say.

"Do you want me to stop?" I licked a stripe upward, tilting my chin so it rested against the bare skin of his lower stomach, and watched him with a wide, mischievous smile.

His eyes locked with mine, dark and wanting as his mouth curled into a lopsided smirk, "Hell no," the answer came out a growl. "Don't you dare fucking stop." I liked the unhinged side of him as he leaned back to support himself on the hood of the car and his other hand slid down to cup my jaw.

I smiled at this touch, reveling in the idea that he's been caught off guard and enjoying how unbalanced he was about the situation. I waited a second longer, giving him the option to back out, but he just watched me, his thumb brushing over my bottom lip with a smug look on his face.

I hooked my finger into the band of jeans, and he lifted just enough to allow me to roll the jeans away from his hips. My tongue wet my bottom lip at the sight of him straining against the fabric of his boxers. I leaned forward, looking up at him and his breath hitched as I exposed him, his eyes never leaving mine.

His grip on my chin tightened as he fought against his control, no doubt hating how little power he had in the situation. I inhaled slowly, preparing myself as he popped free. It didn't matter how many times I'd seen it, *felt it*, I always got giddy at the sheer size of the man. It made my mouth dry, and for a split second I was nervous I had bitten off more than I could chew.

Jensen grinned, knowing exactly what was going through my head as he pushed forward slightly, giving me better access. His cock, long and hard sitting slightly upward begging to be touched. I parted my lips and watched as his entire body reacted in a wicked shudder. Taking him into my mouth with small teasing strokes at first, feeling his body vibrate against mine as my tongue pulled long slow lines to the inside of his shaft.

Jensen's head fell back, a loud groan escaping him as I sucked more of his length between my lips. His fingers tightened painfully, guiding the pace but careful not to be too rough. "Fuck," he whispered, his hips moved in time with my movement, "you feel so good Adeline," he choked out.

With each suck and lick I could feel him slowly coming undone as I smiled around the base of his dick taking him into my mouth full with pride. It was intoxicating to see him fall apart with such ease. His hips jerked sharply at the sensation, being reduced to nothing but a needy, growling mess. Jensen's fingers curled tighter as my teeth grazed the underside of his cock.

"Adeline," he breathed out my name softly.

"Mhmm?" I hummed, mouth full of him and unable to answer his plea for relief. I tilted my head up and his eyes met mine briefly before rolling back as I took him even deeper. He throbbed against my tongue, contracting against the walls of my mouth as he crawled closer to his release.

"The sight of you on your knees—" his words were cut short with the swirl of my tongue, batting my lashes at him as my eyes watered. "You have to stop—" He begged. Unfortunately for him, the sound of his pleading only made me work harder, relaxing completely to take him against the back of my throat. His eyes widened as I took him in, hips bucking forward involuntarily.

"*Baby*," he growled, "seriously... stop," His fingers curled. I only pulled back because he forced me too, his hand in my hair demanding obedience.

I licked my lips sitting back on my knees. The gravel and dirt dug into my skin but looking up at Jensen, leaning over his car was a treat that made the annoyance stinging worth it. He was shirtless and breathless, his tattoos and scars bathed in the dimmest shade of blue from the moon. It was ethereal.

Jensen's chest heaved with each breath, his cock painfully hard as he took in every small movement I made. "I swear to fucking—"

"What?" The question came out a purr.

His eyes snapped to mine, clenching from the innocence of my question and the knowing smirk on my reddened lips.

"If you keep looking at me like that, sitting there like a wet dream. I'm going to lose it." He pushed off the car to hover over me, his hand brushing beneath my chin, ending with a tight squeeze that made my thighs clench together.

"You lose it?" I teased leaning into his grip. "Never."

"You're pushing your luck," he warned.

"Prove it." I pushed to my feet.

The request of being fucked under the stars on the hood of his extremely nice car went unsaid between us as he closed the gap between us. It was obvious what I wanted, my thighs tight, my chest heaving slightly, waiting for him to make the move. I felt more free with Jensen than I ever had in my entire life, seen, touched, held... loved. It was crazy, but I knew I could do anything, no matter how insane simply because of the way he was looking at me at that moment.

Jensen's hand moved from my chin, slowly sliding down my neck, over my collarbone and down over the swell of my breast in my tank top. I could see in his eyes that I'd won, he was just trying to figure out how to make it seem like I hadn't. "You want me to fuck you right here? Under the stars?"

"Please," I asked so politely, watching his face contort into amusement given how stingy I had been earlier.

"Oh we're doing that," he chuckled darkly, his fingers splaying out over my stomach possessively. "Say please again," he murmured, eyes locking onto mine daring me to beg. "Please what?" He prompted, his voice husky.

"*Please*, fuck me on the hood of your sports car under the stars, Jensen." I said dramatically as my gaze flickered up to him, the stars reflecting back in his eyes as a wicked grin formed on his face.

His hand slid to grip my throat gently as he turned me and backed me up against the car. "You're so polite when you want something," he hummed, his fingers quickly finding the condom he had to keep replacing in his wallet, rolling it over his head before wrapping his hand around his hardened shaft and pumping it slowly.

Without pause or even argument against his statement, I pushed my pants over my hips and tossed them away with his shirt. "I know how to get what I want," I whispered, leaning back against the car.

Jensen's eyes darkened as he watched me, spreading my legs slightly, inviting him to step forward and open them wider. "Spoiled," he teased, gripping his dick and dragging it upward between my thighs to brush against my sensitive clothed core.

"You created this monster," I giggled breathlessly as he ushered my underwear aside.

"You're a little brat," he said, rubbing the blunt head of his length against me teasingly. I could feel the cool metal beneath my back and the warmth of his skin against mine, the soft starlit sky above and the ocean crashing against the rocks below. "Is this what you want?" He smirked, sliding the tip of his cock against my wet entrance before abruptly pushing inside me; hard and deep. One hand stayed on my throat while the other gripped my hip to keep me steady on the car.

My head fell back at the sudden intrusion, a spark of heat igniting at the base and coursing through my system as he rolled his hips into mine. Jensen had zero control, he rocked into me mercilessly, the car hood creaking under our weight as he held me in place. His fingers tightened around my throat, gently coaxing my head back further, exposing my neck.

"Look at the stars," he whispered, his breath hot against my ear.

They shone so brightly that for a second I forgot that we were entirely alone. "Fuck," I gasped, as he wrapped his arm around my back and lifted my hips up changing the angle he was thrusting from. Jensen had figured out every curve and corner of my body, knowing exactly where to hit and stroke to drag such needy moans from my lips.

"You look so pretty like this—" he pulled all the way out and slammed into me again, tickling all the sensitive nerves inside of me. "Spread out under the stars just for me." He continued to thrust into me, his pace returning to a brutal speed. The sound of his hips slapping against my skin echoed across the coast line.

I was going to lose myself soon, I could feel the cord tightening within my stomach and it was harder to keep my eyes open than ever before.

"Keep your eyes open, Adeline," he ordered, noticing the struggle as the pleasure racked through me. "Watch the fucking stars and come all over my dick." He reached between my legs and started pressing hard circles into my clit, knowing exactly how to push me over the edge. His other hand grabbed at the collar of my tank top exposing the tops of my breast as my nipples slipped from my bra and pushed me into the hood just enough to keep himself balanced. "Now," he snapped, "come now."

I never stood a chance against the tone in his voice as he ordered the orgasm from me. My body was writhing beneath him in pleasure, my thighs clenched tightly and my hands scrambling for purchase on his tense biceps. His body responded to mine convulsing around his shaft as his name fell from my lips over and over. Jensen buried himself deep inside, letting out a low guttural groan as his body flexed and he ground out his own release.

"You win," I gasped out, the pleasure still tickling at every nerve ending. "That will always be better than driving fast..." A smug grin formed on my face when he started to laugh, leaning down to press a kiss to my lips as he pulled out of me.

He disposed of the condom, returning to help me sit up on the hood, his hands lingering on my hips. "You're the most perfect girl," he praised, kissing my cheek softly below my eye as it fluttered close. His hand brushed a few loose, sweaty strands of hair away from my face.

The words were there, on the tip of my tongue, and I almost said them simply because of how beautiful he looked. His cheeks were flushed, his chest heaving with labored breaths as he came down from his high. How was I ever supposed to leave this behind? The feeling caught in my throat as I pushed a smile to my face.

"I know," I said instead with a giggle as he bombarded me with punishment in the form of more kisses.

JENSEN

> **A present**

We had gotten the photos back from the photographer for the new calendar, and the shot of Van and I was insanely embarrassing, but Adeline would die for it. Van hung over me with two water bottles squirting it into my upturned mouth, both of us drenched in water and covered in sand.

> **I'm printing this and hanging it on my wall.**

> **Don't you dare.**

"Mom?" I dropped my baseball bag at the front door, shoving my phone away and wandered through the house exhausted from the midday practice before tomorrow's series started. It was going to be one of the hardest ones we'd have to play this season, but we all believed that if we overcame this, pulled out a series win. The rest of the playoffs would be a wash.

"Here!" Mom yelled, from somewhere in the house.

"You know this house is too big if I can't find you after searching three rooms," I said, finding her on the floor in her office surrounded by paperwork and two open laptops. "What are you doing?"

"Running a billion-dollar hotel franchise, Kai," she grumbled, flipping over her phone when it started to ring.

"Not important?" I asked, lowering to the ground, being careful to avoid all her work, and sitting with her. I'd spent years of my childhood doing my schoolwork on the floors of hotels and offices across from her while she ran her business. It had always been our time together.

"Not more important than you," she said, looking up from her work. "Shouldn't you be at physio?" She asked, brushing her hands through her hair.

"Doc moved me around to make space for Josh before tomorrow's game. I'm low priority," I responded with a soft smile.

"Your knee hasn't been sore?" She asked like I knew she would. I shook my head and it was the truth. Three years ago I hurt it playing recreation hockey and it never healed properly. We only did therapy to keep it loose for ball.

"What's with the small talk?" I tapped her foot with mine.

"I can't ask my son normal questions now?" She tilted her head to the side.

"When have you ever?" I laughed leaning back on my arms.

"Don't give me attitude boy," she scolded with a soft laugh. "I should be asking you what's with the impromptu visit."

"I can't visit my mom now?" I countered and she threw a pen at me. "Alright, alright. I need to hash something out."

"I feel used," Mom smiled but rose off the floor to grab an old notebook from the top drawer of her desk. "We haven't pulled this out in a while." She waved it at me and sank back to the carpet. Mom's approach to a problem was always logic, while Dad was the guy I went to when I wanted a yes or some good old toxic positivity.

"Last time was when I had to make a decision about what I wanted to play," I said.

"Hockey or baseball," she said, flipping it open. "I'm glad it was baseball, hockey gear stinks and you always have such a lovely tan."

"Okay, this time it's a little more serious than a tan," I sighed.

"Is this about the very pretty, very intelligent girl you brought into my house last Sunday?" Mom scribbled across the top of the page.

"You can't write stuff until I tell you the problem," I scoffed and she just raised an eyebrow at me. "I mean it is about her but..."

"If you're just about finished tip-toeing around the conversation..." she teased. "What's wrong?"

"I like her." I shrugged and it caused her to laugh.

"Is that all?" She teased.

"Come on, Mom," I wet my bottom lip. "I mean like it started because she's hot—"

"Malachi," she huffed.

"It's true, you've seen her..."

"Choose a different adjective," she said calmly and went back to writing notes.

"She's beautiful," I said, my tone softening and not my choice, it was something that happened when I allowed myself to think about her like that. Beautiful was correct but it was a heavy word in my mind associated with heavy feelings. "We were having fun, we're supposed to be having fun."

"You brought your... booty call to my house?" Mom looked up at me and I threw my hands up in surrender. "You are not my child." She rolled her eyes at me. "I disown you," she joked.

"It *started* like that," I reminded her. "I think we both know it's not that anymore considering I'm sitting on your floor."

"So what is the problem, because all I'm hearing is you're toying with a very beautiful, incredibly intelligent girl's heart and if that's the case, I'm closing this notebook and beating you over the head with it," she said, and that time she wasn't joking.

"Keep writing," I laughed, scooting back on the carpet. "She plays rugby and she's good Mom, *really* good. It's almost scary how natural she is at it."

"More problems, less compliments, Kai." Mom rolled her hand in a circular motion to hurry me up with an annoying smirk on her face.

"The problem is she got scouted, for another professional team."

Mom looked up at me finally and the humor faded away. I wasn't stupid and the reason I wasn't was because neither was she. We both knew what that meant and I watched as she put together the pieces of my crumbling heart. Up to that point I hadn't been brave enough to say it out loud, silently sleeping with it to try to get over the sting of her possibly leaving but telling my Mom. The look on her face. No glue, cement or nails could hold me together anymore.

I loved Adeline Sarah, and I would be an idiot if I ignored it any longer.

"So your problem is, your casual fling—" Mom rolled the words off her tongue and they hit me like a dagger. "—Is traded out of Harbor."

"That casual fling is going to fly out of Rhode Island with my heart in her back pocket." I dropped my head to stare at my hands.

"It sounds like you've already come up with a solution," Mom said after a long beat and I looked up at her confused. I had definitely not solved anything... *what the fuck was she on about?* "Letting her go, being sad about it and not doing anything to stop it."

Oh, "Sarcasm, thanks Mom." I sighed.

"Malachi, over the course of your life you have never quit anything without a serious conversation and this notebook." She held it up, "it's got notes in it all the way back from kindergarten when you decided that soccer wasn't the sport for you. It took us two weeks to decide that you wanted to quit."

"This is different," I said.

"Exactly, and whoever is sitting in front of me right now is not my son. Because he would never just give up on something because it was too hard." Mom pushed. "What are the pros of her leaving?"

I swallowed down the urge to argue, "She's been working toward this for her entire career, it's all she's wanted. It's her dream."

"And cons?"

"It means I'm not," my tone was heavy and cold. I was upset but not with Mom, with my own foolish heart for getting us into an impossible situation.

"Give me a real con and stop being dramatic." Her smile was soft and encouraging.

"It's in California," I said and ran my hand through my hair.

"Long-distance relationships can work, Kai. They do all the time," she was quick to swoop in with an answer. The issue was, we couldn't do long distance. Even now my fingers were tingling, absolutely itching to get my hands on her. It had been less than twenty-four hours since I saw her last and all I wanted to do was be close to her. Facetime and weekend visits would be hell.

"Not for us," I said because I knew.

Mom didn't flinch at the conviction, her dark eyes watching me carefully before she spoke again, "I need you to be very honest with me for a second," she said and I didn't even blink, my entire body stilled. "Do you love her?"

I didn't say a word, saying them out loud would make them real, true... tangible. Right now they were just words bouncing around in my mind like a rogue tennis ball. But they were honest, raw and honest. Fear wasn't an emotion I experienced often, I just found the adrenaline in every scary situation, but to love someone? That was fucking terrifying.

"You know what you need to do," Mom said after a beat.

There were unspoken ideas ricocheting around us.

"I can't just leave," I said after mulling on it for a while.

"Why not?" Mom chuckled. "You're taking one class a semester to play baseball, maybe it's time you graduate for real and find a new thing to *love*."

"Aren't Mom's supposed to warn their sons against chasing girls across the country or something?" I said, prompting her to give me a reason for why I was being dumb and reckless.

"None of this," she looked around at the office, "would exist if your father had listened to his mother when she told him exactly that. He followed after me because I knew my dream, and I knew how to get my hands on it. There's nothing wrong with your dream being Adeline. You've never been one for staying put in anything, you love what you love, and I'm proud to say that you love with everything you have." She set the notebook down. "Look at your time with the Hornets. You only had one reason to take more classes this year and it was simply because you loved playing with them. It had nothing to do with baseball. You just wanted to be around your friends."

There's nothing wrong with your dream being Adeline.

"What the hell would I do in California?" I laughed, it was ridiculous to even be entertaining the idea. Mom looked around at her office with a bewildered look on her face. "Oh, yeah. Right..." The new hotel in San Francisco. It had always been the plan to follow her into the business, it wasn't exactly my dream to wear a suit every day but I knew the ins and outs and had more degrees than I needed to be qualified to do it.

"You're too smart to be this slow, Kai." She smiled, leaning forward to pat my face with her hand. "You're looking at the situation like it's the end all, but it's not. Nothing in life is that serious unless you make it so."

"I'm serious about this Mom." I said, practically cutting her off.

"Then do something about it." She nodded and I knew that was the end of the conversation.

SARAH

"Do you think they'll actually show?" Rhea shimmied into her shorts, pulling them over her spanx and adjusting them around her thighs. Her dark hair was pulled back into two messy buns on the side of her head. Game days were her favorite, and it was easy to tell by the way her eyes sparkled.

"Jensen takes his bets pretty seriously," I said, tying my cleat in a double knot. "We should be more worried about this team today. The Jags aren't messing around."

"Tenzie is back—"

"Wasn't she suspended for metal cleats?" Sunday was braiding Kaia's hair into two neat rows beside me.

"Kenna has the scars to prove it," Kaia added. "Just watch each other's backs and if she tries anything shady we deal with her."

"Your definition of dealing with her will end up with you in jail so just be vocal about the misconduct if it rises and let Cosy handle it." I warned her and Kaia rolled her eyes. "I mean it."

"I heard you," Kaia patted Sunday on the thigh and stood up rolling out her shoulders in her jersey.

"You hearing me and you listening are two different things, Kaia." I stand up, shaking out my legs to fix the creases in my shorts as I tighten my ponytail. She watched me carefully as I cocked my head to the side. "Today is going to be hard, don't get hurt. Please."

"Don't give me those puppy dog eyes, Minty. It's illegal," Kaia said, shaking her head and looking away from me.

"You forced my hand," I said, I was only trying to keep her upright and out of trouble for as long as I could, "promise me." I poked.

"You are a thief of joy," she said but shook my hand, rolling our palms together in a smooth movement that linked our pinky's tightly. "I promise..." she started to back away and I instantly knew what was coming out of her mouth, "to never die..." she changed her words at the last second and went running from the locker room.

"You can't *Team America* me and run away, Kaia!" I called after her, and we all flooded from the cramped locker room onto the pitch. The bleachers were vibrating with energy that matched the rapid rate of my heartbeat.

Kaia was already chatting with Coach as we lined the side of the pitch and started to warm up. I knew that she was amped about today, it was going to cause trouble if she wasn't able to reel it in but I always knew she spotted my new agent in the stands and she'd do anything for me.

I stepped onto the field with the team, following through the warm-ups with Sunday at my side while she remained with her head in the clouds. She lost her balance once or twice during her scoop stretch and ended up on the ground laughing as I hauled her to her feet.

"Oh my god," she said, her eyes widening at something over my shoulder. "They came."

I turned on my heel as the rest of the team flanked us in awe. Not only had Jensen managed to get nearly the entire Hornet's team to join him but he had several of the Hogs in toe, including both Black brothers and Loveday, all three shirtless and painted head to toes in Hillcats colours.

The Hornets team wore similar getups, using their gifted rugby jerseys as bandanas or armbands. Every single one of them was sporting either a letter of the Hillcats name painted in bright orange on their bare chests, or a number that corresponded with a player. Ella was carrying a box and one by one the guys pulled out Pom poms that looked roughly handmade and lopsided.

She gave me a little wave as Arlo laid out a blanket for her on the bleachers, giving her a hand up and leaning against the side with a disinterested expression on his face. Brighton was talking to Judd both wearing backwards Hillcats hats, their array of tattoos peaking out beneath the blue body paint as Boone helped the guys line up to spell Hillcats correctly.

"Are they missing an L?" Cosy sounded confused.

"No it's Arlo," I said, pointing to him still standing with Ella. The chaos of the situation combined with one two many naked men was drawing the attention from both sides of the field. They might actually turn out to be a good distraction as long as it was the other team they were disturbing.

"Boone's been working out." Rhea's head tilted to the side.

"He stopped drinking," Kaia said, "It's annoying." It meant that he wasn't as fun, at least not when she needed him to be, in those dark moments when she just needed a clown.

I didn't care about any of them though, because Jensen was staring at me with a goofy look on his face and Hillcats bandana wrapped around his neck. He was painted with my number and gave me a wink before turning back to his team.

"Why are they in a huddle?" Cosy asked nervously.

"That can't be good," Sunday said.

"Ladies, time to play a game!" Coach interrupted before we had the chance with a clap of her hands. The Jaguars had brought a crowd of their own and before long the bleachers were alive with noise which felt intense with pressure as the game began.

The ball came off Sunday's boot and ripped through the air as Kaia surged through her attacker toward it. It bounced wildly, tipping to the right and staying in bounds but slipping between the fingers of the chaser.

The action caused the Jaguar to miss the ball completely and allowed Kaia to wrap herself around it, flipping the play and stealing the ball. Rhea wasn't far behind and took up her flank, clearing the left side so she could get a few uncontested yards before being thrown to the ground.

Kaia pushed the ball out, her body covered by the attacker and a struggling Cosy who was fighting against their props unassisted until Megan flew in to help from around the right side. Sunday scooped up the ball in record time, her legs moving faster than the attacker as she goose-stepped to the right, surging forward into open field with Rhea and myself on her tail to assist.

"Sunny!" Rhea called out. The ball popped out and flung back into her arms roughly as Sunday was tangled up around the waist and spun out of the play. The next two attackers took on Rhea from either side, smart enough to know that if they tried it alone they'd never take her down and if they missed their chance she would be gone. But Rhea was smarter than both of them, waiting until the last possible second to push the ball out, sending it flying through the air like a torpedo into my arms as Kaia bulldozed her way across the field behind me to have my flank.

The girl that got loose to follow me was fast, but she wasn't as fast as me. She surged forward trying to get her fingers around my jersey, but I kicked out my leg and darted from her grasp before she could get purchase. I felt the other chaser on my right and pushed a little harder, flinging myself over the line just short of middle and scored the first try of the game.

The home crowd erupted into cheers, the Hornet's doing a very sloppy coordinated chant that was completely inaudible. Kaia wrapped her arm around my middle in a lazy, out of breath full body high five before letting me take the ball back to center.

Cosy was standing lopsided ahead of me and I could see the bruise starting to form on her bicep from being stepped on. "You alright?"

"Beauty run, Minty." She said, not answering my question. Cosy was our team mom, she always had been, always stuffing down her own pain to put on a smile for us. I scanned over her again, finding no blood but knew that Tenzie was playing dirty from the way she was smiling in line across from me.

She was a beast, a solid hundred and eighty pounds of anger that she took out on anyone she could. Luckily she was slow and the only time she got her hands on any of the smaller players is when we made a mistake.

"Play clean, play fast!" Cosy yelled, reading my mind as the ball was kicked, wasting no time putting us back in motion. The game became chippy after Sunday scored a third try with another conversion bringing the game to a tie. It was more of a fight than we'd ever expected.

I carried the ball, checking over my shoulder for help but Rhea was too far behind and caught up with another body when I collided with Tenzie. Her arms wrapped around my legs, pushing me off the ground a solid two feet before Cosy came up behind me to support the huddle and shove her back a step into her own player. I tried to chuck the ball to Kaia the moment I saw her but Tenzie had other plans, she loosened the hold causing me to fall backwards unbalanced and hit the ground. Cosy tried to move in for coverage but her cleat was already ripping the skin of my inner thigh.

Screaming out I yanked as hard as I could to pop the ball free and push it out on the ground for Kaia who grabbed it quickly and took off as fast as she could through the break. Cosy followed, only doing her job as Tenzie ripped away from me and I rolled clumsily off the ground to get back into the action.

I could feel the blood pooling down my thigh as I forced my body to ignore the searing pain and caught up to the action just in time to see Kaia score.

"Looks like you need a sub, Sarah!" She called to me, jogging backwards with a smug look on her face.

"Yeah fuck you, Tenzie!" I hollered at her, pulling my shorts down over the wicked scratches left behind by her cleats, hissing as the fabric made contact and hiding it as best I could from Coach. We had one half left in the game, there was no way I was being taken out.

The girls huddled together, passing water around when Kaia's eyes landed on the smudge of blood and dirt between my legs. "My eyes are up here, Killer." I joked with her but she had the look of murder in her eyes.

"Was it her?" She snapped over the sound of Coach talking us through what needed to happen to hold our lead. "I'm going to fucking kill that bitch."

"Later," Rhea said, her voice more commanding than normal. "First we win, Minty has eyes on her, we can't turn this match into a bloodbath."

"What we can't do is let that ogre get away with playing dirty," Kaia argued, her knuckles white as it tangled into the side of my jersey.

"Beat her above the board and we'll slash her tires in the parking lot later," Rhea yanked gently on one of Kaia's braids making her look at her. "We'll make her pay, I promise."

Rhea was the only one good for it. Kaia knew that, if Rhea made a promise. No matter how ridiculous, or sometimes even illegal, she was the first to sign up for trouble and always followed through.

"Okay don't make us all complicit in your crimes please?" Cosy furrowed a brow as she whispered.

Once the second half started the blood kept spilling. Tenzie was on me constantly, leaving me very little room to do anything besides push the ball out to the next set of hands. I spent more time on the ground than I had all last season, and my body was starting to feel the effects of the abuse. I got up off the ground as Rhea pushed her way over the try line. Coach was trying to get me to come in off the field but the game had two minutes left and I wasn't giving up just because she was trying to put me down. We were up, but it wasn't enough. There was still time for them to tie the game and we couldn't let that happen.

"Run a chicken," I yelled out. It was a play we did to distract the opposition and create holes, it didn't work often but it would work now because they were so hyper-focused on putting me in the dirt.

Sunday stepped up to my side as the kick was made and like lightning crashing the adrenaline exploded under my skin. I took off as fast as I could, pushing those sore muscles to their limit to collect the ball before it hit the ground. Pocketing it I sidestepped out of the attackers grasp and took off into the empty pocket left by Tenzie who had been distracted by Sunday for a damning split second.

The crowd was on fire as I walked the ball to center and tapped it on the ground, kneeling down with it between my legs to catch my breath. The new minted cheerleading squad were dog piled screaming and cheering, paint smudged across their chests and smiles bright as they screamed.

"If that didn't impress your agent, I don't know what will." Kaia stepped toward me and helped me off the ground. "Put that ball through the posts and let's get drunk."

JENSEN

"I don't think I'll ever get used to the bruises," I said, opening her apartment door for her as she carefully navigated herself. She was keeping her weight off her bandaged thigh, and from what I could tell, it was starting to bleed through again. I had offered her the sweats in the back of the car, helping her slip into them after the game and dramatically carried her up the path to the elevator while she protested that she could walk just fine.

Kaia had argued against the rescue mission from the locker room, trying to get Adeline to go to the Hollow to celebrate, but I hadn't seen her one on one for nearly four days and I was taking what I wanted. Kaia could fight me later about it.

"How about a bath?" I asked her as I set her duffle on the island. She stripped from hoodie with a tiny hiss but nodded. "Stay, don't get anymore naked." I warned as I backed away to her bathroom. I ran the water hotter than I could stand but she'd still complain it was cold.

When I got back to her she was downing a shot of whiskey with a pained look on her face in her sports bra. "I am unbelievably sore," she said, pouring another. "I'm bringing this with me," she declared as I knelt in front of her to help her from her shoes and sweatpants. Her legs were a mess with fresh, glaringly sore bruises that ranged in shades of purple. It took a second but in a feeble attempt to keep it painless I pulled back the ruined bandage to expose the nasty imprint in her skin.

"You can do whatever you want after that performance." I kissed her tattoo, grateful that it was her other thigh that had suffered the attack. The paint on my arms and chest had dried painfully and my entire body was itchy as I moved to get her out of her spanks and bra. I scooped her off the ground, carrying her to the bathroom and lowered her into the tub.

She slid forward without a word, setting the bottle on the edge of the tub but I shook my head. "I'll turn the water blue," I laughed but she pouted at me and it was enough to have me stripping from my sweater. The water was too hot but I stifled the groan as I sank down behind her.

As predicted, it turned a murky color but she didn't even notice as she snuggled back against my chest and closed her eyes. The apartment was quiet except for the soft sounds of our breathing tangled together for a long while. If she was finding relief I didn't want to bother her, I was content to just wrap my arms around her chest and hold her close.

"How's your thigh?" I asked her after a while.

"It'll be fine," she mumbled. She sounded less tense than before which helped me to relax a little more against the back of the tub. Every second spent with her was a blessing, I'd never thought it was even possible to feel so attached to another person the way I had become with Adeline. "I have to talk to you about something." I felt her stiffen and knew what was coming.

"Please don't break up with me in a bathtub full of blue water when I have a semi..." I chuckled but my heart was racing like a horse. Adeline looked up at me and shook her head.

"I'm not breaking up with you," she scowled but I could hear the tiny laugh leave her throat. "Why do you think I'm breaking up with you?" Her voice strained with hurt at the end and suddenly I felt like an asshole for assuming.

"Talking is usually a bad sign," I said, pushing a few pieces of her hair away from her face and cupping her cheek as she stared up at me.

"It's not that—" She stopped, inhaling a long breath before talking again. "I'm being traded to a team in San Francisco."

It took everything in me not to say *I know.*

"Hey, that's incredible." I did what I could to keep my voice cracking under the sadness I felt trying to be happy. "I'm proud of you. This is big."

Leave it to me to fall in love with a girl moving across the country.

"Yeah," she said quietly, confusion lacing her tone. "It's pretty crazy..." she slowed down, "how come you aren't upset?" She asked bluntly.

"It's your dream, I'm never going to be upset about you getting to live it." I swallowed the urge to tell her I loved her and her leaving was going to kill me.

"Even if I have to leave? California isn't close," she reminded me like I didn't know.

"I'm aware of the geography of the United States, Belle. The thing is since the day I met you, this has been your life. Rugby is what you want, what you need. I'm not going to stop you from chasing that dream." I said to her, each word chipping away another piece of my heart. She stared at me blankly and for the life of me I couldn't figure out what was going on in her pretty little head. "What?" I finally asked after a long stretch of silence.

"I just…" Adeline stopped, her words dying on her lips.

"Want me to be pissed off, angry? Sad?" I said, wetting my bottom lip. "If what you need to hear is that I don't want you to go, it's a lie. Your dreams are important, Adeline, and I'm never going to stand in the way of them, but…"

"But what?" She perked up, and it stung. I didn't want to be the reason she had an excuse to stay. If that's what she was looking for I didn't want to be that guy. The man that stifled, *The* Adeline Sarah.

"But the truth is I am sad," I confessed. "Of course I am. A few months ago I would have laughed in your face if you told me I would be sitting in a tub with the most beautiful girl trying to be a better man."

Her expression softened, "And now?"

"I don't want to be the reason you don't do this, and I'm a big boy. I can be sad and supportive. I'm capable." I explained.

"I don't want this to end," she said, turning in my arms and kneeling between my legs with a soft groan. "There's still a few months left in the season and maybe you can come with me for my trip to meet the team?"

"You don't want to bring Kaia?" I stopped her.

"Distance isn't going to destroy my friendship with Kaia, I want to spend as much time with you as I can before this blows up in my face and I'm reminded I can never have both things." She said with a sadness that stung my vulnerable heart. "I have to sign the papers, finalize everything…"

"You've got me until then," I said, ignoring how much the statement hurt. I wasn't going to spring my solution on her until she asked me. I knew deep down, if Adeline really wanted me in California with her, she'd ask.

JENSEN

Van pulled the truck up to the outdoor paintball facility, and everyone hopped out. I grabbed Adeline by the waist and lowered her to the ground with a kiss to her head.

"I'm excited for today, I wish you told me it was your birthday sooner," she hummed, staring up at the welcome sign. Her hair was loose around her face and her eyes were bright with excitement. After our hard conversation, she had been avoiding the topic altogether while I tried to find a way to keep her in my life a little longer than just the few months she promised.. For now, all I wanted to do was keep that smile on her face at least until I could make a promise I could keep.

"Presents are overrated, I'm just glad you were able to come today," I said, taking her hand and leading her inside. Everyone had come, nearly the entire team and some stragglers. I had told the guys not to bother with a party, with everything going on in the Nest... with Cael. It felt wrong to be out enjoying ourselves. But Arlo had delivered word from Cael that if we didn't do something he'd risk recovery and bolt from the hospital to make sure it happened himself.

"Wouldn't miss it for the world." She stayed in step with me, and I got her a pair of coveralls and got her suited up with a paintball gun. I watched her tug her long dark hair into a low ponytail before she stepped into the coveralls. "I've never played paintball before," she said looking nervous.

I stepped forward, reaching down to take the zipper from her, "don't worry," I lowered my voice as I pulled it over her chest to her collar while she locked her big hazel eyes on me. Getting her more dressed went against every fiber of our relationship, but at least I could have some fun with it. "I'll talk you through it." I whispered.

"What a gentleman," she giggled.

"Don't let him sweet-talk you," Van said, tying a bandanna over his mullet. "Out there..." he looked through the dirty glass window to the vast field behind the shitty brick building we were standing in. "Loyalty means nothing to him."

"Seriously?" Adeline looked between the two of us with that same infectious smile on her face.

"Last year I had twenty-two bruises coming out of this," Dean said, from behind us. "They were all from him."

"You were just going to send me out there without telling me you're a professional?" Adeline scoffed.

"They're just messing around," I tried to lie. The truth was, I loved paintball. The rush of running around, hiding, winning. It was my favorite thing to do for my birthday. I was just lucky that the guys always indulged me.

"We are not," Dean argued. "Just watch your back, he'll do anything to win."

"Even if it means taking out the rookie," Arlo added as he fixed Ella's goggles on her face.

"If you guys are finished putting the fear of god into my girlfriend, can we play?" I asked, zipping up my own coveralls and scooping my gun to get onto the field.

"Losing team buys dinner," Ella said, walking past me as I held the door open. "And we're drawing captains, you aren't cheating," she said, patting my chest gently.

"I don't cheat." I rolled my eyes as everyone else passed through the door into the field.

"Yes you do." Van slapped my cheek, "We just let it slide because you're an only child and it's easier to let it go then fight you on it."

"Wow, alright..." I shook my head and followed them to where Dean was already tossing names into his phone to randomly draw.

"Don't worry you won't get picked last," I pressed my chest to Adeline's back and whispered in her ear.

"Arlo and... Van." He said, jogging back to toss his phone away.

I waited as the two of them looked over the roster of people available, knowing one of them would pick me first—

"Addy," Arlo said, cutting off my thoughts.

"Don't worry." She turned to me with a wicked smile that begged to be kissed off her perfect face. "You won't get picked last."

"Ha, ha."

She was wrong though, and as if they were trying to fuck with my head, I was in fact picked last. Van begrudgingly took me after Arlo stole Baker. Now we were on opposite teams, and I hated that. It felt like a cruel joke.

"Don't you go easy on me," Adeline said, shifting on her feet between Arlo and Dean. She looked oddly tiny between the two, and for a split second I was genuinely worried that today might have been a bad idea.

"Wouldn't dream of it," I winked.

"Lover boy," Van snapped at me, "get your head out of your ass and pay attention," He called me over to where he, Ella, Silas, Todd, Mattheson and Josh stood. Our team wasn't horrible. Ella would outlast most of Arlo's team. It was Dean that would stand in our way.

"We have to take out Deano first," Van said like he was reading my mind. Josh grumbled.

"If we lose because you can't shoot your boyfriend, I'll take you out right now," Ella teased him, pointing her gun at his boot.

"I know how to win, just don't hit him in the face…" Josh said, looking over his shoulder.

"No promises." Van shrugged and laughed when Josh's expression went dark.

"We have the terminator on our team this year, there's no reason for us to lose." Silas was tugging at the straps on his knee guards as he spoke. "I'm not paying for dinner, *again*." He said, straightening out.

"Take it easy on Adeline, it's her first time," I said to them and they all nodded in agreement.

The fifteen-second horn sounded and sent us all scattering for cover, the start horn would follow and no one would be safe until there was only one person left standing. The giant field was covered in patches of long grass and areas of pure dirt or mud, the perfect landscape for all the haphazardly placed junk cars, two large broken down buses and about a dozen structures either recycled or built out of wood. We had been coming here for years, nothing like a little team building that allowed the veterans to get their frustrations out on some rookies.

The first year I was allowed to come they thought they had me cornered and I ended up taking down Arlo, Nick and Silas by myself. Since then whenever we did birthday stuff I picked paint balling. Everyone enjoyed it and I loved the ego boost that came with knowing how good I was.

The horn echoed through the air and the sound of shuffling feet was the only thing that filled the remaining silence. It didn't take long for the first crack of shots being fired to pop out into the sky loudly as I circled one of the destroyed cars to the left side of the field. They had changed the layout a bit but if I was right, Arlo was stashed up inside the tree house. The ladder was squeaky, making it nearly impossible to sneak up on him, but there was a stack of boxes near it piled just high enough to get a decent vantage point on him.

I flipped my gun over in my hand and used the other to hoist myself up on the boxes. I needed to be quick, or someone else would take me out before I even eliminated Arlo. I shuffled across the top of the box, pulling up my gun and staring down the scope, and within seconds a head full of dark hair popped up in my sights. He crouched, turning his back to the window for a fraction of a second. Just enough time for me to pull the trigger.

"Fuck you!" He called out, making noise. "He's over here!" He shot off his gun a few times in the air, standing up straight to get sight of me. "You're a dead man, Jenny."

"If they can catch me," I hopped down off the box into the dirt and scurried away through the massive pipe tunnel to my right. Reyes was easy to find because he was stalking Josh and making too much noise. I popped him twice in the back before finding Baker hiding in a cubby off one of the buses.

Ella swore loudly as Dean found her just before she got to Josh, but luckily loyalty meant nothing and Josh took out Dean without remorse.

"Wow!" Dean hollered, "does our love mean nothing to you?!"

"Take your hissy fit off the field," Josh called out running away from the commotion to keep himself safe.

I watched from the bus trying to get sight of Adeline but it meant she was hiding somewhere. Van, Josh, Silas and myself were left on our team. While the others still had Adeline, Louis, and Johnston. We had successfully cleared out all of their most dangerous players.

Unfortunately for Louis, he was loud, he'd never been good at being sneaky and I heard him before he had the chance to sneak up on me. I whirled around and unloaded on his leg, spraying neon pink paint across his coveralls.

"Where's Adeline?" I asked quietly, as he groaned rubbing his leg.

"She broke off from us early," Louis offered in broken English. "I don't know," he huffed. I aimed the gun at him again, teasingly placing my finger on the trigger only enough to make Louis panic a little. "Hey! I said I don't know, Jenny!" His accent was thick as he started to swear at me in French.

"Oh come on Louis, give her up...." I said again but he only shook his head.

Another round of paintballs echoed through the air and seconds later, Silas's voice could be heard across the yard claiming victory over Johnston only to have his announcement cut short with more shots and screaming.

Louis took his window and ran off darting across the field away from me as I took the other exit. I crisscrossed down through some long grass behind one of the broken down trucks following the sound of yelling and gunfire.

When I broke into the clearing Adeline was laying in the grass, her hair covering her face and her hands wrapped around her body. I waited for a second, looking around, but quickly realized she was crying.

"Fuck," I dropped my paintball gun against myself and jogged toward her, "what happened?" I questioned and was met with the consequences of underestimating my girlfriend.

She was fast, her hand whipped out and there was a flash of paint splattered across my chest right above my heart before I could even reach for my gun. My skin stung where the ball exploded but it was numbed by the wicked grin on her face.

"I win," she giggled.

Fuck.

"I thought you said you never played paintball before," I groaned, rubbing my chest from the close contact shot.

"I didn't say I haven't shot a gun," she said, pushing off the ground and cleaning herself off as everyone came out of the woodwork covered in paint. "Besides, we knew that would work." She gave a high five to both Arlo and Dean who had clearly played their roles very well.

"What would work?" I asked.

"Boost your ego, make you think you won…" Arlo explained.

"See your girl injured, you'd act chivalrous and—"

"Bam," Adeline finished Dean's sentence, pressing the barrel of her gun against my chest.

Ella slow clapped, "it was smart. Rude, but smart. I hate losing."

"It was for the greater good, Blondie." Arlo smiled at her and threw his arm over her shoulder.

SARAH

"Are you sure?" I held up the long dark blue dress, it was made of a light, satiny fabric and patterned with the most delicate gold hydrangeas that climbed over the bodice to my right shoulder. I stared at Jensen in the mirror as he rested on my bed giving me his undivided attention.

"It's perfect." His hair was messy from my fingertips an hour before, and he was still half dressed. We should have been on the road already but he had showed up in a sleeveless t-shirt and a pair of shorts that showed off every pumped tanned and tattooed muscle from his workout. I would have had to be a saint to resist him.

"Please tell me you brought the GR?" I said, slipping the dress into a hanger bag as he pulled on his shirt and got off the bed.

"Only to see that smile on your face," he said, zipping up his shorts. "We're going to be late if you don't hurry up."

"I thought the wedding was tomorrow?" I asked him, fixing my hair in the mirror. His hand wrapped around me, reaching down to palm my thigh as his teeth grazed my shoulder.

"It is, but there's a dinner tonight, and if we miss it Ella will have our heads," he mumbled, peppering kissing along my skin.

"*Your* head," I said, "she likes me. It's your head at stake."

"Mmm," he grumbled, squeezing my thigh tighter.

"And if you don't stop doing that, we're not going to get anywhere fast." I giggled as his fingertips tickled my inner thigh.

"I can think of one place I can get fast," he chuckled.

"Can I drive?" I asked while he was distracted by my skin. He clicked his tongue at the question, digging out the keys and holding them up beside my head as his lips found my jaw on the other side. I smiled wickedly, snatching the keys and turning my head to brush my nose against Jensen's. "That gives us an extra twenty minutes." I whispered and he didn't even hesitate to haul me back to bed.

Once Jensen had gotten it completely out of his system, and I was dressed, *again*. He dangled the keys in my face and we finally got out the door. This weekend would be a whole other ballgame when it came to our relationship. Being around all his friends, the people he considered family for something as important as a wedding. Since we had spoken about California, he had been nothing but sweet and charming. The same loverboy that had wormed his way into my heart all those months ago, but there was something else there now. He was cautious, like he was anticipating the heartbreak before it even happened.

Part of me regretted telling him but the other part was glad I did. Hauling around a secret like that was breaking me down. The weight was too much to bear. I thought it would feel good to tell him but it only made the guilt worse. I wanted to play rugby *and* have Jensen. Was that too much to ask for?

He made me feel seen which wasn't something I was accustomed to in my life. I was always the last thought. And maybe it gave me a complex, maybe it was the reason I pushed so hard in rugby but... I didn't have to push with Jensen. It was effortless attention, meant only for me.

It was in the little details, my apartment always had my favorite snacks, there was always a new set of dice in my dungeons and dragons bag, he had started to keep an extra gym duffle for me in his trunk... he was always one step ahead of me, caring about things that *I* cared about.

And he let me drive his expensive car way too fast because he liked how happy it made me. I giggled to myself, and sped up. The GR took the turns to the Shore cabin like a dream, I barely had to let off the gas for the back end to slide into place, straighten out and take off. I'd never get sick of the engine rumbling to regain momentum, the vibrations that coursed through my veins.

Jensen was relaxed in the passenger seat, the wind whipping through his dark hair. He hadn't bothered to put his shirt back on and the sun nipped at every inch of the tanned, tattooed form. Kaia's words about him being a Greek god, ruffled through my peaceful thoughts.

It was rare that she was wrong.

"What?" He said, with a lazy smile on his face. I turned my focus back on the road.

"It's stupid," I said, tapping the steering wheel and switching gears.

"Adeline," he whispered over the wind.

"I was just thinking that you're beautiful," I admitted.

"Beautiful?" Jensen smirked, his brown eyes lightened by the setting sun. "I've never been called that before." There was a soft blush on his cheeks that demanded attention.

"Yeah." I bit my lip letting up on the gas as the driveway for the cabin came into view. There were already a ton of cars parked in the massive gravel driveway and my eyes went wide at the sight of the cabin. "He really does make it sound small," I said, looking over at Jensen who was pushing his hair back to hide it with a backward hat.

"Modest is Silas's middle name." Jensen laughed, "go on in, I'll grab the bags."

I cut the engine and inhaled slowly, I could do this. I took the stairs inside and was instantly met with thunderous echoes of laughter and chatter. I'd have back up in Cosy for the weekend and could hear her chatting from the front door, my ears leading me further inside.

"You made it," she turned around, her dark red hair curled around her face. She was standing with Zoey, both sipping on something that smelled delicious and sweet

"Yeah, sorry we're late," I said, giving her a small hug. The room erupted again when Jensen burst through the door and chucked our bags on the floor.

"What was it this time?" Cael asked, from the counter.

Jensen came up behind me and threw his arm around me, "this one doesn't know how to keep his hands to himself."

"Oh yeah blame me," he huffed.

"It's always you, Jenny." Arlo dropped the beer from his lips with a raised eyebrow.

"Yeah yeah!" He laughed, "I'm starving, when's dinner?"

"We're waiting on Gramps," Cael groaned like he was dying. It was good to see him in good spirits. Jensen had been a mess for nearly a week after that game. I was selfishly grateful I wasn't there to watch Cael tear that muscle, when Jensen told me I could feel the strain in my own shoulder and winced. I'd never seen him so cuddly, it would have been endearing if it wasn't heartbreaking. Even though there was nothing any of them could have done, it still ripped through the team like an unstoppable storm.

This weekend was a break for them, they'd been training and playing harder than ever. They won the semi-finals but not without bloodshed and the championships would be no different. Jensen came crawling back to the apartment every night barely on his feet but still in search of comfort and I would continue to oblige for as long as I could.

I couldn't think about that right now, it was going to make me sad.

"Is it frowned upon to get drunk tonight?" I asked Zoey and Cosy, only to be met by excited laughter. Three hours later and probably one too many shots half of us were sitting around the coffee table in the living room playing *never have I ever*.

"You definitely have," Van was laid across the floor propped up on an elbow so Zoey could use him as a backrest.

"I never made out with Otis!" Dean argued. "I have standards," he scrunched up his face. "The real question here is why Clem drank for Cael!"

"Otis really?" Van still sounded horribly confused.

"Drunk people do drunk things, and Otis has really nice green eyes," Cael said with a shrug. "It's Jensen's turn," he passed off the conversation to his left.

He was sitting flush against my back with his head resting on my shoulder and let out a low grumble. One of his hands was on his beer and the other one was tucked under my shirt and pressed flat against my stomach. I could practically hear him thinking with how long it took him to come up with something to add to the game's already hilarious turn of events.

"Never have I ever skinny dipped in the lake," he blurted eventually.

Not a single person moved.

"Seriously?" I looked around, "*You guys*? Not even one of you has gone in the lake naked?" I moved to look around at the players that had stayed awake.

"Don't look at me this is only my third time up here," Joshua Logan scowled at me.

"What about the rest of you?" I looked at Van, Dean, Arlo and Cael.

"Never really crossed our minds?" Van shrugged. "We're naked around each other enough..."

"Cael?" I was actually in disbelief that this wasn't a common thing with them.

"There's a first for everything." A wicked grin formed on his face.

"Don't you fucking dare," Arlo warned and Ella started to laugh as Cael stripped from his shirt. "Sit the fuck down."

"Mom's laughing, all bets are off," Cael yelled, backing toward the door.

"Stop encouraging him," Arlo sighed, looking at Ella.

"He's got a point," Van said next, rolling back and causing Zoey to lose her balance laughing. She held her glass up, impressively not spilling a drop as her boyfriend darted after Cael, only pausing to haul Dean up by the back of his shirt.

Dean stumbled backward but followed, bravely flipping off Arlo as he went. Josh laughed gently as the shirt slapped him in the face but rose from his spot and followed the boys outside.

"Sorry Cap, it's kinda funny," Josh said as he disappeared. Both Zoey and Clem were gone before Arlo could stop them and Ella scrambled away from him forcing him to get up and join the fun.

"You too hot shot," I nudged Jensen in the sudden quiet.

"If I'm going, you're going," he smirked, moving too fast for me to stop him as he scooped me off the floor and started toward the back door. The cool night air hit my face, and I instantly curled against his chest with a deep laugh that rumbled his chest. "You started this." The warning was loud as he flipped me over his shoulder to navigate the stairs, his hand pressed up my shorts against my ass.

"I didn't think they'd all get up and get naked!" I giggled, pushing against his back.

"That is exactly when you knew they would do, you're just trying to catch a peak of Arlo!" Jensen dug his fingers into my skin and made me squeal.

"How are you even upright? It's pitch black outside!"

"We know this path in our sleep, now stop wiggling." He gave me a squeeze.

Even backwards, it was easy to tell when the lake came into view because the moon reflected off it and turned everything a hazy blue color along the tree line. Jensen set me down on the dock and kicked off his shorts. I could hear bodies hitting the water behind me but with his eyes on me nothing else needed my attention.

"You guys take everything way too seriously," I whispered but lifted the hem of my tank top.

"Get in the water Adeline." His voice was low and commanding, stepping toward me, I took a step back. Water splashed as two more people took the dive and everyone's light, tipsy laughter echoed across the surface. Jensen's gaze was predatory. "Shorts too. This was your idea."

"Did Arlo get naked?" I whispered and his jaw ticked but his eyes flickered over my shoulder.

"Yes," he grumbled. "You even got Harbor's grouchiest dickhead to have fun. Now, get in the water," he said, snapping each word as I rolled my shorts off. I wrapped my arm around my chest and smiled at him. Stepping back again my heels balanced off the side of the dock and I hung there for a second letting the cold air nip at my skin to cool the heat from Jensen's admiration.

"Okay, okay!" I giggled, pushing off my toes and jumping in. The dark water swallowed me whole as I sank beneath the surface. I went limp for a second and enjoyed the muffled silence before kicking up for air.

"Careful," a hand wrapped around my bicep pulling me away from the dock as Jensen backed up from the shore. I swam backward a little, falling in beside Ella and Van who had enough sense to warn me.

"What is he doing?" I asked, looking at Van.

"Showing off." He laughed, slapping the water. "Does your dick shrink when you're nervous Jenny or is that just normal?" He teased loudly and Jensen laughed uncontrollably but took off at a run to the end of the dock.

Pushing off his toes he curled into an impressive front flip and hit the water with a massive splash of water. He broke the surface, shaking his head around violently like a dog and spraying water everywhere with a crooked smile on his handsome face.

I loved when he showed off.

SARAH

"Morning," I said, wandering into the kitchen to find Ella and Zoey at the island with their noses in mugs of something that smelled incredible.

"Do you need this too?" An unfamiliar warm voice called to me and I turned the corner to fully access the kitchen to see Coach Cody standing in a sleeveless tank, a pair of Hornets sweats and his shaggy hair pressed beneath a hat. For a forty-something year old man he sure was in good shape. The rising sunlight pouring through the massive kitchen windows back lit his strong frame and it took me a whole fifteen seconds of observation before I remembered he had asked me a question.

"Oh yeah, thank you," I said, reaching out for the mug he was holding.

"Coach is making pancakes," Zoey mumbled, setting her head on the counter.

"You know you're supposed to get drunk on the wedding night, not before." He said with a hearty chuckle and went back to cutting fruit on the island next to Ella.

"Hey I'm just sleepy, not hungover…" Ella defended herself. "They got Arlo drunk and in turn…"

"Arlo's always been a horrible drunk," Coach mumbled, sliding a bowl of strawberries and mango across the island.

"Van fell off the bed this morning, and he hit the ground so hard it woke me up an hour before my alarm," Zoey yawned through her sentence.

"And you?" He asked me.

"I'm usually at the gym," I confessed. I was a little hungover but nothing near how poor Zoey felt. "We do practice early during the seasons, so if I don't do the gym at the crack of dawn. I usually don't do it," I said.

"Smart girl. If only I could get the boys on that schedule, it would leave more time for drills." Coach hummed to himself but Ella just laughed.

"You run plenty of drills," she teased, "Are they done yet I'm starving."

"Impatient as always." Coach shook his head and went back to cooking.

"There's a gym downstairs?" Zoey said in a strangled burp that also kind of sounded like vomit starting.

"I don't think it's ever been touched." Ella agreed.

"I was in there this morning, Novak." Coach grumbled.

"Okay, I don't think it's even been touched by *normal* human beings." She slid off her stool. "I need a puke and a shower to rally. I'll be back in twenty. Don't let the vultures have all the bacon, I'll need it to survive today!" She wiggled past me clumsily and disappeared down the hallway.

"I'll have to wake her up in two hours," Ella said, looking over her shoulder. Coach set a plate of pancakes in front of her and looked at me in question.

"I think I'm going to go try that gym out," I said.

"Basement, last door on the left." Coach threw a bottle of water from the cooler on the counter and pointed toward a door behind me. "There's a stereo, you can plug your phone into it," Coach said, it sounded like he was still surprised by the fact that he could. "Room is soundproof so no one will hear it if you turn it up."

"Thanks." It took me all of thirty seconds to find the door. Large, framed in the same oak as the rest of the house but with a sleek gold plate across the front. I don't know why I was surprised when I turned the knob. It was massive down here, rows of machines all in pristine condition. It was a smaller version of the facility at the university and would be the perfect way to relax before everyone else got up.

I found a stereo he was talking about and plugged in my phone, turning it up loud enough to echo across the space before I started to stretch. My body was a little sore from the night before but I wasn't nearly as hungover as Zoey.

I giggled to myself starting a simple circuit around the gyms with what machines I could find and didn't stop until I had successfully sweated out all the booze from the night before. I paused as my phone chime went off through the speakers scaring me half to death and making me drop my weight on the mat in front of the mirror.

> **Are we sneaking off like booty calls now?**

> **I'm in the gym**

> **We have a gym?**

I chucked my phone back on the shelf, if Jensen wanted to find me he would. It was just a matter of time. I went back to my workout, the sweat starting to pour down my back enough for me to strip from my cover.

"You shouldn't do that without a spot," he appeared above the bar as I laid back, the music so loud I hadn't even heard him sneak in. His hair was messy from bed, dripping off his forehead as he ducked beneath it and laid a kiss to my lips.

"Is that all you're good for?" I questioned, staring up at him with wide eyes.

"Have you done your cardio yet?" He asked, ignoring the jab.

"No," I scrunched up my nose, "I have two more sets here."

"Alright," Jensen stared at me, his hands still wrapped around the bar as he hovered over my mouth. "One more," he said, stealing the little expendable air I had with a smirk.

"One more." I confirmed as he pulled away.

"Go for it," he said, lining up so I could finish.

Once I was finished, I tortured Jensen for another twenty minutes on the treadmill. He kept up decently for a man that was hungover, but he was just patiently biding his time for me to ask him for help stretching. He'd come down here with one thing on his mind, that much was clear. The second I stepped off the treadmill he followed, pushing back his sweat-licked hair off his face and trailing his eyes down my body. He stalked me across the gym to the mat, stretching his arms above his head, every muscle flexing tightly. "I thought I was in good shape, but you..." he doubled over, resting his hands on his thighs to catch his breath.

"Me what?" I laughed, sinking to the ground and kicking off my shoes.

Jensen huffed, shaking his head and straightening up, hands on his hips. He eyed me hungrily, the intent in his gaze clear. He dropped to his knees in front of me, hands on my shins, "You work me like a dog, and I fucking love it."

"Like a dog, hey?" I rolled my eyes.

He grinned wider, his thumbs gently rubbing the back of my calves, "Yeah, a very happy dog." He leaned forward slightly, pressing a light kiss just above my knee.

"A very cute one too," I leaned back on the mat as he massaged my legs.

"It took forever to find you down here." His hands slowly crept higher, squeezing my thigh as he went. He looked over at the stereo on the shelf, still pumping out music. "You can't even hear the music from the hall."

"Ryan said it was soundproof." I shrugged with a tiny smile.

His hands paused for a moment, his eyes narrowing before he leaned in a bit closer. His voice was low and teasing, "first name basis with Coach now?" The grin returned when his fingers found a knot in my muscles I'd been trying to work out all week.

"What else did you and *Ryan* talk about?" Jensen asked.

"He made me pancakes!" It was a tiny, funny lie that made him even more worked up as I wiggled under his tight grasp, and despite the sharp pain I was grateful when the muscle started to smooth beneath my skin.

"Wow, who knew it was Coach I needed to watch," Jensen said, pushing harder.

"He was all sweaty from working out to—" The words died on my lips. "Mercy, mercy!" I yelled through gritted teeth, groaning as my back lifted and arched off the mat.

"No mercy, this is payback." Jensen watched on, knowing he had me right where he wanted me. His fingers continued to work the spot until he knew it was completely gone. "You can take it, Adeline. Almost there." He closed the gap between us, his lips brushing my ear.

I pushed my hand into his hair, holding onto him as he got the last remnants of the knot out. His fingers worked harder and better than anything, in more ways than.

"That's my girl," he praised when his finger finally let up. He watched me relax against the mat, catching my hand as it slipped from his hair and locking his finger into mine. He smirked softly, his eyes lowering to take me in spread out beneath him.

"Wow," I huffed with a bright smile, "who knew he wasn't just a fuck boy. No, Malachi Jensen, talks a girl through *everything*." I teased.

He threw his head back and laughed, a deep rumble that echoed through the room before he moved over me and pressed a playful kiss to my lips. "Shut up," he whispered, "I save all my best pep talks for you."

SARAH

"You spoil me," I whispered as he pulled away.

"Someone's gotta take care of you." His other hand slid up my leg slowly, his touch light as a feather.

"I was doing a decent job before you came along," I said but there was no fight in my voice as his lips found my jaw and throat.

Jensen chuckled against my skin, his hand inching higher up my leg. "I bet you were just fine all alone down here too," His voice took on a teasing tone, "no need for me at all."

"You could be useful," I hummed, arching my back against the mat.

His touch grew a little more possessive as he nipped at my jaw, his fingers spreading over my inner thigh. He pulled back slightly, his eyes roaming over my face, "Useful how?"

"I only finished half my cardio," I wet my bottom lip, my whole body on fire from his touch. *Come on Jensen, take the bait.*

His dark eyes followed the movement, his breath hitching. Leaning in closer, his voice dropping to a low murmur as his fingers finally reached their target, sliding beneath my loose shorts, "Can't have that."

I shook my head at him slowly with a tiny lazy smirk on my face, his touch sending shivers down my spine. I gasped, my hips lifting from the mat as his fingers found the wetness between my legs.

Jensen's smirk turned into a satisfied grin as he felt how ready I was for him. His lips brushed against mine as he slipped a finger inside me. "See, useful," he murmured against my lips, his thumb finding my clit and rubbing slow circles around it.

"Very," I gasped as he hit the perfect spot, he knew my body almost as well as he knew his own. His touch was unhurried as he added another finger, his thumb tracing faster circles. His lips searched hungrily over my sweaty skin, nipping and kissing whatever he could find as my heart started racing faster in my chest.

With his free hand, he pushed up the hem of my sports bra, his teeth finding a nipple biting down hard before his tongue swiped over it to soothe the sting. His kisses trailed down between my breast, my stomach and back up as he hooked his fingers inside me and hit that sweet spot perfectly.

He was being deliberately loud and messy. And I loved it. His fingers moved in and out of me at a brutal pace, his mouth working every inch of hot, sweaty skin. "Fuck, Adeline. You're so wet," he groaned.

"You have that effect on a girl," I teased in a breathless moan.

Jensen looked up at me, his eyes dark with desire. He slipped another finger inside me, stretching me perfectly.

"I know," he whispered, before sharply pulling all of them out.

I whined from the lack of contact, watching him bring the fingers to his lips, sucking them clean. I stared up at him, pushing my shorts away as he sat back on his knees. He watched as my legs fell open, his eyes darting down my body.

"I wonder *how* soundproof this room is?" I smirked.

His smirk returned, spreading my legs wider apart with his knees. He undid his own sweats slowly, freeing himself with a dangerous look on his face. A tiny rumble vibrated from the base of my throat as his hand clapped against my center softly. If he wanted me to get loud, he was going to have to work for it.

He watched me, his jaw ticking at the silent response and tried again, harder that time watching my chest rise and fall softly. He was gauging my reaction, trying to figure out how hard he'd have to try when his lips parted.

"Earn it," I purred.

His cock twitched at the challenge. He grabbed both my thighs and pushed my leg up as he pressed against my entrance. Without warning, he slammed inside of me, bottoming out with a loud groan. I folded beneath him, sliding up on the mat from the force as I bit down on my tongue to keep quiet. Jensen watched my body closely, knowing the game I was playing. He pulled out slowly before hammering back inside hard, making my entire body bounce. He set a brutal place, fucking me deeply and harshly on the gym mat. Sweat dripped down his abs as he held my leg up, spreading me wide. Proud of himself when a tiny muffled moan escaped my lips. I used my hands on the mat to keep from sliding, but with every snap I slipped a little higher.

He grinned to himself, the words coming out sloppy and short. "I love the way you feel wrapped around me."

He kept up his pace, determined to break me as his hips moved perfectly, his abs contracting with every thrust. Without warning, his arms slipped around me, damp with sweat as he hauled me up against his chest and lifted us off the mat. My nails dug into his back as he walked me over to the bench with him still completely inside of me. Lowering carefully, he kept me on his lap. The new angle made my entire body shiver with pleasure.

Jensen watched my face closely as I trembled on his lap, biting my lip to stay quiet. His hands gripped my hips and lifted me up with such ease before dropping me down again on his dick. His dark eyes dropped between us, watching his cock disappear inside of me with every rough bounce. He ran one hand up my body, pushing me slightly backward so he could watching himself fucking me. His other hand gripped my hip tightly, pulling me down harder each time I returned. My muscles tensed around him as the fire inside of my belly burned brightly, threatening to wash over me sooner rather than later.

"Too quiet, Belle," he whispered and something broke inside of me. "Scream for me? *Please.*" The begging, low and husky .. completely breathless and overworked, would be the end of me. *"I need it."* He was playing every card and it was working because my lips parted and a curse fell from my lips.

His eyes flashed with triumph as that noise fell from me, immediately giving me what I needed. He snapped his hips up, driving his cock so deep the bench shook

"That's it," I praised, my moans growing louder just for him.

Jensen growled at the soft praise. His hand spanked hard across my ass, warranting a yelp that brought a smile to his face as he started fucking me harder. His hand palmed my breast roughly before moving to the back of my hair and yanking roughly to arch my back against him.

"Fucking Christ, Adeline." His other arm wrapped around my waist holding me steady as my nails dug into his biceps and I slipped into complete euphoria. "What do you need?" He gasped breathlessly.

"Just you," I yelled, the words echoing over the sound of the music over and over.

He gripped my hip tightly, and started pounding into me relentlessly, giving me every last thing he had. His movements became more erratic as his own release bubbled up. His fingers tightened in my hair as he brought our lips together in a desperate messy kiss.

That kiss broke every resolve and the dam exploded inside of me as the orgasm dominated my thoughts and sparked through my nervous system. My core fluttered violently around him as I came apart and my face contorted with pleasure. He growled roughly against my lips, the sound rumbling from deep in his chest as my nails broke the skin on his arm and his cock pulsed inside of me, tensing with release.

I pushed my hands through his hair and leaned back in arms with a pant, sweat coating every inch of our bodies. He was still half hard inside of me as his arms wrapped around me possessively and he caught his breath. "I love when you do that," he whispered, his lips grazing my jaw and neck. His tongue licked at a bead of sweat and if he didn't stop we'd never leave this room and miss the wedding completely.

"What?" I asked, tugging gently on his hair to pull him away.

"When you get all dreamy and sweet during sex. *Just you*," he hummed, pressing a long kiss to my lips and making my heart sore. It wasn't dreamy though, it was just the truth.

Fear was a funny thing when you were in love.

"You're all I need," I responded finally, knowing the weight the words held and still daring to say them. Jensen stared at me, his pupils still blown from lust and his cheeks still flushed from the extra cardio.

"I think I love you, Adeline," Jensen said quietly, the words low and almost mistakable beneath the sound of the music.

"Mm." My teeth dug into my bottom lip. "I think I love you too, Jensen."

JENSEN

"Would you like to dance?" I asked Adeline, my hand extended to her. She peered up from her seat and nodded gently, allowing me to pull her onto the dance floor in a soft circle.

"I shouldn't be surprised that you can ballroom dance too," she giggled as I spun her out and back in against my chest. My hand raked down her spine as I moved us around to the music, the smell of her shampoo tickled my nose and made me hum with need.

"Three years of it," I said, "I can outdance half the team."

"Only half?" Adeline teased.

"You want to know a secret?" I asked her, leaning closer and lowering my voice as Silas and Drew swayed close by. She watched me, waiting for me to continue. "Mrs. Shore made Silas, Arlo and Nicholas all take lessons."

"Arlo King can do the waltz?" She gasped and looked around for him as her fingers dug into the open buttons on my dress shirt.

"And the foxtrot," I added just to hear the strangled giggle that left her. She almost slipped from my grip with a wiggle but I caught her gently, the fabric tangling between my fingers. "Get it together before you ruin this dress," I teased her and she turned back to look at me with mischief in her eyes.

"I bought it to be ruined, Jensen." She challenged.

"I'll remember that," I said, bracing her and dipping her low to steal a kiss from her collarbone and then the top of her breast. I could tell something had been bugging her all day but I wasn't sure how to approach it without ruining the evening. The words she had said that morning in the gym played on repeat in the back of my mind, *I think I love you too.*

My heart had been racing uncomfortably in my chest ever since.

"Do you think Arlo will dance with me?" She broke through the wall of thoughts and my grip tightened on her subconsciously. "Whoa possessive, I was only joking." Her face scrunched together in the cutest way as I stared down at her. "What's wrong?" She asked.

"Nothing, sorry..." I shook free of the crippling anxiety, a feeling I wasn't used to having... There was just so much going on outside of my control and it all suddenly revolved around losing the one thing I never expected to need.

Adeline's grip on my heart was tightening.

"You haven't lied to me once since I met you, Jensen. Why are you lying to me right now?" She poked my chest as I spun her out of my arms and back in. The music slowly died down and I could hear Silas chatting away on the mic but my main focus was the confused stare on Adeline's face.

"Tonight's perfect," I controlled the tone in my voice but I could see that she wasn't satisfied with the answer. "You're perfect."

"Flattery is not honesty," she said. "Is it because of this morning?"

Yes.

"No," I shook my head.

"Are you scared?" She asked me.

"Terrified," I answered, and the hazel in her eyes darkened.

"Of what?" She asked gently. "This? *Us?*"

"The end," I said, giving her the honesty she requested. "I've never had my heart broken, Adeline Sarah. I don't want to know what it feels like, but the dread is setting in that I'm going to find out no matter how tightly I hold on to you."

She stared at me for a moment, her jaw tightening.

"Jensen," she chewed her lip, aiming to say more but out of the corner of my eye I saw something soaring through the air, my hand lifted and caught something soft and lacy without a second thought.

"Nice catch, Jenny!" Cael whistled from the other side of the lawn.

I held up the garter on my ring finger and stared down at her.

"It's really hard to be mad at you for saying stupid shit when you immediately do something hot." She groaned and pressed her forehead against my chest.

Adeline spun around on the dance floor with Dean, her smile bright as the fabric of her long blue dress whipped around her bare feet. The party was dying down but most of the team was still hanging out drinking and dancing. I couldn't help myself when I pulled my phone out and took a few photos of them, tucking them away for later.

"Here," Van handed me a beer as he lowered into his seat. His dress shirt was unbuttoned to the middle and his hair was sweaty from dancing all night.

"Where's Zo?" I asked, looking around.

"She fell asleep an hour ago, it might have been the two nights of going hard in a row. She's not used to it anymore." Van laughed, lifting his own bottle to his mouth. "Addy had fun this weekend?"

"Yeah," I said with a sigh. "We talked about it..."

"Cali?" Van asked, leaning forward on his elbows to look at me but my eyes were still on her. Singing loudly in Dean's face as the music shifted into a song I didn't recognize but loved the way it dripped from her pretty mouth.

"It's her dream, Mitchell. But..." the words refused to come out.

"You're sad?" Van finished.

"I don't get sad," I said, shaking my head. "I don't think I've ever been sad in my entire life and now... every time I look at her I'm happy and at the exact same time... I'm so fucking sad, man."

Van set his beer down, his head tilted up to watch Adeline just a few feet from me. "I get it. That conversation was hard for me and Zoey. It's been fight after fight. She's so scared that if she goes to law school and leaves me in Harbor that something bad will happen. She keeps replaying this scenario that I'll fall out of love with her because I don't see her every day or something."

"I don't think there's a universe that exists that you and Zo aren't together," I said.

"That's what I tell her, but she's scared and fear blankets all reasonable thoughts. All I can do is keep reminding her that she's only going to New York. I'm finishing school next year. The second that graduation is over I'm in the truck, on my way to her." Van huffed.

"How long have you two been together?" I asked him, turning away from Adeline finally.

"Twelve years this October." He said without having to think about it. It was so nice to see him at peace with everything. Van Mitchell had always been a lifeline in the Nest because of his consistent calm nature. "She's mine and a little distance isn't going to break down twelve years of knowing that she is, in my soul."

"How did you know?" I questioned, "Like... that she was the one?"

Van ran a hand through his dark hair and thought about it.

"Believe it or not, Zoey was loud in high school," he laughed.

"Our Zo? No never. She's as quiet as a mouse," I teased, lifting the beer to my lips.

"Ella was quiet, but more intelligent than most of the students. She was quick, athletic and it wasn't that she wasn't friendly or nice. It was that she didn't have time to entertain people that didn't give that same energy back. Zoey did, she went to bat for El more times than I can count." Van explained, though I wasn't sure what that had to do with knowing Zoey was the one. I needed help with my own girlfriend, not a history lesson.

"I never really needed that, most people didn't mess with a guy that was six foot five in junior year but there was one time," Van laughed. "Last week of the baseball season, some guys were trashing me for being one of the low-income kids. I guess having no mom and a blue-collar dad is something to be ashamed of."

I remembered being shocked to hear that when Van was accepted to Harbor's ball program, his dad and sisters moved with him. He had tons of family back home but they were his people and they did it without question. His dad was funny, we didn't see him much because he worked a lot but when we did he was always the life of the party.

"Kids are mean." I added.

"Yeah well, Zoey was so pissed that I didn't stand up for myself that we got in a fight and she went home from the game without speaking to me. In the morning, all three of those assholes woke up to find their expensive cars covered in spray paint, exposing some pretty nasty gossip about them. To this day I can't prove she did it, but that night we were studying for our math final and I knew I loved her when I saw that bright orange paint caked beneath her fingernails."

"She had missed some?" I asked with a smile.

"Her pinky nail," Van hummed. "Zoey showed me that day how much she loved me and I promised to myself that I'd always be that for her."

"You guys are cute," I grumbled. "Doesn't help me much though."

"You're talking about Adeline aren't you?" Van asked quietly.

"I don't have anything to compare it to," I admitted, smiling softly as her laughter filled the space from Dean dipping her low suddenly.

"Love?" Van asked, his heavy brows pulling together in question.

"I've never slowed down long enough with a girl to figure it out," I sighed. "Try everything once," I groaned the stupid saying that used to come out of my mouth at house parties, drunk off vodka and just looking for a new girl to fuck.

"How did you know baseball was your favorite?" Van asked and I looked at him, confused. "You played just about every sport in the book. How did you know baseball was the one you wanted to stick with?"

"It felt like home," I whispered and felt all the splintering pieces of my heart click back into place as I shifted my gaze back to her. *My Belle âme.*

"Fuck I'm so good at this," Van snorted under his breath, drunk as he'd ever been.

"Shut up," I grumbled, slapping him in the chest.

"If she's home Jenny." He tapped his empty bottle against mine, the clink loud and echoey. "Then it doesn't matter. Here, California. You'll be okay."

"You think?" I asked him as he rose from the table, leaning over completely to place a drunken, messy kiss to my cheek. I shoved him off and watched his long body stumble backward.

"I know." Van winked and disappeared to harass someone else.

JENSEN

"Are you sure I shouldn't have worn something... I don't know, nicer?" I asked Adeline, opening the car door. I was in a black shirt, with a dark jean jacket and a pair of nice pants.

"It's the Hollow, it's not like we're having dinner at a five-star restaurant," she said, pushing up on her toes to fix my hair. "And you've already met them."

"I met one," I said nervously, "and it was a chaotic night. This is like having to hold an actual conversation with your two very intelligent older brothers."

"Ew," she laughed. "They aren't that smart, or that tough. Besides, if they try to fight you, Boone is working tonight and he has a boy crush on you so he'll probably back you up." She patted my chest.

"Probably?" I stilled, "What do you mean, *probably?!*" I called after her as she wandered into the Hollow's front doors. "Adeline!" The door closed in my face and I yanked it open to follow her inside. Taylor and Zane sat at a table near the back of the bar, intimidating as ever, both of them glaring at me.

I looked over at Boone who dropped the towel he was using to dry cups with to give me a thumbs up. *Super encouraging.*

Adeline was already ordering some drinks from the blonde kid I had met the other night, Wren maybe? He was dressed in a uniform tonight and looked less than impressed about it but was still managing to flirt with my girlfriend.

I slid into the stool separating the two of them, and he took his leave to get our drinks. Adeline eyed me with a tiny smile, knowing all too well that I was too nervous and wound up to be dealing with her shenanigans. I leaned in, kissing her cheek and ignoring the fact that both her brothers were watching us, waiting for me to say hello.

Adeline first.

Adeline, always.

"Jensen, right?" Taylor said as I straightened out. "We met at the pop up."

"Taylor, and Zane," I acknowledged them respectfully. Seeing them all together was weird. They looked similar, in a way most siblings did. All sharing certain traits but clearly there was a significant age gap between her and them. She had mentioned once or twice about how she had come along, she called herself a *'fix it all'* baby. Claiming she was the one they had to fix the marriage but that was never the case.

"I thought dad was coming?" Adeline said, her voice sounding disappointed but not surprised.

"Stuck in Osaka," Taylor said. "I warned you not to get your hopes up."

I looked over at her and her jaw ticked like she was holding on to her emotions by a thread so I weaved my fingers into hers beneath the table in her lap.

"Maybe we can make the trip for Christmas this year," Zane offered.

"There's too much going on for that and I'm not wasting money to go visit a man who never puts in an effort," Taylor abolished the idea before Adeline could voice her opinion.

"Whatever, Tay. Get the stick out of your ass," Zane groaned.

"I don't have time to babysit either of your feelings about Dad, just... grow up." Taylor rolled his eyes. "He's always going to be flaky and this isn't something we need to be discussing in front of Adeline's flavor of the month."

"*Boyfriend,*" Adeline snapped, finding her voice with a vengeance. "And Zane's right, what is wrong with you today?"

"It was just a long day at work..." Her tone seemed to curb his attitude a little as he sipped on his beer and went quiet.

"You're the son of that hotel millionaire," Zane snapped his fingers and Adeline groaned "I knew I recognized your name. My husband and I stayed in your hotels last spring when we travelled to Italy."

"The locations there are by far the nicest," I tried to hold a steady conversation as Adeline's finger dug into my hand beneath the table.

"Quit being weird," she said to Zane with a tiny huff.

"So why are you playing baseball if your career is basically a shoo-in?" Taylor asked, the tone in his voice accusatory like he was trying to make me seem less than what I was.

I shifted on my stool. "Because I'm good at baseball," I answered easily. "Really good."

"Yeah but if you haven't gotten drafted yet the chances are low you go pro." He challenged.

"Not necessarily, I've had offers but I wanted to play with the Hornets." I explained.

"Why?" Taylor asked and I heard Adeline huff but I just rubbed my thumb over the back of her hand. He was trying to rile me up and I knew it was the right of her older brothers to do so. Ask questions that might be uncomfortable or weird and even with quiet being my default setting I wasn't afraid to speak my mind, or stand up for something I had faith in.

I smiled at him, collecting my thoughts.

"Because I wanted to get the most of my time with my family, with my friends. I'm young, my life is just starting and yes I'm entitled to my parents fortune, but it doesn't make me *entitled*. I value hard work and loyalty. My team has one game left to play and to most of the guys on that field. This championship means everything, so I'm going to put my best in and I'm not going to leave them until they say it's okay to go. Because I don't take my privilege for granted, I use it to my advantage."

Zane clapped his hands leaning back in his chair as Taylor eyed me for a long time. "He's good," Zane laughed, "I like him."

"Didn't need your approval," Adeline groaned, taking her drink straight from Wren's hand as he circled around.

"Wouldn't have asked us to dinner if you didn't want it," Zane mimicked in a similar voice and it was clear who was closer in age. Taylor's jaw was still clenched tightly as I drank but it wasn't a harsh glare anymore, it had softened into a mild annoyance. I'd take that.

The rest of dinner was spent fielding questions from the both of them. What my life looked like before Adeline, what my family was like, who my friends were, what classes I was taking. They barely spoke to her, every once and while

Zane would make an off handed comment and the two of them would start bickering back and forth until Taylor put an end to the fight by clearing his throat. By the time I had grasped the full scope of their family dynamic both brothers were excusing themselves from dinner to get back home.

"You survived!" Boone slammed two shots down on the table. Adeline jumped from the sound, a giggle dripping from her that made me wanna melt into her completely.

"What is that?" I stared at the amber liquid.

"Peach schnapps and Fireball." Boone looked at the overfilled shot glass proudly.

"That sounds incredible," I said at the same time that Adeline warned not to drink it. I tapped mine against his and lifted it to my lips with instant regret. Whatever was in the shot glass was *not* either of those things, but pure homebrewed cinnamon moonshine.

I gagged but swallowed it down as Boone slammed his empty shot glass on the table laughing. "They never learn," he scoffed, scooping my empty glass in his fingers and patting me on the back as he went back to the bar. "Good job tonight, kid!" He hollered as he went.

"Take me home?" Adeline asked after I got the brutal coughing out of my system.

"You drive, whatever was in that just put me well over the legal limit of being alive," I coughed again, the threat of a vomit very real. Adeline giggled, pulling the keys from my back pocket.

"Thanks for putting up with them tonight," Adeline said, stripping from her shirt in front of the bed. Her reflection in the mirror behind her was glorious. Her perfect ass hugged tightly in a pair of dark lace underwear and bathed in what moonlight was pouring through her massive apartment windows.

"Don't move," I said to her, laying across the bed in my shorts as she undressed.

"What are you doing?" she asked, crossing her arm over her bare chest and tilting her head to the side. In that moment she looked unreasonably soft, but not fragile, never that. Adeline was carved from marble.

"Committing you to memory."

Her playful expression softened and she let her arms drop to her side with a tiny exhale. I stared at her in awe, she was so beautiful it radiated across my chest in bursts of warmth.

"Give me my phone," she wiggled her fingers toward the bed where she had thrown it when we came into the apartment. I reached across, grabbing for it with a confused look on my face as she unlocked it.

When she turned away from me I swallowed tightly to muffle the whine that threatened to leave my throat. I wanted to trace my hand down the soft curve of her spine and connect all the freckles along her back until I couldn't keep my eyes open anymore.

I moved on the bed to rest on my elbows and watch as she positioned herself in front of the mirror taking photos with her phone. I tangled my hands into the sheets trying to be patient as she took them but all I wanted to do was touch her.

There was a peaceful haze that settled over me and even though tomorrow would be the hardest game we'd ever play, I wasn't worried. If every single thing went wrong and we came out the other end short of the championship, I'd be okay. I had found another place to store my soul, staring up at her in the moonlight. I knew she was it.

Adeline was where I felt at home.

"There," she said, setting the phone back on the bed. My phone vibrated next to my hand and I looked over at it to see a message from her.

You earned some new ones.

I smiled down at the phone, flipping through the few she sent, knowing they were just for me. Chucking it aside, I leaned forward, wrapping my hand around her thigh and pulling her onto the bed. She collapsed in a soft puddle of skin against my chest with a sad smile on her face.

"Which one is your favorite?" She asked, just like she had before.

"Mine," I replied without hesitation, only that time I wasn't talking about the photos. I brushed the pad of my thumb over her bottom lip and gently kissed her, soaking up all the sadness in her bones.

"I officially signed the deal this morning," she whispered when I pulled away.

I stared at her, swallowing down the fear trying to tell me that it was the wrong decision. That maybe I was moving too fast, holding on too tight but my heart raced every time I saw her, and whether I liked it or not Adeline had brought the strings to our relationships and had been tying the knots since the day I met her.

Ones I had no intention of untangling.

"When do we leave?" I asked her, holding my breath when her eyes widened and her body tensed.

"I'll probably go meet the—"

"No, when does the season start?" I rephrase my question for her.

"What?" Adeline pulled back from me, placing her hand on my chest but I grabbed her wrist, pressing it to my lips and tugged her body back flush with mine.

"When do we need to be in California, Adeline?" I asked her, giving her palm a kiss.

"August fifteenth." She said, her brows still pinched together tightly.

"Alright that gives us some time after the season is done to get moved, I think we should skip an apartment and go straight to a house and before you argue you should see my bank account—"

"Jensen!" Adeline snapped.

"What, *baby*?" I couldn't stop the laughter that bubbled up from me at her sudden outburst. "A house is more practical and has better investments. We'll be there for a little while and I'd rather own.. " I rambled until she stopped me.

"What are you talking about?" She sounded like she was on the verge of tears when I grabbed her face and squeezed.

"I'm coming with you," I said.

"You can't just—" I kissed her hard to silence her argument.

"Contrary to popular belief, *I can.*" I said when I pulled back, "I made the decision a while ago. It's my last season with Harbor, and there's a new hotel going up in San Francisco."

"Harbor is your home, Jensen. You shouldn't sacrifice that to watch me chase my dreams," she said softly, her throat bobbing to keep from crying.

"No, no. Harbor will always be my home, and I have spent my entire life trying everything once in search of that feeling but I never had a dream, Adeline." I kissed her nose, my thumb brushing over her cheek, "not until I met you."

Her lips parted to argue, and again I stole the air from her, not willing to listen to whatever dull argument she was ready to start. "I'm not going back to text messages and rain checks," I said to her. "I want early mornings, late nights, gym dates, and long baths with you."

She sighed and I shook my head at her.

"I want every rough touch, every hard kiss, and to talk shit with you *face to face,* Adeline Sarah." Her face lit up at the words, it was exactly how we loved one another. "No long distance."

"Touch rough," Adeline said, threading her fingers into my hair with a tug.

"Kiss hard," she reminded just how so with a crushing kiss that melted her to me in a pile of rampant nerves that neither of us could control.

"Talk shit," she pulled back breathlessly and scowled at me with tears in her eyes, "you're fucking insane."

"Only about you." I whispered and I meant it.

"Are you serious about this?" She questioned carefully. Scared that I wasn't.

"Yeah, Adeline. You're where I belong."

JENSEN

"Are you nervous about today?" I sat at the table with Josh and Louis, just trying to mind my business while the press ran the final game junket on all the players. Most of Portland's guys sat down the hall from us doing the same thing.

Adeline had come around to the Nest with me that morning to help Zoey make signs and do August's hair with old temporary blue hair dye she had lying around. She fit in so effortlessly with them all that it was hard to remember a time when she wasn't there. I was just so stupidly in love.

"Sorry, what?" I asked, rolling a small piece of ripped paper between my fingers.

"Today? Are you nervous about the game?" The reporter asked again. She was a tiny thing with an innocent, bright smile.

"A little, but nerves are good for the game," I tried to answer as diplomatically as I could without sounding like a total asshole. I wasn't nervous at all. Mostly just excited. To be honest, typically at these things they left me alone. It wasn't the catcher they wanted information from, it was the pitcher, the first baseman, the coaches.

I usually just goofed around.

"What are some of your favorite pre-game snacks?" One of the social media girls asked Louis who looked at Josh confused. Sometimes the girls still talked too fast for him to understand, and his sad puppy dog face always made me laugh.

I turned to him, explaining what she meant in French and he clued in quickly.

"What about you?" She asked me next, leaning in close.

"Chicken wings." I said without hesitation, but my mind was between Adeline's thighs. Most of the time these junkets were full of either extremely serious questions or goofy ones that were almost harder to answer. Anything to do with routines, food, or favorites. It was for socials so the answers they were looking for were funny, buzz things that made people interested in the sport because of the player.

I was generally better at answering the stupid questions over the serious ones.

"And you Josh?" She asked.

"A sandwich and a banana." He answered dryly with a smug smile on his face. For a man so beloved by the female crowd you'd think he'd have more suave with them off the field.

"Fun," she said, trying to add something more to his answer that wasn't boring. Once she moved on from our table, Josh grumbled something under his breath making me laugh.

"Relax," I whispered to him. "They just want to make you seem human."

Josh turned his death glare on me, "How much longer do we have to do this?"

"We've got at least two hours," I told him and he swore. There was a reason we were sat at the same table, if anyone could make Josh seem personable it was me.

"This is your last season with the Hornets, today is your last game. Any feelings about that?" Another short, chubby man asked, practically stepping on the girl.

"Careful," I said and he looked to his left, finally noticing her. There were far too many in this room today. "Pride," I answered him, popping the small paper ball in my mouth. "It's been a long five years with these guys, and a lot of us are done with the team this year. We want to make it count today."

"And after?" The female reporter asked. "There's rumors you signed with a team in San Francisco."

"Something like that," I smiled at her before flicking the wet ball at Van and hitting him in the forearm with a small wet tick.

He looked down at it with a disgusted look and flipped me off secretly as he continued to answer the question he was asked. Eventually the room died down and the reporters dwindled leaving us all sitting there, staring at each other burnt out for the morning but ready to play that evening. The air was tight, almost buzzing with energy as Coach shooed us all back up to the Nest for lunch.

Drew, Clementine and Mrs. Shore had put together a massive lunch for us, that half of us picked at because of the nerves but it was nice to sit around the table one more time. After lunch I dragged Adeline up the stairs to find a quiet place to kiss her silly.

"I've never been in here without Todd watching us like a hawk," Adeline giggled, curled around me in my bed. It would be one of the last times I'd be in this room and I couldn't help but feel a little sad about it. "I always thought it was weird you didn't just live at home with how close it is to the stadium."

I laughed, pressing my face into her hair, "I didn't originally. Mom had to convince me that it would be good. I was happy to live at home." I huffed, "She was right though. It was good. Living here is different, the Nest makes everyone family."

"Yeah," Adeline hummed. "Are you nervous about today?" She asked.

"No." I shook my head. "Games like this, like today. They're my favorite."

She shifted in bed, resting against my chest so she could look at me with her judgmental hazel eyes, "are you sure?" She asked, checking a little more thoroughly that time. It wasn't about the game though, she was asking how I felt about everything else.

"It's going to be hard, not just on me but everyone too. Today means a lot of different things to everyone. It's a once in a lifetime win for some, it's a chance to be draft eligible for others, for some of us it's a goodbye."

Adeline swallowed tightly.

"A happy goodbye, Belle. Not a sad one." I cupped her face. "I can't stay in this room forever, eventually I have to grow up and I'm grateful I get to do it with you."

Before she could say anything else her name was hollered through the house by Zoey interrupting what little alone time, we were getting that day.

"Hey!" She popped her head in the door, "There you are. I'm doing Ella's hair, do you want me to do yours?" She asked her as Adeline gently looked back over her shoulder.

"Do I get ribbons too?" Adeline asked with a bright smile.

"I thought you'd never ask!" Zoey squealed and put her hand out, "Come with me!"

Adeline didn't move right away, her face turning back to mine. "If I don't see you before the game," she whispered, giving me a small kiss, "I love you."

The *I think* portion had finally faded away and the certainty in her voice made me vibrate with unbridled affection toward her.

I squeezed my fingers into her skin involuntarily and surged forward, sinking my teeth into her bottom lip as I stole another kiss. "I love you," I repeated back as she pulled away. "Hey," I called out as she slipped off the bed. She turned back to look at me, her hair wavy and crazy around her perfect face. "One more?" I asked and she came right back.

"One more." The second kiss was longer, sweeter and left me a little breathless when she finally pulled away.

"I got you a surprise," I pointed to the dresser and she smiled.

Sitting on top was a folded jersey and two bags of gummy cola bottles just for her.

"You spoil a girl you know." She scooped her jersey off the dresser, my phone number freshly plastered across the back. "Seriously?" She threw her head back laughing, her cheeks bright pink with amusement before she scrunched her nose up at me. "It's perfect," she hummed and disappeared after Zoey. "Good luck!"

> **If you win I have a treat for you**

> **Baby, you are the treat.**

"In you come, boys, no more delaying." Coach stood at the door of the stadium staring at us all in a huddle. I shoved my phone away and pulled at the collar of my suit walking up, suffocating on the pressure that was coming down on our shoulders. I swear the whole team sat in the parking lot for nearly twenty minutes before any of us dared to move. Holding my breath I stared up at the iron bars in awe, no matter how many times we did that walk. It never got old.

I held my breath to steady my heart and take in the moment.

Harbor Stadium had been my home for the last five years.

"You coming?" Van leaned against the door when I came back to focus and I nodded, following him with a smile. I had told him that morning about what was going on and in true Van fashion, he was nothing but proud of me.

"You'll make a cute house wife, Jenny." He teased, throwing my clean ball pants at me from the dryer.

"I'll be working, I'm not just going to be her ball boy." I shook my head.

"I don't know, that sounds kind of fun." Van shrugged, folding his pants. "What did she say?"

"She thinks I'm insane," I said, with a laugh. "What do you think?"

"I've just been waiting for you to catch up, man. I'm glad you found some happy."

Cael had the party mix blasting in the locker room by the time we caught up with everyone, Arlo and Nicholas were huddled with Josh going over plays as the rest of the players stripped from their suits just trying to keep the energy in the room high. Seeing Cael navigate the room, stuck in his dress clothes sucked for everyone but he was taking it in strides.

"Hey, Cody." I called out to him, tapping his locker with my hand. "Get changed. You can't go out there like that."

Cael looked at me, his jaw clenched tightly as his eyes landed on his untouched locker.

"Just because you can't play doesn't mean you don't get dressed," Van agreed from beside me. He was uncharacteristically quiet as he shifted in his fancy shoes, his blonde hair pushed back off his tight face.

"What the fuck are you waiting for?" Arlo barked and Cael instantly moved toward his locker laughing nervously from the intrusion. Arlo watched over his shoulder for a moment, giving a tiny nod to both Van and I.

"Do you think that was a smile?" Van leaned down to whisper to me.

"That was definitely a smile." I hit him on the shoulder and started to get changed.

Coach cleared his throat, flanked by Silas and Ella at the front of the room.

"The last game is always the hardest, boys," he said, looking around the room. "It's the end of season for some of you, for others it's the end of your career with the Hornets but that doesn't matter because that's tomorrow's business. Today, you get together and you show Harbor what it means to be a family, you show them exactly how fucking good you are at being a team. Walk out on that field with your chests out and your heads held high. You have gone through hell to get here today," Coach's glance stopped on Cael and Josh across the room as his hand raised to his chest. "You've overcome challenges as boys and came out the other side as men. Portland fucking knows how hard you're going to fight for this so do not let them down, you fight for that win tonight and when you think you can't fight anymore, you get back up and try some more."

"Yes Coach." The room erupted.

"I don't talk about her much because frankly none of you boys need to see a grown man cry but," Coach cleared his throat. "Rae would be proud of you."

He tapped his chest with two fingers, and we all mirrored it, holding it a little longer than we usually would have. Taking in the silence and letting it wrap around our nerves.

"Bring it home, boys."

JENSEN

Josh stood in front of me on the pitchers mound, dripping in sweat from the lights after four hard-fought innings. "Harris is fucking killing us," he rolled the ball in his glove.

"How's your elbow?" I asked him and earned a death glare. "Doc told me to keep an eye on you, answer the question."

"It's fine," Josh snapped. "I don't know how to beat him on the mound," he said, his eyes darting around as he tried to come up with a solution.

"Your best pitch is a cutter," I offered, "Use it."

"I haven't thrown one in months," he huffed. *Because it hurts to do it.* I stared at him for a long second. We were running out of options.

"I thought your elbow was fine?" I poked.

"It is." His eyes narrowed on mine, the lights of the stadium buzzing brightly above us as a reminder that we were constantly being watched.

"Then throw the cutter," I said quietly, backing off the mound and pulling my cage down over my head. Harris approached the box and swung out his shoulders with his bat as Josh set up on the mound. I watched Josh, the same way I watched him every game. Counting his every breath, waiting for each finger to tap the stitching around the ball, check left, check left and right. Always more confident in his shortstop than his second baseman.

But the right had been checked twice lately. His faith was breaking.

I stood up calling a time out and the ump gave me a dirty look as I said it again louder that time. Coach was quick to follow, storming the field as I bombarded Josh.

"What the fuck is wrong with you?" Josh snarled as we both approached and Coach's face told me he had a similar question.

"It's not your elbow," I said.

"Yeah I fucking know that, Jensen!" Josh got louder, only for Coach to put a hand out.

"We don't have time for cryptic," he warned me.

"He's looking for Cael," I said in a quiet hiss.

"No I'm not," Josh scowled but his jaw ticked uncomfortably and I knew I was right.

"Four breaths, five fingers, check left twice, right once. Pitch." I repeated the actions back to him. "It's what you've done all season, until Cael got hurt. Now you check right twice. It's making you unbalanced."

Coach stared at me and then at Josh, his mind turning.

Without a word, he waved down our third base coach, Peter. "I need you not to argue with me right now, but give your jacket to Cael and put him out on the line."

"What?" Peter scoffed.

"Just do it." Coach barked and Peter took off toward the dugout, stripping from his jacket and handing it over to a confused Cael. Josh stared at me, his anger rolling off him in waves.

"Now pitch." I jabbed and for a second I thought that Josh might hit me but he only looked over his right shoulder to find Cael.

"Fuck you, Jensen," Josh said, but a small smirk formed on his lips.

He hated it but it worked, Harris wasn't a match for the three balls that came at him. Josh had struck him out.

"There we fucking go!" I yelled across the gap and Josh just shook his head.

He managed to cold snap the entire inning, not a single run went out. Only two hits and both were flies.

"How did you know that would work?" Dean asked me as I stripped from my mask.

"I didn't," I said, with a shrug. "We're all creatures of habit, Josh more than anyone. He just felt off balance without Cody behind him."

"Good call." He slapped me on the back and went up to hit.

Two fights and six runs later, we were exhausted, just dragging our feet to finish the game on a high note. Portland had two bases full, and if we shut them down here, it would all be over. The championship would be ours.

I turned around and looked back at the stands, Zoey, Adeline, Drew and August all sat with nervous faces watching on. There was a pack of empty cola bottles in her lap and she was stress eating her way through the second one.

She saw me looking at her and scowled, "*pay attention,*" she mouthed before blowing me a kiss and leaning over to listen to what Zoey was saying.

Win or lose, my life was pretty fucking great.

I turned back to Josh, his dark eyes determined.

However, I didn't want to lose. I wanted to win, for me, for Josh. For all of us.

I waited, watching Josh go through his motions, and when he threw that final pitch, I knew it was over before it even slapped into the back of my glove. My palm stung, flickers of painful fireworks exploding across my muscle as I shot from the ground in celebration. Gloves flew off in every direction, and the entire stadium roared to life the second the out was called. The entire team surged toward the middle of the field, but I put on the brakes before grabbing Josh and offered him a wicked grin instead.

"Damn good job," I said before being lifted off the ground by Van and spun around in the air over his shoulder. I ruffled my hand through his hair, screaming alongside him as the rest of the team began to celebrate in the infield.

Josh turned, waiting for Dean who shoved into and out of a few sloppy hugs before wrapping his hands around Josh's face and kissing him hard. The team erupted in cheers as the two of them flashed across the massive LED screens around the stadium.

Cael whistled loudly while being jostled, his face plastered with the biggest smile we'd seen from him in a long time. Confetti exploded above us, dripping over the stadium in blue and gold snowflakes.

"I can't believe that fucking worked!" Cael said to me as Van finally dropped me in favor of Zoey. She ran across the field and crashed into him as he lifted her to his chest.

"Me either," I yelled back over the noise. "Who knew he liked you enough to have it affect his game," I joked and Cael started to laugh.

"I'm going to miss you, man," Cael said, his smile a little shaky.

"What, you don't know how to use the phone?" I teased, understanding his cagey behavior around people leaving. He laughed, shaking his head. "Idiot, come here." I held out my arms to him, and he wrapped me up in a tight hug, kissing my cheek roughly as I messed up his hair.

"That's my cue," he huffed, letting go of me and spinning me around to see Adeline standing a few feet away in the chaos. The jersey hung off her body, showing off every loveable curve and her hair was pulled back into two loose, messy ribbon adorned braids.

"Did it hurt?" I said to her and she shook her head.

"That's Kaia's line," she laughed.

"Answer the question." I stepped forward, narrowly getting tangled up by the dog pile that started to my left. "When you fell from heaven, did it hurt?"

She shook her head gently at my teasing, "Do I know you?" She smiled so hard it created lines around her eyes.

"I could have sworn we've met before," I whispered as I surged forward and wrapped her up in my arms. She yelped as her feet left the ground and she buried her face in my neck, peppering my sweaty skin with light kisses. "I'd know those pretty little noises anywhere."

"You know, I think I figured it out," Adeline said, leaning back in my arms with her hands flat to my shoulders.

"Figured what out?" I grumbled playfully, stealing the sweat from her jaw with a tiny kiss and nip.

"What do you love more than chicken wings? You said '*ask me later.*' But it's baseball, it's this." She said so confidently I almost didn't want to tell her she was wrong.

I shook my head softly, and her brows knitted together angrily.

"What else could it be? You're just being obtuse." Adeline scowled.

"*You.*" I said without hesitation, kissing her pouty bottom lip.

"Me? That was months ago," she shook her head in disbelief.

"That's why I told you to ask me later."

"I didn't mean—you know what, never mind, shut up and kiss me."

She raked her hands over my head and tangled her fingers into the messy hair at my nape, pulling me closer and taking what she wanted without waiting. I squeezed her tightly against me, my fingers digging into her thighs as she swiped her tongue into my mouth and deepened our connection.

"There's a party at Delta!" Dean yelled in passing, throwing championship hats at everyone who looked at him.

"Meet at home first," Arlo barked, his arm flung over Ella's shoulder. "Do your press, shower. One hour." He ordered.

We found ourselves laying around the deck with drinks talking over the game. Once we had gone through the round of questions from every reporter on this side of the country, we showered and did as we were told.

Arlo was late and Dean had already started to get restless about it.

"What do you think he wants?" He asked. "He can't possibly want to go over the game already? We have all summer."

"Sit down," Josh reached for him, as he paced on the deck.

Like clockwork, the moment his ass was on the bench, Arlo came around the side of the house with Silas in tow. Both were smiling as they took the steps up to stand on the deck in the middle of all of us.

Ella sat with Zoey against the opposite wall, her head resting on her shoulder as she watched Arlo with so much love in her eyes and it only made me turn my attention back to Adeline. She looked up at me, stars glimmering in her eyes, seated between my legs on the ground and raised her eyebrows in question only for me to shrug.

"You're going to let me get through this or no one is going to Delta but I have something I need to say," Arlo said roughly, causing Silas to chuckle. "What?" He scowled.

"You could have started with hello or a good job," Silas just shook his head gently.

"Good job..." The words sounded painful.

"Alright Buddy, A for effort..." Silas patted his back.

Arlo shifted uncomfortably, he never had been good at the whole speech thing but still managed to pump one out every game night for the last five years. The guys all watched on quietly as he worked himself up to it.

"Silas and I were here when the Nest went up, just two idiot kids running around a giant mud pit looking for trouble anywhere we could find it. We watched them frame every wall, lay every tile, paint every wall. We were there when Mrs. Shore picked out the furniture, and there, when she had to pick out a new couch because Cael pissed on it."

"More than once," Silas grumbled and as Cael and I started laughing.

"We grew into men here and watched all of you do the same. From Cael's high school graduation, to Van's appendix exploding, and even Zoey's first time being black out drunk." Arlo said.

"The bathroom never smelled the same," Van noted and the rest of us agreed.

"It hasn't always been easy, we all suffered our fair share of heartbreak and loss but we always did it together," he said, smiling at Cael. "We slipped up, we fought, we shared bruises and cruel words."

Cael stared at him, his jaw ticked at the thought of his mom.

"But, the Nest was never quiet, and that could be annoying but the sound of family filling the halls was all I ever craved as a kid. So before you all run off and start your own families and I'm left to raise a new era of fucking idiots, I just wanted to say thank you," Arlo said.

Cael rose from where he was sitting, untangling himself from Clementine, and paraded his long legs across the deck. Arlo didn't even flinch when contact was made, he just let Cael hug him. Van laughed, pushing from his spot and joined wrapping his arms around Silas to pull him against the other two. One by one we all joined and soon we were just one big huddle of arms and laughter.

"You guys, this team, for years to come... will always be the heart of the Hornets."

EPILOGUE
JENSEN

"Let's go get wasted," I huffed and kissed Adeline standing on the porch.

"Carry this," Cael said, slamming a crate of CDs into my arms as I turned. One last walk to Delta. I shifted it in my arms as Adeline caught up to Zoey, who was carrying a bottle of rum and stole a hearty shot.

Van fell into line with me as Cael argued with Arlo about song mixes ahead of us and Dean whispered a conversation to Josh behind. Silas had Drew on his back leading the swarm of Hornets down the hill to an already raging Delta.

The party erupted in cheers and congratulations as we made our way up the stairs and inside. Everyone fanned off, getting drinks and taking the chaos in strides but once it calmed down we all found ourselves in the backyard where we belonged.

"Is that for me?" I laughed wildly at the crooked paper sign that hung from the upstairs deck. Dean had sloppily painted over *Hornets Win!* To make it say *Goodbye Jenny* and it was the sweetest thing he'd ever done for me. "It looks like you painted in the dark! I love it," I said, turning to him as he threw his arm over my shoulder.

"Anything for you Jenny," He rubbed his hand into my hair and crashed his lips against the side of my head in a messy show of affection.

I made my way down, finding a place in the grass and Adeline balanced on my lap as she took another shot, handing the bottle to her left for Dean.

"Party's here!" Kaia and Rhea appeared from the side of the house, Rhea was hauling a keg in her arms and Kaia was wearing Cael's crop top. I turned to look at him and he shook his head with a sigh.

"Who invited the strays?" Van asked jokingly, standing up to help Rhea. Kaia wandered over to where we all sat and sank down on her heels in a squat in front of Cael.

"What's up, pussycat?" Cael smirked, leaning forward as she settled in the grass.

"I heard you got hurt," she said, and Cael's smile faltered. "Here." Her hand curled around to the back of the crop and she pulled it up and over her head of messy dark hair. Holding it out for him in nothing but a thin patterned sports bra she waited for him to take it.

"You need it more than I do." She said, shaking it for him to take.

Cael stared down at the relic, that crop had seen war. Tears, screaming, fights, car accidents, bathroom floors and back alleys.

"You won it fair and square." Cael shook his head, his blue eyes flickering back up to Kaia.

"You earned it back." A smile formed on her face and Cael reached out to wrap his big hand around the fabric. Kaia held on for a second longer, violent mischief written across her face, "but don't think this means I won't come for it again."

"Bring it on." A Cheshire grin grew on his face and he quickly stripped from the t-shirt he was in to wear the crop. *Fuckboy* splattered across the chest, he glowed a little brighter with it back resting against his heart. Adeline looked down at me and smiled with a little cute pout over their interaction as Kaia stood, taking a solo cup from Van as he returned.

"What the hell is dad doing here?" Cael went still as Coach came around the corner with a four pack in his hand.

"I forgot that smoke show and you were related." Kaia chewed on the rim of her cup. "Is it weird that I want to fuck your dad?"

"Get in line," Adeline giggled and I dug my fingers into her side.

"Is that beer?" Arlo asked.

"Hey boys," he stopped and set the beer on the unused beer pong table. "Have you seen Silas around, I wanted to speak to him."

"Oh, this is going to be good," Arlo laughed, a sick smile forming on his face.

"Ryan?" Silas came down the stairs, handing a second drink to Drew who was staring between them like she might have to stop a fight.

At least Cael was just as confused as the rest of us.

"You wanted to talk today, here? About what?" Silas scowled, the wind fluffing up his dark hair.

"Maybe somewhere not everyone is staring at us?" Coach said.

"Sorry Ryan," Ella piped up. "If you wanna have a conversation at Delta you do it over the table." She pointed to the beer pong table, seamlessly in cahoots with Arlo as always.

"I'm forty-nine years old. I'm not playing beer pong, Miele." Coach scoffed.

"You play or sit there grumpy," Silas said, liking Ella's idea as he moved around the yard. He pointed to the beers Coach brought. "Those for us?"

"Yeah," he sighed. He piped his head back and muttered something before looking back at Silas, there was a first for everything. "Set it up," he groaned.

"How about we go get some food." Zoey looked over at Drew who gave a nervous smile but joined her inside.

"To the death!" Dean yelled and everyone around them cheered as Silas popped the caps off the beers and filled the cups equally for the two of them. Coach stripped from his sweater, chucking it at Arlo with a dirty look on his face as he rolled up his sleeves and positioned himself at his end of the table.

Silas didn't even give him a chance to breathe before he pocketed a ball in the back row of cups. "What do you want to talk to me about?" He asked him as Coach downed the first cup with a disgusted look on his face.

"Are you sure you don't want to do this in private?" He asked him and Silas narrowed his eyes on him.

"Throw the ball, Ryan," Silas demanded.

Coach threw it and sank it with ease. "It's about your mom."

"Oh, I know." Silas tossed back his cup and chucked it into the grass, "You two think you're so fucking sneaky," he laughed. "You aren't."

"Wait…" Van looked over at Cael who was staring at his father in shock, while Arlo couldn't stop smiling

"Don't be like that, Silas," Coach tried to reason as he collected the ball and cup, downing it.

"Be like what?" Silas was getting a little sloppy with every toss. But still they went shot for shot, never missing a beat until there was only one cup left. Coach tried to keep control of the situation, but Silas couldn't have cared less.

"You're acting like a little kid," Coach said.

He stared at him, a pissed-off smile forming on his face. "Are you fucking my mom, Ryan?"

Coach stilled, his hand wrapped around the ball. "Don't talk about her in that context," he warned, and everyone that heard in the vicinity went dead quiet.

"What the fuck?" Dean mouthed, leaning forward.

"Wait, Mrs. Shore and Coach?" Van's eyes grew wide, "There's no way."

"This is a nightmare," Cael gagged.

"This is the best day of my life," Arlo started laughing and Ella just shook her head at him with a smile on her face.

"You're screwing my mom behind my back!" Silas scoffed.

Something flipped in Coach, he went from nervous to annoyed and the familiar look of controlled rage settled over his features but a nasty smirk curled to the left side. "Do you wanna keep calling me Ryan, or we can try out Dad?" He teased, sinking the last ball into Silas's cup.

All hell broke loose, and for a second I thought Silas might actually hit Coach but Arlo got between them and Silas was laughing like a madman.

"Yeah well, I fucked your sister." He snapped and Cael threw his head back with a long huff of air.

"I thought that was a fever dream," he groaned.

"You did *what*?" Coach snapped and Arlo suddenly had to work harder to keep them separate.

Silas flipped him off and Coach just shook his head.

"If you break her heart, I will make sure you never step foot on a field ever again," Silas growled but for some reason the entire conversation still felt normal, like they weren't actually mad. Just... caught off guard.

Honestly, I could see it, Mrs. Shore was a fucking babe.

Everyone was involved, laughing and hollering about the entire interaction, but eventually Coach managed to bring Silas closer and apologize for not bringing it up sooner. It was still tense but the air was cleared of any secrets, and it allowed everyone to return to their celebrating.

"Do you want your present?" Adeline whispered to me in the chaos.

"A present?" I looked down at her and nodded. "Is it you naked? Because wow I could go for that right now."

"You're insatiable," she giggled, slipping her hand into mine and dragging me up out of my chair. We took the path back to the Nest, where it was so quiet in comparison to Delta. All I wanted to do was get my hands all over her but I needed to be patient because she was too excited about her gift for my wandering hands. She dragged me over to her car and popped the trunk, "close your eyes."

I listened, coming to a stop in the gravel. Everything smelled better after our win, it tasted better, looked better, and right now the smell of fresh-cut grass and an impending storm filled my nose.

"Okay," she said, sounding excited. I opened my eyes, and she was holding a large picture frame.

"There's no way," I said, stepping forward, my eyes flickered between her and the present. It was the original jersey, still in pieces but laid out to display it perfectly against a navy blue background. "You framed it?"

"This is a special piece of history," she giggled, "One day I wanna be able to tell our kids the story of how you destroyed that while it was still on my body."

I shook my head no as she said it and it only made her laugh harder.

"Okay, maybe not the kids, but definitely anyone else that will listen." Adeline beamed with pride. "We can put it up in the living room."

"Deal," I stared down at it in disbelief and realized that her pride over the shredded jersey only made me love her more. "We're going to have to test the durability of your rugby jersey."

"A matching set?" She gasped, "That's the most romantic thing you've ever said to me."

"I fucking love you." I reached over the frame and cupped her face, bringing her lips to meet mine.

ACKNOWLEDGEMENTS

O ne more time, you ready?

The end of the Hornets, the end of an era. The beginning of something new, something exciting. I've grown so much since releasing Bad Honey in 2024, it feels like that was a life time ago when it was literally just last March. Five books in two years is actually nutcase behavior and yet every single one of you stuck around. I can't begin to explain how grateful I am for all of you. The other day a conversation was had about why we write books and I had a moment of grief wash over me that I wasn't expecting because *she* shouldn't have been there, but she was.

Lorraine loved to tell stories, about herself, about anyone she met, about the restaurants she visited, the movies she saw, the books she read. She was the person that taught me how to tell a story and make people listen to you tell it. I'm stubborn, to a fault sometimes and I let my own fear of this career keep me from it for too long. So long that the one person who told me once a week that I should be writing and publishing my stories, died before she could see me do it. I'll regret that forever. You guys not only accepted me, but helped me preserve the memories I have of her forever. I don't have words for that. Which sucks cause I'm an author and I should.

Five books is lot for one person to write alone, I would have been able to do it without Aaron. He's honestly the only person who sees the real me on a day to day basis and still puts up with my bullshit. He's a national treasure, a Dad to our kids that neither of us had when we were young, a feral grumpy crow wrangler, a best friend to everyone that meets him and one of the smartest people I know. We've been together for sixteen years now, through thick and even thicker times but we managed to grow together and learn together. Every day is an adventure with him, I never know what's going to come out of his mouth. I like to relate people in my life to the character in my books and there are pieces of my favorite people in these characters. Sometimes he's Arlo, other days he's Cael. But if I'm honest, he's the Dean to my Josh. And of all the stories, that one is the most important. Thanks for being my safe space, my pink motel. I love you.

Beta Team unite, over the last two years the beta team has changed, welcomed new faces, sadly said goodbye to others as life kicks us around but one thing has never changed, my love for you all. These books wouldn't even make it to the shelf if it wasn't for your input and discussions. You shape every single story with me, side by side. I hope that I never have to write a book without any of you because it just wouldn't be the same. Mattie, MK, Rory, Ale, Jess, Lizzy, Aiku, Tiffani, Hannah, Jes, Sarah, Netty, JJ, Thea, Anna, Teagan, and anyone else that's been here over the years. *Thank you.*

Rory, my Eddie. I've said just about everything I can say over the last two years. You are so brilliant and kind beneath those sharp lion teeth. From the moment I met you I knew that I'd never be the same, you're one of my favorite bully's and I just know it means you love me. Please never leave me. I wouldn't survive this world without your light.

Mattie, my Matty, my Cas. Thank you for always creating a safe space for me. From the day we met until now, you've been there, protecting me from land mines I couldn't see. Thank you for taking care of my heart when I just can't bare to hold it anymore. For teaching me new things and for always sharing your music. I love you more than Frank loves beating the piss out of people for no reason. (And I love you more than Dean loves pie and more than I love Cassian Andor.)

Ale, my Dustin, my Ted. I know alot of the time I'm a mess, and you are too, but that's the beauty of you and I, we get to be a mess together. Thank you for teaching about your culture and always taking the time to translate Bad Bunny songs for me, I truly cannot explain how much your massive heart means to a little chickadee like me. I love you. Probablemente esto no tenga sentido, pero ten paciencia. Te amo, y ninguna distancia lo apagará. Siempre te veré como inspiración para ser amable y cortés. Mi luna.

Bec, my mother from another life. Thank you for being so patient with me. For never telling me that I'm too much or moving too fast, but instead just putting on your running shoes and keeping up with me when I need a running partner. You are the magic in my veins, I love you more than wine on a school night.

Jayj, my baby, my misery, my Sunday. Thank you for being a constant shock to my system. For teaching me that we aren't our lowest points, that no matter what life throws at us we can survive it with a fucking smile on our faces. Thank you for never giving up on me, even when I'm terrible at answering messages or tik toks. Thank you for believing in me the way Bubbe does, every single fucking day. I love you more than you know.

MK, my Jensen, my Kaia. I have no idea how I did any of this before you bulldozed into my life with so much support and love. You are a forced to be reckoned with, a fucking hurricane on a sunny day and I never want to receive you any other way. You told me that I shouldn't cry writing these because I've done them a billion times but as an author I take pride in one upping myself every single book. So how dare you. Bad Honey brought you into my life, and it brought Honey Undone into everyone elses. You inspire me every single fucking day and I'm so grateful that I get to say that. Looks like our mantra came true. 2025 was our bitch, it just took us a second to get there. I love you, Killer.

Forever, and ever. My Twinkle Toes. This is a special report from your very own Drunk Tuck Duck, thanks for being there every single fucking day of my life. For never backing down, for always reminding me that I'm a badass. For being the balance in my life when everything gets too hard. My sweet ocean obsessed, dinosaur crazy bby girl. You are the epitome of Dean Winchester's heart. The version of himself that he protects from the world, that childlike desire to run away from home and start somewhere fresh. There for you are my heart. I could not survive this life without your steady pace.

And to the Nest, which no matter where we are in the journey will *always* be the Nest. The readers that have been here from the beginning and the ones that are just joining us. Thank you for bringing the best kind of chaos into my life. For sending me videos, pictures, screenshots and screaming. Thank you for sharing your stories with me and keeping the circle of Lorraine going in doing so.

You're my family now, and forever. Dean Winchester said it best, remember that family cares about you, not what you can do for them. Family's there through the good, the bad - all of it. They got your back, even when it hurts. That's family. That's the Nest. I'm grateful for every single one of you in different ways and it would make this book about forty pages longer if I sat here typing away but I have a rugby series to right and the girls are waiting for me.

www.ingramcontent.com/pod-product-compliance
Lightning Source LLC
Chambersburg PA
CBHW020516080526
44583CB00013B/617